V

THE HAYMARKET SERIES

Editors: Mike Davis and Michael Sprinker

The Haymarket Series offers original studies in politics, history and culture, with a focus on North America. Representing views across the American left on a wide range of subjects, the series will be of interest to socialists both in the USA and throughout the world. A century after the first May Day, the American left remains in the shadow of those martyrs whom the Haymarket Series honours and commemorates. These studies testify to the living legacy of political activism and commitment for which they gave their lives.

Secular Vocations

Intellectuals, Professionalism, Culture

◆

BRUCE ROBBINS

V

VERSO

London · New York

First published by Verso 1993
© Verso 1993
All rights reserved

Verso
UK: 6 Meard Street, London W1V 3HR
USA: 29 West 35th Street, New York, NY 10001-2291

Verso is the imprint of New Left Books

ISBN 0-86091-430-5
ISBN 0-86091-630-8 (pbk)

British Library Cataloguing in Publication Data
A catalogue record for this book is available from the British Library

Library of Congress Cataloging-in-Publication Data
A catalogue record for this book is available from the Library of Congress

Typeset by Leaper & Gard Ltd, Bristol
Printed and bound in Great Britain by Biddles Ltd,
Guildford and King's Lynn

Dedicated to the memory of my father
Eugene Robbins
1924–1990

Contents

Preface

The critic's starting point, Gramsci writes, should be "'knowing thyself' as a product of the historical process to date." This book applies Gramsci's words to intellectuals of the cultural or literary left over the past three decades. It examines the "historical process" that has done the most to form and transform intellectuals in these years, the process described by Alan Wald as "the deradicalization of twentieth-century American intellectuals, a middle-class stratum increasingly tied to the professions."[1]

Many others have seen this process in much the same way. "The intellectual is either shut out or sold out." "Seldom have the management of minds and the conduct of business affairs converged so." "The near total absorption of intellectual life by the universities marks the decline, if not the obliteration, of 'the intellectual' as a distinctive social type." "Today nonacademic intellectuals are an endangered species." In the decades since the 1960s, and especially within the past ten or fifteen years, the disappearance or decline of the intellectual has been announced repeatedly.[2] This decline or disappearance is usually ascribed to the increasing role of the universities in intellectual life, to the increasingly specialized division of labor, or to an increasingly dominant professionalism (the general term that will cover both of these), which is held to divide culture and its interpreters into different institutional compartments and non-communicating areas of expertise. There are no more intellectuals today, we are told, or else there soon will be none, largely because there is no longer room for them in our compartmentalized, commodified, bureaucratized society. Society today makes room only for professionals – credentialed carriers of institutionally defined expertise who sell their commodity on the market, academic or otherwise, and are thus constitutionally incapable of carrying on the

ix

intellectuals' public, independent, critical functions.

Have intellectuals, judged to be public, independent, and critical by virtue of stepping boldly outside their specialized competence, been replaced by professionals, characterized by their willingness to remain comfortably within their competence? This book tries to see through and around the received notion of a one-way journey from the intellectual to the professional. It breaks open the opposed pairs of intellectual and professional, oppositionality and expertise, public and private, in order to ask whether critical consciousness and social institutions are ever indeed so neatly opposed to one another. Taking as its central exhibit the institutionalizing of culture in the humanities, it argues the inadequacy of the familiar polysyllabic sociologisms – "specialization," "academicization," "professionalization" – that are usually brought forward in order to produce the illusion of the intellectual's fall. The book argues, in brief, that nothing so simple as a fall has in fact taken place.

There is of course an element of personal apologia in this argument. In order to believe that what we do is meaningful, as our persistence in it suggests we must believe, some effort to understand how oppositional work is conceivable within a professional framework seems required. Otherwise, it might seem as if the cultural or academic left, to which I belong, exempts itself from its own analyses, claiming an inexplicable immunity to the determinations it finds analytically everywhere else, and is unwilling to account for the fact of its own existence. Yet I do not want to claim that such an effort can be fully successful. When lower-middle-class values join with an elite education to produce some form of academic leftism, as they have for me and for many others, it cannot be assumed that the resulting perspective is capable of understanding itself historically. Though I try to reveal the drama, dignity, and public significance of certain scholarly work and certain scholarly careers, the embarrassments of possessing expertise in a deeply unjust society cannot be wished away.

The structure of the book may be summarized as follows. Chapter One exposes certain ambiguities within the ideology of professionalism as they work themselves out in the 1966 Western *The Professionals*. Against the view of professional ideology that emerges from the male-centered Western genre, it plays off the complications of feminism's richly troubled encounter with professionalism. In Chapter Two, I discuss the specifically *cultural* left, that is, the uses and limits of concepts like culture, literariness, and the aesthetic as grounding for politically adversarial practices and institutions of intellectual work. Marking the move *away* from culture among critics and theorists, Chapter Three takes up "rhetoric" as one ground or object of knowledge put in play over the past decades so as to replace or transform the culture concept within the academic disciplines of the humanities. These objects of knowledge belong at once to the discipline and to a broader public history, I argue – a history that is mediated through the discipline's efforts to renegotiate with the public its own boundaries and purposes.

Recognizing the personal, even existential, motif that overtly or covertly animates the topics of intellectuals, the suggestion that what is at stake is not merely ideas, but the possibility of living out one's ideas within a given set of circumstances and a given mortal span, Chapters Four and Five take up two salient examples of the intellectual as a figure of the meaningful life: Raymond Williams and Edward W. Said. Each of these central figures of the cultural left is exemplary in acting outside the academy as well as within it. Each, I argue, has wrestled with the ideology of professionalism in a manner that is also exemplary.

Finally, Chapter Six examines the grounding of intellectuals like James Clifford and Gayatri Chakravorty Spivak in the light of the new globality or internationalism of cultural life, and more specifically against the backdrop of attacks on "multiculturalism" in educational institutions. In a time when worldliness demands recognition of the "Third" as well as the "First" and "Second" worlds, if it does not require that the Three Worlds theory be scrapped altogether, this chapter asks whether the unfashionable term "cosmopolitan" can be renewed as a figure for a multiculturalism that does not stop at the particular, and that self-consciously respects the value of intellectual and professional work.

I have incurred more debts in the long writing of this book than I can possibly mention here. Among those friends who have challenged and corrected, lost patience and found time, I owe special thanks to Aijaz Ahmad, Paul Bové, Jim Clifford, Audrey Fisch, Marty Gloege, Ken Hirschkop, Marjorie Howes, Gerhard Joseph, Carol Kay, Tom Keenan, John McClure, Richard Ohmann, Andy Parker, Fred Pfeil, Dana Polan, Andrew Ross, Edward Said, and Ella Shohat. I am grateful to Stanley Fish, Catherine Gallagher, and Jeff Williams for lively public disputations, and to Nancy Armstrong, Lauren Berlant, Barbara Johnson, and Tova Perlmutter for asking questions I couldn't answer. Jonathan Arac, Gerald Graff, and Michael Sprinker read the entire manuscript in draft and were extraordinarily generous with their commentaries, suggestions, and support. My colleagues in the Rutgers English department and in the *Social Text* collective have also been wonderfully helpful and inspiring. Elsa, Sophia, and Andreas put up with it.

Portions of this book have appeared in earlier versions in the following publications: "Cultural Criticism" (with Gerald Graff), in Stephen Greenblatt and Giles Gunn, eds, *Redrawing the Boundaries of Literary Study* (New York: Modern Language Association, 1993); "The East is a Career: Edward Said and the Logics of Professionalism," in Michael Sprinker, ed., *Edward Said: A Critical Reader* (Oxford: Basil Blackwell 1992, pp. 48–73); "Comparative Cosmopolitanism," *Social Text*, 31/32, double Issue on Postcolonialism (Summer 1992), pp. 169–86; "Othering the Academy: Professionalism and Multiculturalism," *Social Research*, 58:2 (Summer 1991), pp. 355–72; "Interdisciplinarity in Public: The Rhetoric of Rhetoric," *Social Text*, 25/26, double Issue on the Public Sphere (Summer 1990), pp. 103–18; "Espionage as Vocation: Raymond Williams' Loyalties," in Bruce Robbins, ed., *Intellectuals: Aesthetics, Politics, Academics* (Minneapolis: University of Minnesota Press, 1990), pp. 273–90; "Oppositional Professionals," in Jonathan Arac and Barbara Johnson, eds, *Consequences of Theory*, Selected Papers from the English Institute (Baltimore: Johns Hopkins University Press, 1989), pp. 1–21; "The History of Literary Theory: Starting Over," *Poetics Today*, 9:4(1988), pp. 767–81; "Professionalism and Politics: Toward Productively Divided Loyalties," *Profession 85* (New York: Modern Language Association, 1985), pp. 1–9; "English as a National Discipline," *Harvard Educational Review*, 55:1 (February 1985), pp. 127–31; "Modernism and Professionalism: The Case of William Carlos Williams," in Richard Waswo, ed., *On Poetry and Poetics*, Swiss Papers in English Language and Literature, 2 (Tübingen: Günter Narr Verlag, 1985) pp. 191–205; "Homelessness and Worldliness," *Diacritics*, 13:3 (Fall 1983), pp. 69–77; "Modernism in History, Modernism in Power," in Robert Kiely, ed., *Modernism Reconsidered*, Harvard English Studies No. 11 (Cambridge, MA: Harvard University Press, 1983), pp. 229–45.

The attempt of leftist intellectuals to pretend that the avant-garde is serving the wretched of the earth by fighting free of the merely beautiful is a hopeless attempt to make the special needs of the intellectual and the social needs of the community coincide.

Richard Rorty

None calleth us to labor.

Ralph Waldo Emerson

L'intellectuel moderne aurait-il une telle phobie de l'État, et l'État de l'intellectuel, si l'un ne détenait pas les secrets de l'autre?

Régis Debray

From *Luftmensh* to "Cultural Elite": Intellectuals in the *New York Times Magazine*

The cultural elites respect neither tradition nor standards. They believe that moral truths are relative and all "life styles" are equal. They seem to think the family is an arbitrary arrangement of people who decide to live under the same roof, that fathers are dispensable and that parents need not be married or even of opposite sexes. They are wrong. . . . I know it is politically correct to be dismissive of those who speak of moral values. But political correctness is a form of intolerance. . . . Talk about right and wrong, and they'll try to mock us in newsrooms, sitcom studios and faculty lounges across America. But in the heart of America, in the homes and workplaces and churches, the message is heard.

Dan Quayle

"Quayle Attacks a 'Cultural Elite' in Speech Invoking Moral Values," the *New York Times* reported on June 10, 1992. The then Vice-President's appeal to moral values was quickly taken by many as a piece of cynical electioneering, artfully staged so as to woo back the Republicans' conservative base from Ross Perot while allowing George Bush (as the *Times* pointed out) "to strike a bipartisan tone" – in other words, to avoid the appearance of unseemly philosophical intimacy with people like the Southern Baptists whom Quayle was addressing.[1] But the success of the speech could not be so easily explained away. If Quayle had managed, as a *Times* commentator noted four days later, "to impress his views more sharply on the public consciousness than any other candidate for top office this year," it was because his speechwriters had found a formula for his opponents whose premises are almost universally acknowledged – even by those opponents themselves.[2]

Consider how economically the brief phrase "cultural elite" embodies a logic that is acknowledged far beyond the radical right. As the phrase asserts that self-styled leftists (one must assume that

1

there exist no cultural elites of the right) are perched on a privileged rung of the social hierarchy, it insinuates that they are at odds with their supposed anti-hierarchical principles – in effect, that they are a bunch of hypocrites. On the other hand, they are also a *cultural* elite, and the adjective cultural labels them as something more, and worse, than merely a group concerned with the preservation, interpretation, and transmission of culture. It suggests an elite whose privileges are based not on skill and accomplishment in the real world of production, but only on the acquisition of culture, which is to say on something unproductive, unreal, or at least unverifiable, a matter of minority taste and arbitrary fashion. Estranged from the solid values of ordinary people, therefore, while it is also neglectful of their economic needs, not to speak of the greater urgencies of the "disadvantaged," culture can only be intended to bolster the interests of the elite itself. First and foremost, according to this logic, culture is what the elite requires in order to establish its own rule, the rule of esoterically self-congratulating, self-promoting opinion. In effect, the cultural left is a professional left. Cultural means it is irrelevant to the real problems of the working majority; professional means it is protected by its expertise against anyone who might contest it from the outside, hence unaccountable to that majority. In both respects, it is false to its own supposedly democratic, change-the-real-world principles. In brief, it is a contradiction in terms. The cleverness of the phrase cultural elite lies in the disappearing act it performs on its opponents. If that's what the left is, it implies, then no real left exists.

This logic of guilt by professional association is still clearer in Dinesh D'Souza's *Illiberal Education* (1991). While denouncing the fondness of university teachers for Marxism, D'Souza pauses strangely to complain that in its respect for culture, and especially for other cultures, the academic left has forgotten the poor and suffering. The subtitle to his book says it all: *The Politics of Race and Sex on Campus*, but not (even in the name of Marx) the politics of class. "Universities should retain their policies of preferential treatment," D'Souza concludes, "but alter their criteria of application from race to socioeconomic disadvantage."[3] Those who have overvalued culture, including cultural expressions of racial and sexual difference, while undervaluing "socioeconomic disadvantage," D'Souza implies, have really been looking out for their own socioeconomic advantage: "this sort of analysis helps the literary professionals to claim a specialized field for themselves. Through professionalized jargon, however meaningless, critics assert their claims to special expertise

2

and consequently to special recognition and privilege" (181). The left is identified with culture, and culture is identified with professionalism; the result is the oxymoron, and the embarrassment, of a left identified as professional.

This syllogism is by no means confined to conservative think-tanks and their well-funded harangues against "political correctness." In respectable academic journals and in anarchist anti-academic pamphlets, in the struggling little reviews of a would-be postmodern counterculture and at the bland center of middlebrow opinion managed by the *New York Times Sunday Magazine* – across the cultural and political spectrum, the logic of the indictment is everywhere. Most strangely, it is the same logic that many, perhaps most, of the intellectuals of the left themselves seem to follow when they turn their attention to their own professional status. "Power based on knowledge is," according to the authors of *Power in the Highest Degree* (1991), "a basic form of class power. Modern-day experts are only the latest in a long succession of specialists who have spun knowledge into gold – in every age and every part of the world."[4] Professional status thus becomes political self-betrayal. For Shelby Steele, the sad fate of the civil rights and women's movements of the 1960s was professionalization:

> Reform ... also means recognition for those who struggled for it. The movement's leaders are quoted in the papers, appear on TV, meet with elected officials, write books – they come to embody the movement. Over time, they and they alone speak for the aggrieved; and, of course, they continue to speak *of* the aggrieved, adding fresh grievances to the original complaint. It is their vocation now, and their means to status and power. The idealistic reformers thus become professional spokespersons for the seemingly permanently aggrieved.[5]

For Russell Jacoby, the academicization of former student activists and intellectuals has meant both the cooptation of the 1960s generation and the disappearance of US intellectuals as such. The villain of *The Last Intellectuals* (1987) is in its subtitle, "The Age of Academe": "In the end it was not the New Left intellectuals who invaded the universities but the reverse: the academic idiom, concepts, and concerns occupied, and finally preoccupied, the young left intellectuals."[6] In much the same vein Cornel West writes: "I am disappointed with the professional incorporation of former New Left activists who now often thrive on a self-serving careerism while espousing rhetorics of oppositional politics of little seriousness or integrity."[7]

3

Now if there *is* a logic linking "careerism" to "rhetorics of oppositional politics," as West intimates, this would be a strange fact, and it would seem to call out for investigation. Of all the ways to make a career, this is surely the least predictable. Assuming the worst possible motives on the part of the individual careerist, it would still be interesting that careerist motives should have to be camouflaged by "rhetorics of oppositional politics," rather than by some other sort of camouflage. And if camouflage-by-oppositional-politics is happening widely and systematically, then there is clearly more to the institutional process of career-making than meets the innocent eye. But when it is announced that the New Left has been absorbed into the universities or that intellectuals have become difficult to distinguish from professionals, the point is rarely that universities, professionals, or careers may need to be thought about in a fresh way. What is usually meant, both left and right, is that this new thing is a monster to be repudiated and ridiculed.

Ridicule seems especially hard to avoid when the full logic of the phrase "cultural elite" is invoked, when the emphasis falls not just on the replacement of intellectuals by professionals, but on a replacement of real or class politics by cultural politics, by aesthetics. "The attempt of leftist intellectuals to pretend that the avant-garde is serving the wretched of the earth by fighting free of the merely beautiful," as Richard Rorty succinctly put it in 1985, "is a hopeless attempt to make the special needs of the intellectual and the social needs of the community coincide."[8] And more recently, arguing over cultural politics with Andrew Ross in the pages of *Dissent*, Rorty concluded as follows:

> I think it is important to note that ... in the triad of "race, class and gender" it is class that is currently losing out. The English department left has lots of thoughts about race and gender, but almost no ideas about class. In particular, it has no ideas about the political problem posed by the desertion of the Democrats by their traditional working-class constituencies ... – a desertion that has, in the United States, immensely increased the ability of the strong to do what they like to the weak. The English Department left is acting as if it has a lot better things to do – a lot higher forms of consciousness to have – than thinking about this problem. But until that problem is solved, the strong and the selfish will, in this country, steadily increase their power.[9]

Rorty's call for academics to participate directly in party politics is a powerful one, even if it does not engage with the long and pertinent history of arguments on the other side of the question – to

4

take a recent example, arguments by the National Organization of Women. But suppose we are moved by Rorty's appeal. What then do we make of the fact that, in calling for engagement against Bush and Quayle, then still in the White House, Rorty agrees with Quayle's premises? For Rorty, like Quayle, implies that widely publicized conflicts in the domain of cultural politics are really no more than the absurd, selfish posturings of an "English Department left," a "cultural elite" that is more faithful to its narrow professional self-interest than to any larger political project. To me, this agreement suggests that both are right – right at least about the existence of a category of non-traditional intellectuals, difficult to name or describe without adopting in advance a viewpoint for or against it. And it also suggests that in dismissing this category, one of them is making a serious political error. Quayle has something to teach Rorty, I think, about the political significance of the so-called "cultural elite" now that the family and sexuality, tradition and standards, lifestyles and moral values, have become crucial issues of political debate and decision-making, and crucial elements of how people identify themselves politically and of how they are mobilized. The former Vice President is correct in seeing critics of the cultural status quo as his enemies, as *real* enemies, and whatever stands in the way of the rest of us seeing this is therefore a real obstacle to political change. This is one reason why I want to address those who, like myself, feel the force of Richard Rorty's political appeal. And I want to argue that to play along with the right's authoritarian populism about culture, to allow our indignation to be diverted (as happened in the Senate hearings over Justice Clarence Thomas) into anti-professionalism, is indeed an error. Which entails, to begin with, a willingness to look at the historical conjunction of the left, culture, and professionalism as something more than an opportunity for an easy laugh.

Since the Berlin Wall came down in 1989 and the Bush/Quayle government began wildly searching for new enemies – a habit we cannot be confident the Clinton administration will be able to break – the tendency to resurrect earlier versions of "the left" and to measure the diminished present against them has been an oblique way of acknowledging a new and burdensome uncertainty as to what the expression "left" might signify, to its opponents as well as to itself. With the disintegration of the socialist states and the intensifying of North/South confrontation, with the increasing importance of knowledge and information to the economy, the decline of union radicalism, and the rise of political movements in the name of race, gender, environment, sexual orientation, and so on, the meaning of a metaphor based on Parisian seating arrangements two hundred years earlier can no longer be assumed. This book will rephrase Quayle's and Rorty's joint polemic, therefore, as a series of questions: how is it that professionalism and a special concern with culture should have combined to produce something that can be labeled, however invidiously, an "English Department left" or a "cultural elite"? Does this phenomenon indeed mark the disappearance of "intellectuals" or "the left"? What are the politics of professionalism in the US today – and what are the politics of the critique of professionalism?

The immediate political context for these questions includes the Great PC Offensive that followed (not coincidentally) the Gulf War of 1991, when exposing supposed threats to "free speech" in the professional enclaves of the academy enabled the news media to forget their own recent, total surrender to the information control of the military.[10] And it extends into the election campaign of 1992, with its anti-institutional rhetoric of "family values" aimed at unseating the left from those institutions in which it had acquired some influence. But the premises that Quayle's "cultural elite" speech shares with Richard Rorty's jibes at the "English Department left" obviously go back further, and so does the conception of this book. I began to write it, I think, when I encountered, in the mid-1970s, the work of Raymond Williams and Edward Said. These two examples of what I did not call the "English Department left" were an immensely powerful inspiration to me and my generation, and yet their power seemed a benign mystery, having nothing to do with how anyone thought about English departments or universities or institutions, untheorizable not just to others, but even to themselves. Public figures as well as academics, each seemed to challenge the understanding of them, and of the separation between their political lives and their professional lives, that was unquestioningly accepted both in the academy and in the popular press. This book tries to take up that challenge.

Over the past decade the *New York Times Magazine* has run a number of articles on old intellectuals and new academics, on figures like Stanley Fish, Henry Lewis Gates, Jr, Catherine McKinnon, Cornel West, and Richard Rorty, on the yearly Modern Language Association convention, on conflicts over the canon, and on other signs of fashion and faction in the humanities. Without announcing themselves as a series, these "human-interest" stories amount to a collective presentation of the new academic radicals to a broad reading public. A look at one or two of these articles is thus a good way to begin examining American common sense, such as it is, about intellectuals, professionalism, and culture.

Let us examine, then, an article by James Atlas called "The Changing World of New York Intellectuals," published by the *Times Magazine* in 1985. The article reports the disappearance of the New York intellectual in a narrative that has since become familar:

> Since the 50's, intellectual life in this country has been largely concentrated on the campus.... The predominance of universities in the nation's cultural life has just about done in the type of self-educated, sporadically well-read intellectual who flourished in the 40's. The academy has become increasingly specialized. Some of the most influential English departments in the country ... are dominated by the arcane disciplines of structuralism and deconstructionism, modes of literary discourse imported from Europe and virtually inaccessible to the lay reader. The general, free-wheeling essay that was a favored genre of the New York intellectuals ... is nearly extinct.[11]

The article ends on an explicit note of nostalgia: "To have come so far, and to see the vocation that represented the dream of one's youth in danger of extinction is a bitter thing indeed" (76).

Like many other writers on the subject, Atlas quotes the Yiddish term "*Luftmenshen*," or "'air men,' without visible means of support" (25), to describe the principled poverty that is taken to distinguish true intellectuals from the professional journalists, literary scholars, and so on who have come later. Intellectuals seemed to live on air, and thus by poetic extension seemed as free as their ethereal element. As Karl Mannheim had put it in the 1920s, they were "free-floating, detached." Now, assimilated into institutions of one sort or another, they are salaried, pensioned, tenured, and they write accordingly. The *Luftmenshen* have been grounded. They have become an elite of specialists.

Atlas does not need to be told that no one really lives on air. Why, then, does he make use of the *Luftmensh* metaphor? The answer may be that, by playfully throwing up its hands at the mystery of how some people manage to get by, this metaphor distracts attention from a serious, indeed a paralyzing, incapacity to say how the New York intellectuals actually earned a living, or even *that* they did. Atlas quotes William Barrett (in *The Truants*): "Without jobs and without prospects, the young were not chained immediately to the wheel of career.

and profession" (25). Here the *Luftmensh*'s distinctive otherworldliness seems to be his reward for renouncing "the wheel of career and profession." But two sentences later, Atlas writes: "To read and talk all day was considered a respectable profession." Here intellectuals seem to be respectably riding the wheel along with everyone else. Which is it? Did intellectuals constitute a profession, or on the contrary were they the one exception to "the wheel of career and profession"? In ordinary speech, the term "profession" is used to mean a label one can attach to oneself without dishonor as well as the occupation by which one earns one's livelihood. This looseness of common language permits the issue of whether the New York intellectuals were or weren't professionals to be evaded, at least for the moment. Then, a bit later, Atlas gives another quotation (from Leon Wieseltier), again with apparent approval: "No one can afford to be an intellectual anymore. The culture doesn't support it as a profession" (70). According to this view, once upon a time being an intellectual *was* a profession, with full financial and social support. But in this case, the word *Luftmenshen* would *never* have been an accurate description of intellectuals.[12] And what has died out of the world, it would then appear, is not after all a figure of heroic otherworldliness. The conclusion gives this point still another twist: "the intellectual vocation – at least as I imagined it – is largely obsolete, an archaic profession; the intellectual has gone the way of the cobbler and the smithy" (73). Like the cobbler and the blacksmith, the implication is, the intellectual was once a self-supporting, proudly independent artisan. He is another casualty of the relentless, tragic process of capitalist modernization.

The incoherence of all this is noteworthy, if only because it illustrates how little respect some defenders of the intellectual have for standards of intellectual argument. The notion of the intellectual as an archaic, pre-industrial craftsman would not find much support in the historical record, if Atlas cared enough to look there. But there is a more important point. Having defined the intellectual as a *Luftmensh*, possessor of an ideal impoverishment that is opposed to the compromised vassalage of employment, Atlas (and many others) can say neither that the intellectuals *did* work nor that they *didn't*. For if they didn't work, then what were their sources of income? And if they did, then how did those sources of income escape the social servitude, suffered or inflicted, that even the most irregular employment can be assumed to involve? In short, how could they possibly be employed and yet *remain* intellectuals?

Irving Howe, Atlas tells us, wrote reviews for *Time Magazine*. But

8

Atlas says nothing about the possible inhibitions that this large and aggressive corporation might have brought to bear upon work it published. (The information is available; James Agee, for example, had a great deal to say about the effects on himself of working for Henry Luce.) Nor does Atlas suggest that being obliged to sell one's freelance writings on the open market might not be everyone's definition of absolute personal freedom. Even if it is his own definition, it would seem appropriate to say as much, so that the cost of the intellectuals' supposed surrender to institutions like the university could be impartially compared to the cost of submitting to the laws of supply and demand. Why is working for a university less "independent" than working for *Time*? Paul Starr, reviewing still another attack on the academy funded by a right-wing institute, observes ironically:

> it is a curious thought that conservatives comfortably ensconced in well-endowed, nonprofit institutes are more disciplined by the marketplace than are liberal professors comfortably ensconced in well-endowed, nonprofit universities. If virtue were so predictably aligned with the market, both would be in trouble – and Vice President Dan Quayle would have nothing to worry about from television sitcoms that have, after all, met one of the market's most exacting tests.[13]

Atlas notes that the New York intellectuals tended to marry women who had money. There is no word about what gender arrangements like these might have to do with intellectuals and their politics. The *Luftmensh* is offered as gender-neutral. Yet the concept takes certain servitudes for granted. In *Anti-Intellectualism in America* (1963), Richard Hofstadter defines the intellectual, once again, against the professional:

> The heart of the matter – to borrow a distinction made by Max Weber about politics – is that the professional man lives *off* ideas, not *for* them. His professional role, his professional skills, do not make him an intellectual. He is a mental worker, a technician. He may *happen* to be an intellectual as well, but if he is, it is because he brings to his profession a distinctive feeling about ideas which is not required by his job.... At home he may happen to be an intellectual, but at his job he is a hired menial technician who uses his mind for externally determined ends.[14]

By locating the intellectual in the home, Hofstadter says more about the genderedness of the concept than he apparently means to, and thus also says more than he means to about the professionalism to which he opposes it. Is the professional workplace simply a site of tyranny, of "externally determined ends," hence inherently hostile to the intellectual? There is of course a peculiar inconsistency in proposing this idea within one's own published, professional work. If work is the tyranny Hofstadter says it is, then what tyrant in his own workplace (Columbia University) would be telling him to say so? And if it were so tyrannical, *why* would it be telling him to say so? Leaving aside this inconsistency for the moment, let us note another. One can only think of the workplace as tyrannical if one hypothesizes some other space, like the home, which can be seen as a site of freedom and autonomy, congenial to the intellectual. But one can only see the home as this alternative space of freedom from the tyranny of the workplace if someone else is slaving away at the chores that need to be done there. What is assumed by this familiar definition of the intellectual as against the professional, in other words, is a sexual division of labor in which cooking, children, and other encumbrances are someone else's business.

Let us be clear. There is no "home" in this sense, no place where thought can be free of all material encumbrance and social entanglement, and it is time to stop trying to return there again and again. And, by the same token, there is also no "work" in Hofstadfter's sense. If Hofstadter can speak of work as he does in his work, then work cannot be the totally alienated, "externally determined" place he claims it is. In order to take the true measure of the real but relative freedoms we have, we have to stop positing spaces of freedom which, like domesticity for Hofstadter, inevitably mask someone's servitude. And we must look closely at those supposed spaces of tyranny, like the professional workplace, which have been seen as antithetic to the intellectual. No principles of gender justice can allow the intellectual to be defined within this antithesis. Not disembodied freedom, but diverse embodiednesses and incomplete servitudes have to become the common sense view of intellectual work.

And this is so even though professionalism has often seemed an obstacle to feminism's own radical politics, and even an obstacle to embodiedness. The lives of the professionally successful, Virginia Woolf writes in *Three Guineas*, "make us of the opinion that if people are highly successful in their professions they lose their senses.... Sight goes. They have no time to look at pictures. Sound goes. They have no time to listen to music ...".[15] What is purchased by this sacrifice is something less than ideal political agency.

For if Mr. Chaventry and the gentlemen who agree with him believe that "at a disadvantage and under suspicion" as she is, with little or no political or professional training and upon a salary of about £250 a year, the professional woman can yet "build a new and better world," they must credit her with powers that might almost be called divine. (85)

The angel in the house, like the intellectual, is expected to be disinterested and disembodied. As the etymology of the adjective "meretricious" suggests, to be a woman who earns money (*meretrix*) is to be a harlot. Woolf foresees with clarity what the male left will therefore conclude about women who do become professionals. "If you succeed in your profession the words 'For God and Empire' will likely be written, like the address on a dog-collar, round your neck" (81). What is to be done then?

Behind us lies the patriarchal system; the private house, with its nullity, its immorality, its hypocrisy, its servility. Before us lies the public world, the professional system, with its possessiveness, its jealousy, its pugnacity, its greed.... Had we not better plunge off the bridge into the river ... ?" (86).

Faced with this choice – not between servitude and illusory freedom, but between one real servitude and another – Woolf chooses: "to depend upon a profession is a less odious form of slavery than to depend upon a father" (20).

This position has been eloquently updated by Jane Gallop in *Around 1981* (1992). "The word 'institutionalization' sounds like some form of incarceration," Gallop writes.

The academicization of feminist criticism is generally discussed as if it had happened against our will.... This sort of aggressive dissociation clouds our understanding of how we got here. None of us just woke up one day to discover that she had a Ph.D., a full-time academic job, much less tenure....

I do not want to celebrate our being in. Being in something that is a transmitter of elitist values. Being in a discourse that is constituted, at this point in time, as marginal to the larger culture and society. But I do not want to bemoan it either. I want to understand why we are located here, how we got here, what we sacrificed to get here, what we gained: all as preliminaries to the question of how do we do the most good, as feminists, as social and cultural critics, speaking from this location.[16]

If these questions do not make it into the *New York Times*, it is not because they are not clearly and forcefully expressed, nor because Gallop's perspective is not subtle and fair-minded.

What does make it in, then? Among other things, a fluent vacillation between a weak-minded idealism and an equally weak-minded cynicism. "Intellectuals," Atlas writes in the *Times Magazine* article cited above, "have always composed an adversarial elite; it's in the very nature of the job" (25). This sentence displays an impressive but characteristic inconsistency. To the extent that being an intellectual *was* a "job" for which one got paid, Atlas cannot really believe it was "adversarial." Hence he rushes headlong into self-contradiction: "Intellectuals," he writes on the same page, "like everyone else, tend to follow power." Which is it: oppositional or sycophantic? Atlas swings helplessly back and forth from one extreme to the other, and he does so because he is unable to think of the oppositional and the professional as anything but absolutely opposed extremes.

To conceive of intellectuals as professionals is to put critical thought in social context. To put thought in social context is to accuse it of self-interest; that is what social context usually means. But self-interested thought, from the point of view of the ideal, is no longer thought at all. And by the same criterion, it is certainly not critical or radical or adversarial thought. This is the fatal logic of the intellectuals' disappearance: the more intellectuals are seen as grounded in society, the less they are seen as truly critical or oppositional, hence the less they are themselves. The less they are themselves, the more they can only seem to be glimpsed, for the last time, in the act of vanishing.

In principle, this vanishing act should not be credible, least of all to anyone of the left. Leftist theory in all its many varieties assumes that society is not a monolithic whole but a site of dynamic, conflicting groups and forces. Hence a social category like the intellectual can perfectly well be "grounded" in society without losing its "adversarial" potential to further or obstruct social movement. Gramsci's concept of the "organic" intellectual and Alvin Gouldner's theory of the intellectuals as a rising "New Class," to take two examples, assume in their different ways, with Woolf and Gallop, that the intellectual is both grounded and (at least potentially) adversarial at the same time.[17] Why, then, has the narrative of the intellectuals' disappearance had so much resonance on the left as well as the right?

One reason lies in conflicting claims to territory among the left's diverse constituencies – feminists, racial minorities, environmentalists, the white male working class, and so on. In proposing that the species which comprised and virtually defined the public sphere is now extinct, those who tell the end-of-the-intellectual story are clearly defending the rights and privileges of a certain constituency within the public sphere. More precisely, they are trying to retrieve a public voice or position that was once preeminent and unquestioned, but is so no longer. The argument that intellectuals in the independent, public sense no longer exist has also been an argument, in other words, by which the arguer, who remembers the greatness of intellectuals past, shows in so doing that he himself (it almost always is a he) retains a true intellectual's public voice and truly, legitimately speaks for the public. In a paradox worthy of Groucho Marx, he implicitly claims to belong to a category that he is asserting no longer has any members. At the same time, he claims priority over the specialized professionals, feminist academics, and so on, who, he is implying, have usurped its place. In the name of the public, this line of argument has been an attempt to restrict and thereby control the public sphere.

Biassed though it may be in favor of those who claimed to speak for the public before the 1960s, this argument may well carry weight among those who have come of age since then as well. Professionalism, specialization, academic self-enclosure clearly have much to answer for. Their crimes and misdemeanors are especially evident to those who grew up among them, and who would willingly believe therefore that in this respect the past, even the recent past, was somehow superior. The need for critical distance from the present favors apocalyptic narratives like "the-end-of-the-intellectual," even if they oblige us to suspend disbelief in a once-upon-a-time when intellectuals flourished in a state of prelapsarian autonomy and unselfish public concern. Narrow professional self-interest is also more visible than the so-called public interest. Our everyday skepticism predisposes us to believe those who denounce the former, forgetting to inspect their hidden claims (advanced in and by the denunciation itself) to represent the latter. We are less skeptical of rhetoric like the revisionist Groucho-Marxism above, which tries to control entry to an exclusive club by announcing that the club has closed its doors.

Another reason for the appeal of the narrative that leads from the *Luftmensh* to the cultural elite lies in the adjective *cultural*. The new candidates for membership in the intellectuals' once-exclusive club, those associated with identity politics and the so-called "new social movements," have often (though by no means always) staked their

13

claim to speak for the nation in terms of culture, or cultures in the plural. In so doing, they have of course come up against closed-club resistance in the name of a singular, capitalized notion of culture. There has also been resistance that asserts the priority of class over culture. But whether the complaint is that the new professionals have allowed culture to push out real politics or on the contrary that the new professionals have degraded and abandoned culture, in both cases their predecessors *depend* on culture (in the singular, capital C sense) as their founding intellectual and professional rationale.

In Atlas's narrative, the height from which intellectuals have fallen is not always defined as "adversarial" politics. Without seeming to notice, Atlas switches key terms in midstream. Quickly and unrepentantly forgetting politics, he asserts that what truly defines the former greatness and uncompromising purity of the New York intellectuals, what unifies their adversarial and their conservative members (as well as their adversarial and conservative stages), is not after all a commitment to politics, but a commitment to culture. "Everything was judged by the same intransigent standard: it either was art or it wasn't" (53). "What unites the intellectuals of the older generation, both of the left and of the right, is their suspicion of popular culture" (70). "For the old New York intellectuals, high culture was more than a category; it was a belief" (76).[18]

By surreptitiously replacing politics with culture, Atlas offers an implicit solution to the self-contradictoriness of the *Luftmensh*. How can the intellectual be located or grounded in society and at the same time remain an intellectual, that is, remain adversarial? To be adversarial politically is of course to be interested, if not necessarily self-interested. To be adversarial *culturally*, on the other hand, is to transcend both interest and self-interest, and to pass back into that special domain that has been called, since Matthew Arnold, disinterestedness. Culture, art, the aesthetic: these words define a distance from the sordidness of the material, utilitarian, power-ridden world where livings are earned, a distance that is also a possession, however, a stock of capital that the educated can invest. This capital of distanced knowledge aims ultimately, but not practically or immediately, at the transformation of that utilitarian, power-ridden world. It is an adversarial mode of knowledge, but not a confrontational mode of knowledge. It is a knowledge, therefore, which intellectuals who are already distanced from that world can trade on so as to survive in it.[19] Caesar can be rendered his due in the consciousness that there is a realm beyond his, and Caesar can be induced to pay for the discipline that propagates this consciousness. It is no wonder that the self-image of all intellectuals, including those of the left, has been so strangely yet strongly bound up with the terminology of culture – that left intellectuals, who have no time for disinterestedness as a principle of social explanation, have nevertheless so often been a *cultural* left. As suggested by the quotation from Richard Rorty above, the cultural or the aesthetic (for Rorty, the category-shattering sublime as opposed to the merely beautiful) serves as an attempt by intellectuals to reconcile their self-interest as possessors of knowledge with the welfare of society as a whole. (Whether this attempt must or deserves to fail, as Rorty implies, is another question.)

Like the concept of the intellectual, this concept of culture is a nineteenth-century invention. It was elaborated, as Raymond Williams showed in *Culture and Society*, in specific contrast to the industrial division of labor, specialization, and professional work. Again like the concept of the intellectual, however, the concept of culture can no longer stand opposed to professionalism – if it ever could. For if intellectuals are grounded in culture, as the source of their livelihood, they are not alone or unique in this. The same narrative of decline-from-culture that targets the intellectuals also targets those professionals who are taken to represent their fallen, diminished, decadent successors: the teachers of the humanities.

In an article on T.S. Eliot in the *New Yorker*, Cynthia Ozick offers another version of the familiar narrative which presents the professionalization of literary criticism as the Fall of the freelance intellectual from the heights of Culture.[20] In 1929, she writes, Edmund Wilson couldn't stomach Eliot's Anglo-Catholicism.

> Twenty five years later, when the American intellectual center had completed its shift from freelance literary work like Wilson's – and Eliot's – to the near-uniformity of university English departments, almost no one in these departments would dare to voice such unfastidious thoughts about Eliot. (121)

According to Ozick, Eliot's repulsive opinions, including his anti-Semitism, mattered to the independent intellectual whose only allegiance was to culture, but they will not matter, indeed will disappear from view entirely, in the technocratic emptiness of "English lit."

No sooner has Ozick announced this Fall, however, than she announces another one. Commemorations of the Eliot centenary in

1988, she observes, had the "subdued and bloodless" feeling of "a slightly tedious reunion of aging alumni." She herself writes as an alumna, recollecting the "exultation" of her own youth, or that of "anyone who was an undergraduate in the forties or the fifties (or possibly even in the first years of the sixties)" (119). She recollects these undergraduate memories against an academic climate for which, as she declares: "High art is dead. The passion for inheritance is dead. Tradition is equated with obscurantism. The wall that divided serious high art from the popular arts is breached; anything can count as 'text'" (152). "Undoing the canon is the work of a later time – of our own, in fact, when universal assent to a central cultural standard is almost everywhere decried. For the moderns, and for Eliot especially, the denial of permanently agreed-on masterworks – what Matthew Arnold called 'touchstones,' a notion now obsolete beyond imagining – would have been unthinkable" (120). "Elitism ruled," she remembers.

> [I]n some respects, I admit to being arrested in the Age of Eliot, a permanent member of it, unregenerate. The etiolation of art seems to me to be a major loss. I continue to suppose that some texts are worthier than other texts. The same holds for the diminishment of history and tradition: not to incorporate into an educable mind the origins and unifying principles of one's own civilization strikes me as a kind of cultural autolobotomy". (124)

Ozick's narrative of the Fall from the Age of Eliot cannot be reconciled with her earlier narrative of the Fall into the University. In the first sequence, which runs from Edmund Wilson in 1929 to the academy in the 1950s, culture is apparently betrayed by professionalization. The implication is that from the 1950s on Eliot's anti-Semitism could slip by without comment precisely because culture had been subordinated to the bloodless technical machinery of academic criticism. In the second sequence, however, which runs from academic criticism in the 1950s to academic criticism today, the subordination of culture in the 1980s is clearly contrasted with an earlier state of affairs, also academic – Ozick's own undergraduate years – in which culture had *not* been subordinated: when there *were* "permanently agreed-on masterworks," when "literature could genuinely *reign*" (120). Once again, which is it? Did culture disappear when it passed into the academy in the 1950s, or on the contrary did it "reign" in the academy of the 1950s, thanks to Eliot's influence there, only to disappear into

16

the "secularism" and "nihilism" of the theoretical, multicultural 1980s?

How is it that culture, which was supposedly betrayed and abandoned when intellectuals became professionals, now crops up again *inside* professionalism, if only in order to mark the summit from which a new descent can begin? Grounding in culture is apparently something that the intellectual and the professional have in common. And this is not hard to understand. For without culture, early professional humanists would have been hard pressed to explain why society should pay their salaries. Not by coincidence, one means of making this case to society – one might call it a case for professional legitimation – has been the narrative of cultural decline, much as we find it in Ozick and, for that matter, in T.S. Eliot. "The culture of professionalism," Burton Bledstein remarks, "tended to cultivate an atmosphere of constant crisis – emergency – in which practitioners both created work for themselves and reinforced their authority by intimidating their clients."[21] This sense of crisis was provided by T.S. Eliot's vision of history as decay and degeneration and of the present as an urban-industrial wasteland where we totter on an unnameable brink, desperately shoring up history's ruins with the fragments of distant cultural monuments. Eliot's success in the academy did not depend only on a formulation of apocalyptic pessimism that happened to strike the right chord in the disillusioned post-war generation; it was a useful means of letting society know what it needed (culture) and who could provide it (those who could make sense of the footnotes to *The Waste Land*). For would-be professionals of the first half of the century, struggling to displace the gentleman-scholar's tasteful, unhurried, independently funded appreciation of the finer things, Eliot's despair was enabling and invigorating. It declared in effect that their more rigorous and earnest professional activities were urgently required. If the society of the present is fallen and degenerate, then it hungers, however unknowingly, for acquaintance with values, ideals, and achievements that by definition are not accessible within it – except to a corps of experts specialized in retrieving such knowledge from the culture of the past.

Eliot's specific historical thesis of a "dissociation of sensibility" around the time of Cromwell is no longer taken very seriously by literary critics. But indifference to his explicit catastrophism and even to Eliot himself coexists quite comfortably with a story of culture's decline into a degraded present, a story that Eliot's catastrophist narrative legitimates. Once this reverential attitude toward the cultural heritage had established itself within the unconscious tact of the profession, or once the profession had established itself around it, humanists could take their pick among any number of competing hypotheses about particular historical events, or even choose to do without one. When Leavis set out to professionalize British literary studies, Lawrence served his purpose as well as Eliot: it mattered little finally *which* tradition had been lost, a Catholic hierarchical order or the blood instincts of the English countryside, so long as the loss of *some* tradition set its elite salvagers apart from their benighted, traditionless contemporaries. And the same role could be played, obviously enough, by leftist visions of pre-capitalist "organic community," whether distanced in time or (as in Third Worldist pastoral) in space.[22] I will have more to say below about the awkward adjustments of literary professionalism, over the last fifteen years, to the study of living, conflictual, popular cultures of the here-and-now, whether Third or First World, and about the professional continuities overriding the apparent chasm between Culture and cultures.

Despite these recent challenges, the story of the Fall from Culture still retains considerable force as a legitimating myth for the professionalized study of vernacular literature. Yet it has also always been shaky, and even self-contradictory. For if culture is defined as the wholeness of a valued past, set against the fragmentations of the modern city and the division of labor, then a professional discipline that takes culture as its object must seem to have fallen from culture, to be untrue to culture, to be in a state of contradiction, from the very moment it *becomes* a discipline, that is, one discipline among others within a division of intellectual labor.[23] This is one major reason why academic critics have tended to tell stories about themselves that very much resemble Ozick's and Atlas's "end-of-the-intellectual" story about them. In such stories, with some combination of pride and self-loathing, academics see themselves as fallen from culture. To see yourself as fallen from culture turns out to be a very effective way of arguing that in fact you represent culture.

A recent contributor to the official journal of the Modern Language Association, *PMLA*, describes this as

a time when we are routinely, and perhaps deservedly, vilified – both from within our own ranks and from outside academe – as being obsessed with "accreditation lists" and self-promotion and self-validation and other vapid manifestations of cynicism, opportunism, and status anxiety. About the best we can manage, it seems, is to shrug off such criticism as "anti-intellectualism" (or, worse still, as "journalism") and get on with our portfolio building and our networking.[24]

In the name of what values does this insider make his denunciation? One can reconstruct them from his lexicon of derision. Terms like portfolio, networking, status, and self-promotion belong to the world of consumer capitalism; their other side is thus culture – culture, that is, conceived in the tradition of Arnold and Emerson as the antithesis of commercialism, profit, and individual or collective self-interest. It is easy to miss how very self-interested such denunciations are. But consider the narrative expansion of the same premise in Brian McCrae's *Addison and Steele are Dead: The English Department, Its Canon, and the Professionalization of Literary Criticism* (1990). "To achieve autonomy, professional groups forfeit their public role, their influence outside the professional group," McCrae writes, and this is the cause of his complaint about the present: "the a-public nature of English department criticism." English department criticism is no longer public, hence no longer truly cultural, for commitment to the social whole over any part has always been essential to culture. In offering this narrative, however, McCrae himself is standing in for culture and the public. In his account the noble height from which we have now fallen is defined by Addison and Steele: "Addison and Steele were public men."[25] It is his critique of the present that bestows value upon the eighteenth-century object of his research; it is because their public-ness is missing from the present that it is now useful, and not mere antiquarianism, to recall them. And, in a piece of self-promotion that is noticeable if also normal and blameless, the researcher claims the value bestowed on the object of research. If Addison and Steele were once "public men," and if public-ness has now slipped away from their successors, then the critic who remembers and represents Addison and Steele today is also in some sense a public man, and this is a very important thing to be. Public-ness is transmitted from the object criticized to the professional critic, who claims implicitly to be serving or representing the public even as he also claims that his own profession has become "a-public." At the same time, he suggests that the profession cannot after all be entirely "a-public," since he belongs to it.

This self-interested rhetorical turn might be described as professional self-legitimation. Self-legitimation at the cost of self-flagellation: the formula is not unprecedented. In his analysis of the Puritan jeremiad, Sacvan Bercovitch suggests something quite similar. The jeremiad, Bercovitch argues, was a form of self-critique whose denunciatory fervor was directly proportional to the high sense of mission from which the increasingly worldly Puritans were declared to have fallen, a mission which the denunciations had the effect of re-affirming.[26] In much the same way, the concept of culture has defined a sense of mission from which professionals and intellectuals alike are held to fall away by the very exercise of their competence, by the inescapable activity of assuring their worldly survival. The traces of their continuing existence – publications, conferences, letters of evaluation – constitute evidence of their apostasy. And yet the narrative which tells them they are fallen, translating material survival into a story of gradual spiritual self-negation, is also a procedure that helps them survive in the world. It is a way of giving oneself an enviable sense of meaning and purpose: a vocation.

Professionals who attack their professions, assuming they will thus be credited with the most altruistic motives, are perhaps less motivated to see the professional self-interest and solidarity implicit in their attacks than an outsider would be. My own perspective on this phenomenon, which is not that of an outsider, is of course open to interrogation. But it finds some support in at least one of the *New York Times Magazine*'s pieces on contemporary intellectuals. When the *Times Magazine* ran its profile of Richard Rorty, it made a big point of his contention "that philosophy, as traditionally conceived, is an empty and obsolete game that might as well be called off".[27] If Cornel West, among others, could praise Rorty for his "anti-professionalism," however, the *Times Magazine* reporter, T.S. Klepp, was not taken in by the professional modesty of the argument that "philosophers have no special knowledge" (117).[28] For Klepp, Rorty's professional rhetoric is only as paradoxical as the jeremiad, which is to say that it is ultimately functional: "His work is devoted to ending the stalemated, self-enclosed professionalism of academic philosophy but often seems so absorbed in it as to run the risk of being absorbed *by* it" (117). In a society that never cared much about philosophy to begin with, as the article notes, to knock philosophy can be a way of rescuing it. "Rorty's efforts to end professional philosophy can keep professional philosophy going for years . . . he has reinvigorated philosophy by writing its epitaph" (124).

The *New York Times Magazine* may well be right about professional philosophy. Rorty's proposal that "philosophers should evolve into unspecialized culture critics with a striking resemblance

20

to New York intellectuals" (117), that is, into more public figures, is a daring gambit; it sacrifices a good deal of professional autonomy, and makes most professional philosophers cringe. But in the longer term it might well advance philosophy's interests – its professional interests. As I will be arguing throughout this book, this sort of effect is not confined to philosophy, or to critics of a discipline who also maintain a residual loyalty to it. It is how disciplines work, how they manufacture vocations for themselves, how they shift from one vocation or paradigm to another.

They do so, as I will also be arguing – this is why it is appropriate that this point should emerge in the *New York Times Magazine* – in speaking in public, of the public, to the public, and to some extent for the public. The jeremiad effect is also evidence that disciplines are never as isolated, specialized, autonomous or private as they think or fear they are. Rorty's public argument that his profession is socially useless is not, after all, antiprofessional. In trying to renegotiate the profession's relation to the public, it leads his fellow philosophers toward greater social usefulness, toward a more public role, and thus toward various professional rewards. Like McCrae's argument that his profession is "a-public," it is also an oblique assertion that professions *are* public, and can be so in different ways and to different degrees. Again like McCrae, Rorty implicitly offers himself as an example of that social usefulness or public meaning which he says is missing from philosophy. It is by virtue of this multifaceted public-ness (which becomes still more complex when one considers his polemic about the public and the private) that Rorty also becomes an example of what I mean by secular vocations.

There are several understandings of the phrase secular vocations that I am anxious to avoid. Coming upon words like "mission" and "vocation" in a title, the reader may experience a certain sinking of the heart. The author is going to make a pitch, you feel; you are going to hear the sort of high, pious, cloudy language at which it is impolite to yawn, but from which you can expect nothing solid. As when Kenneth Burke writes, for example: "To live is to have a vocation."[29] Or when Benjamin Barber answers his question without any hesitation: "Does the university have a civic mission? Of course, for it *is* a civic mission. . ." (emphasis added).[30] If everyone always already has a vocation, if having one is the same as being what you are, then having or being one cannot be a topic worthy of much further discussion. In that case a vocation would be as inconsequential a thing as, in Henry Kissinger's view, the external and absolute standard of truth or morality to which intellectuals should always be faithful: "Intellectuals should make themselves heard by putting forward their perceptions of what is right. Then let the politicians worry about what is possible."[31] Telling intellectuals to hold to an ethical standard, however impractical that standard may be, can only serve to distract attention from the practical engagement with worldly power that Kissinger himself as an intellectual so notoriously abused, and that other intellectuals are thus encouraged to disregard or abuse as well. Intellectuals are invited to give Sunday sermons that politicians, along with everyone else, are free to ignore.

The contrary understanding of vocation, which is probably more widespread, suggests not that everyone has one, but that nearly no one does. Ideals so peremptory and absolute have passed out of the world, one frequently hears; they have been replaced with the meaner, mercenary motives of a corrupt professionalism. James Atlas, in his *Times Magazine* article, quotes Hilton Kramer, founding editor of *The New Criterion*: "The counterculture discredited the intellectual vocation" (52). There can be no calling without a Caller. Without belief in truth or justice in some transcendent sense, the argument goes, there can be no vocation, and belief in these forms of transcendence has collapsed, eaten away by philosophical relativism and by the routine arbitrariness of a professionalized society. Individual belief has given way to institutional opinion.

This situation is usually described only to be deplored. In a sweeping version of the same narrative, tracing the evil back beyond 1960s counterculture to the Enlightenment, Paul Johnson argues, for example, that "secular" intellectuals have substituted their own illegitimate authority for the transcendent truth of "revealed religion" and "the collective wisdom of the past, the legacy of tradition." His book begins as follows:

> Over the past two hundred years the influence of intellectuals has grown steadily. Indeed, the rise of the secular intellectual has been a key factor in shaping the modern world.... With the decline of clerical power in the eighteenth century, a new kind of mentor emerged to fill the vacuum and capture the ear of society. The secular intellectual might be deist, sceptic or atheist. But he was just as ready as any pontiff or presbyter to tell mankind how to conduct its affairs.[32]

More rarely, the lack of transcendent foundation has been welcomed, as when Rorty urges, in the name of disbelief in transcendence, that intellectuals should dispense with grounding of any sort. If culture is the wrong way for intellectuals to argue that what they do is in the public interest, there is no right way. Rorty describes the search for legitimation as "scratching where it does not itch." The last words of his essay warn society against "bothering to ground itself."[33] In this case, as in many others, Rorty's version of pragmatism seems to consolidate the "critique of metaphysics" with solid common sense. In the vocabulary of pragmatism, "legitimation is but a phantasm of an interpretational authority sustained by little more than layers of fiction, desire, and exhibitionistic theatricality."[34] In another vocabulary, all attempts at grounding are self-interested fictions, imaginary authorities set up in order to win some advantage for oneself over others. Intellectuals, philosophers, non-experts: we must all admit we are equally, democratically groundless.

I am not interested in deploring or denying the end of transcendence, but I am not convinced that this leaves no alternative other than welcoming it. One can show, for example, that the issue is less that of taking sides for or against philosophical absolutes than of understanding a set of ongoing social practices. Consider the self-contradiction lurking in the current attack on "political correctness" in the humanities, which associates supposed disrespect for Western civilization with a relativistic loss of standards. Whatever else PC may be, to the extent that it is real, it involves not the neglect of all standards but the creation and imposition of new standards – standards regulating speech about race and sex, the scope or inclusiveness of curricula, and so on. Far from institutionalizing relativism, professional scholars have been in the business of fashioning and refashioning standards, norms, values. As of course they have been in the business of producing individuals who hold ethical, epistemological, aesthetic, and political beliefs, and whose attachment to their work is inextricable from those beliefs – in short, who have a sense of vocation.

This is to say that no distinction between vocation and profession can be sustained. Donald Davie, speaking of Stanley Fish, remarks: "for professionalism in literary studies he has a respectful tenderness that I cannot share, preferring for my own part the less easily institutionalized concept of 'vocation,' of 'calling.'"[35] In explanation, Davie says: "I was educated by men and women who in their own time and place were 'mavericks'" (43). The problem here, as with culture, is how to maintain the rarity of the valued term. For what was supposed to be rare and transcendent, what was supposed therefore to resist institutionalization, namely culture or the "maverick," is precisely what was institutionalized. It is because culture and "the maverick" have been institutionalized and generalized that, as our intellectual instincts tell us, the outside is the only place to be. Thanks to culture, the disciplinary object which provided the ground or rationale for criticism's activities, every literary critic could be a permanent outsider. Criticism itself as an institution became a *bande à part*. It can hardly be a coincidence that so many of its individual members should come to share the "less easily institutionalized concept of 'vocation,' of 'calling.'" Describing "a vocation that will always to some degree resist translation into the language of the unconverted," Wayne Booth writes: "at some point in our lives each of us caught the bug of self-driven learning, and we want to spread it to the whole world."[36] Unfortunately, the collective phenomenon (everyone "catches" the same "bug") cannot be reduced to unique individual motive or ideal ("self-driven"). It is because it is anti-institutional that vocation is so well institutionalized.

When I speak of vocations, therefore, I do not speak of pure, individual ideals set apart from impure institutions and collectivities. And when I speak of *secular* vocations, I do not mean vocations that audaciously set themselves up in the place vacated by divinity and that thus exercise or claim a comparable authority. It is true, of course, that the modern concept of vocation has its roots in theology, and it is true that professionalism has taken over some of its associations with religious or charismatic authority.[37] Such associations are sometimes erroneously celebrated,[38] but more often are used, still more erroneously, to discredit professionalism as such. Philosopher Bruce Wilshire speaks characteristically of professions as "archaic initiational and purificational practices which establish the identity of group and individual member through exclusion of the unwashed and uncertified, for example, undergraduate students".[39] Yet the common view of professions as unwarranted secular replacements for religious authority is an error both about the past and about the present. As Fredric Jameson points out, when "the twin affranchisement from the bonds of tradition that is the result of the French Revolution and the development of the market system" permitted people "to hold their professional enterprises at arm's length," the "'Romantic lie' of ... inborn vocations" vanished forever. From this moment on, "to wonder what to do with your life is already to commit yourself in advance to a certain ontological dissatisfaction with any of the ultimate possibilities."[40] In Jameson's account, vocational authority is

24

always provisional, incomplete, and open to expressions of discontent. From a sociological perspective, Anthony Giddens says much the same thing. Giddens offers another useful corrective to the cliché by which secularization, or professionalization seen as a variant of it, is a simple substitution of one authority for another, without change in the nature or extent of the authority.

> The expert, or the specialist, is quite different from the "authority," where this term is understood in the traditional sense. Except where authority is sanctioned by the use of force (the "authorities" of the state and legal authority), it becomes essentially equivalent to specialist advice. There are no authorities which span the diverse fields within which expertise is claimed – another way of repeating the point that everyone in modern systems is a lay person in virtually all aspects of social activity.[41]

"I do not think that writing history is in any sense a sanctified vocation," writes historiographer Peter Novick, "or that it deserves to be spoken about reverently."[42] The first proposition seems incontrovertible, the second much less so. Reverence, or something very like it, is as necessary to those who want to change the world as to those who worship at its established altars. Professional historians, by which I mean both certain individuals and a professional aggregate, have had much to do of late with explaining how the world has been and must still be changed; surely they are deserving, therefore, of some of that reverence. But even if they weren't, my point would remain: the point that arguments like the (brief and hasty) one in the previous sentence, arguments about the public value of work in a particular profession or discipline, are ways of checking, disputing, recalculating the degree of reverence that is deserved. However inadequately, they help to hold it publicly accountable, and thus offer it the possibility of legitimacy. This is an instance of secular vocation: not an unearned sense of self-importance, not an unquestioned or unaccountable authority, but that part of professional discourse which appeals to (and helps refashion) public values in its effort to justify (and refashion) professional practice.

If there is no ultimate foundation or grounding, the activity of seeking after and contending over groundings and foundations does not therefore grind to a halt. In Claude Lefort's words,

> modern democracy invites us to replace the notion of a regime governed by laws, of a legitimate power, by the notion of a regime founded upon the legitimacy of a debate as to what is legitimate and what is

illegitimate – a debate which is necessarily without any guarantor and without any end.[43]

The debate over legitimations does not stop with the recognition that the space of an ultimate judge must remain empty. On the contrary, it becomes more self-conscious, more troubled, more dramatic. It does not become less important; it becomes more interesting. The persistence of this debate within one's work is what is meant here by vocations that are secular.

This is not just a question for a few temporarily embattled professions and disciplines. As former Vice President Quayle's speech will remind us, the "cultural elite" is both a real political target and a metaphor for all that has gone wrong with America in the past generation. (A similar correspondence might be observed between varying interpretations of "the intellectual" since the Dreyfus Affair and varying narratives about the fate of Europe.) When the *Sunday Times Magazine* reports on the new academic radicals, there is almost always some amused listing of their expensive possessions: a Cadillac, a Jaguar, a swimming pool in the backyard, a fashionable wardrobe. The news, presumably, is that they have abandoned a monastic ideal of disinterested asceticism – in brief, the vocation of culture – for professionalism in the mercenary, entrepreneurial sense. But why should this be newsworthy, one may ask, to a general public composed in large part of people who believe in the entrepreneurial system and who have no overriding commitment to the ideal of culture? Part of the answer is that the Fall from Culture is also an exemplary tale of upward mobility and ethnic assimilation. In the same *Sunday Times Magazine* stories, there is also a peculiarly pointed attention to class. Witness the treatment of Miltonist Stanley Fish and Marxist Frank Lentricchia. James Atlas, in another essay, quotes Fish: " 'You come from a background where there were no books, the son and daughter of immigrants,' he says. In such a world Milton was a first name." And then he describes Lentricchia: "Frank Lentricchia has a swimming pool in his backyard. In his work, though, he writes openly and with unashamed ardor, in the autobiographical fashion of the day, about his Italian-American origins, his grandfather in Utica, his working-class Dad."[44]

The word "though" in this sentence sets off Lentricchia's ethnic, working-class background against his swimming pool, symbol of professional prosperity. We are apparently expected to feel that his prosperity conflicts with his background, or betrays it, in much the same way that the professional status of the academic radicals is seen as conflicting with or betraying "Western Civilization" (in the view of the right) and "60s activism" (in the view of the left). In the public eye, it is as if the betrayal of one were the betrayal of all three. And as if all three – ethnic, working-class culture, Western civilization, and 1960s activism – were betrayed by a process that one might be tempted to call "Americanization" – upward mobility, assimilation, the acquisition of professional respect and the consumer tokens of success.

This composite public view is confused, of course. Ethnic, working-class culture is not, for example, what the Hilton Kramers mean by "Western Civilization," and a story of the Fall into professionalism that begins in three such different Edens cannot really be describing the same postlapsarian world, or worldliness. But this confusion also has a valuable political edge. It hints that something is wrong with "Americanization," that something may have been right in 1960s activism, that perhaps there is some deeper connection after all between Culture capital C and cultures in the uncapitalized, plural sense. And that the provisional terminus of the narrative in professionalism might not be quite as bad as it seems.

It is because this narrative is rich and politically ambiguous, rather than simply confused, because it is a critique of what has been happening to America as well as a collective *Bildungsroman* of the academic radicals, that it deserves to be fought over. One needs to say, for example, that Frank Lentricchia's working-class, Italian-American origins are not necessarily betrayed or abandoned when he becomes what he becomes. The "though" in that sentence can be read differently; though Lentricchia has a swimming pool now, it suggests, in his success he remains faithful to where he came from. That is, his "work" remains faithful. And not as an exception, but as one instance of a new rule: "the autobiographical fashion of the day" apparently *prizes* critical writing that returns to ethnic, working-class, and gender experience. If we can see this, then we can see the further possibility that the professional success was not so much a dramatic break with an ethnic, working-class past as an intellectual putting to use of that past, the establishment of a series of unprecedented *continuities* between the university teaching of culture and the culture of ethnic, working-class people. One can even see that the professional success may have come not despite but *because* of the past: because what had not been seen as culture at all – cars, baseball, love-letters, and Italian grandfathers – found or made a place for itself, alongside Frost and Milton, within the professional

27

teaching of culture, thereby giving new energy to that teaching. But if we are to see ethnic, working-class culture as a source of energy and value inside professionalism rather than a hostile force outside it, just as professionalism itself is a part of America's political and cultural destiny rather than a detour from it, then we will have to start thinking about professionalism in a different way.

1

The Ambiguities of
The Professionals

Time and again the experts assigned to an environmental review were none other than those associated with the plant owner or operator – technical guns for hire, with their target the community most directly affected by the facility under review.[1]

1. "A few daring men, specialists . . ."

In Richard Brooks's 1966 Western *The Professionals*, four men are hired by a rich American businessman to rescue his Mexican-born wife, who has been kidnapped by the leader of a Mexican revolutionary band and imprisoned in their desert stronghold. The businessman, Grant (played by Ralph Bellamy), tells them that a battalion could spend a month trying to get her out and still not succeed. But "a few daring men, specialists," just might pull off the rescue.

These four men do not of course belong to the same social class as doctors and lawyers. In what sense, then, are they, as the title tells us, "professionals"? First of all, they are professionals in that they are – that is, have just become, by being hired – mercenaries. They fight for money, rather than for some other motive of their own, like revenge, bloodlust, justice, patriotism, or conscription. Their proficiency is for sale, and it is the buyer/employer who provides the task or goal. No pre-given goals or motives of their own are pertinent other than making a living.

Secondly, they are professionals in that each is a highly competent specialist in some skill necessary to their joint operation. The leader, Fardan, played by Lee Marvin, is a weapons and tactics instructor, a seasoned veteran of the Cuban and Philippine campaigns. The one black man, Jacob Sharp (played by Woody Strode), is a scout and tracker who is also handy with the longbow. The Robert Ryan character, Ehrengard, is a wrangler and packmaster whose know-how

29

with horses is meant to get them across a hundred miles of desert. Dolworth, the Burt Lancaster figure, is an explosives expert.

Beginning with the opening sequence, when each is briefly seen exercising his speciality (in Lancaster's case, leaving a woman's bedroom by the window) before they join up as a team, the audience is treated to the familiar thrills of esoteric and unconditional competence. The varied skills of the four professionals solve the filmmaker's aesthetic problem of differentiating the characters, giving each an identity that permits the spectator to "identify." And this identification takes the form of absolute trust in absolute power. Professional specialization marks a comforting site where the spectator's confidence in the character's performance can be total.

Is this because the narrower the activity, we believe, the greater the possibility of mastering it? More likely, it is because the specialized characters join together to form a team, a whole greater than the sum of its parts, and it is this whole, rather than any of the parts, that is most strongly identified with. Their heroics are harmonized; their individual expertises are vividly individualized only in order to be as vividly assimilated to a shared goal. Here then is a third sense of professionalism: cooperation in a common effort which ensures collective efficiency. Someone will have just the right skill for any contingency, any weakness in one will be compensated by another. And, in so doing, this cooperation forms the image of an ideal (all-male) social collectivity. Membership in the collectivity is defined by a partial, peculiar transcendence of self. Individuality persists, but only in the form of specialization; any self-interest at odds with or separable from the common interest of the group is effaced. In the film, the result seems to be a transcendence of the individual life itself. The unprofessional collectivity of the Mexican revolutionaries supplies the decisive contrast. Like the band of four (and unlike Grant's hypothetical "battalion"), the Mexicans are unofficial; like the battalion and unlike the band of four, they are not a select few. Numerous and dedicated but unspecialized and therefore disorderly, they seem to derive such organization as they have from their charismatic leader alone. Infinitely replaceable by others, therefore, their bodies fall without leaving any noticeable gaps. The specialization of the "handpicked" professionals, on the other hand, seems by a strange economy to account for the fact that all emerge at the end alive. Professionalism confers on them a version of immortality.

The complementary pair of teamwork and specialization combines with the absence of prior personal motive to produce the definitive and the most problematic aspect of professionalism as articulated by the film. Since the professionals themselves do not define the ultimate purpose of their enterprise nor determine its value, and since the subordination of individual preference to the goals of the group is a precondition of its efficiency, there seems to be little or no room within professional life for ethical choice or even self-consciousness. Ethical responsibility, and even more so political responsibility, is assumed to be located elsewhere, at some higher level (the motives of the employer or of society as a whole) where the professional need not, should not, and perhaps cannot allow himself to be distracted by it. As far as the professional is concerned, ethics are to be provisionally suspended for the duration of the job. Or so it seems. As we will see, the problem is in fact staged at the very heart of the film.

The professionalism of *The Professionals* offers distinct and proven pleasures – distinct from those of mere gun-slinging, and proven at the box-office. The same pleasures are offered by the many Western and adventure genre films it resembles (from the same period, for example, *The Magnificent Seven*, *The Wild Bunch*, *The Dirty Dozen*, and *The Green Berets*, and since then the formula has not disappeared). These pleasures suggest that, for all our intermittent bitterness against elites, experts, expertise, and so on, American culture also feels a helpless fascination for professionalism in these senses. We may honor individualism and rugged self-reliance, or well-roundedness and humane cultivation, or an ethical benevolence that treats people as ends rather than means, but these familiar virtues are often upstaged in our entertainment and on our pulses by specialized technical know-how, synchronized teamwork, and a neutral detachment from personal motive on the one hand, from moral questions and problems of ultimate purpose, on the other. In describing the force of these images, it is hard not to import the vocabulary of religion. Whether the power of the professional seems to emanate from specialized narrowness or, alternatively, from ethical abdication (mimed in the spectator's own invitation, whether accepted or not, to abandon critical consciousness), it is a power that allows us to relax in unquestioning, quasi-religious belief. Through it the supernatural, even the divine, seems to manifest itself within the everyday world of work. The four horsemen are apocalyptic both in the sense that they beget a bloodbath and, more significantly, in that they seem to be emissaries of the divine on earth, a revelation of where we do our weekday worship.[2]

The rise of the professional virtues to this state of reverence can be measured by comparing two bits of ethical common sense: (1) " 'Tis no sin for a man to labour in his vocation"; and (2) "It's no sin to win." The first quotation, spoken with self-conscious irony by Falstaff in Shakespeare's *Henry IV Part I* (1598), mocks a fundamental premise of Protestantism's emerging work ethic, which drew all sorts of unscrupulous and self-interested activities (like Falstaff's "vocation" as highwayman) under its protective umbrella. The second quotation, spoken with chilling sincerity by a spectator interviewed on television after what was hailed as a US victory in the 1984 Olympics, restates the work ethic, now extended into the domain of play and leisure, not in order to satirize it but in order to celebrate it, while defending it against a lingering guilty conscience. There was of course an excellent reason why the US victory might seem stolen, if not sinful. Athletes from the former Eastern bloc who normally took a hefty percentage of gold medals were absent in 1984 in protest at the US invasion of Grenada. It is just such complicating circumstances that the work ethic rules out of bounds, as "external" to the task or contest itself. Therein lies much of its power.

Together, the two quotations retell the story that Max Weber lays out in *The Protestant Ethic and the Spirit of Capitalism*: the story of a theologically supported rise in the valuation of work, accompanying and enabling the rise of capitalism. According to Weber, the idea of self-interested work as a "calling" or "vocation" first borrows its power and moral sanction from divine providence in its Protestant interpretation. Then it progressively jettisons the guilt-producing consideration of ends, purposes, and sanctions, religious or even secular. Thus work becomes an end in itself, the self-justifying pursuit of worldly prosperity for its own sake: both an ethic and the end of ethics.[3]

This cultural curve is also a story of differential power. Weber's analysis of how capitalist acquisitiveness has draped itself in the sanctified robes of the Protestant calling is primarily concerned with the psychic cost to the capitalist class itself, but of course the cost does not stop there. In the early nineteenth century, as E.P. Thompson shows in *The Making of the English Working Class*, labor became the slogan which the rising middle class used to unite diverse opposing forces under its own leadership. Marching under this banner, the hard-working bourgeois could claim to represent all "working men" in a common struggle against the idle, indolent, parasitic aristocracy.[4] But beginning with nineteenth-century observers like William Morris, it became possible to see and say that this claim merely masked control by the owners of capital (whether hard-working or not) over the labor of those who possessed only labor. And in this century it has become possible and indeed necessary to say that this masking is not restricted to capitalism. Feminists have pointed out the masculinist bias implicit in the idealizing of production under any social system that accepts a gendered division of labor.[5] The first person interviewed in Studs Terkel's *Working* (1972), a steel worker, describes in a pungently disabused phrase the enthusiasm for work shared by middle-class radicals and socialist state ideologists alike: "singing to tractors." "It's the intellectuals' utopia," he says, "not mine."[6]

In short, the sanctification of work has been exposed as an ideology in the simplest and most negative sense of the word: as a way of spurring on the less privileged to sober, conscientious industry for the greater profit of others.[7] If professionalism is not identical to this ideology, it certainly overlaps with it. In *The Professionals*, it is no accident that the language of professionalism should be used flatteringly by the tycoon, Grant, as he rattles off the CVs of the mercenaries. Among other things, professionalism is a way in which the Grants of the world get people to do their dirty work for them: it offers measured amounts of admiration and autonomy, sometimes but not always accompanied by relatively large amounts of money, in exchange for the unconditional use of the other's skill, the complete surrender to the employer of the employee's control over the ends to which that skill will be used.

It also has more recent and more subtle ideological functions. Unlike certain other forms of work, professionalism casts off from the Enlightenment mooring of production (mixing one's labor with nature), drifting into the dark relativity of a contemporary society based on nothing more solid than consumption, service, information. It offers what support it can when older authorities fail. On the other hand, it also provides our newly relativized social authorities with an epistemological foundation. Thanks to a supposedly direct, unmediated relation to the object or substance of his expertise, which is either nature (the human body for the doctor) or second nature (the body of laws for the lawyer, the reigning paradigm of medical science for the doctor), the expert is the one, perhaps now the only one, who is supposed to know. At the same time, professionalism makes epistemological and social authority seem, by means of education, democratically accessible to all, at least potentially. It appears to reconcile relativism with certainty, actual hierarchy with hypothetical democracy – above all, unrestrained self-interest with the general, collective welfare. Dressing up unequal power and profit in the disguise of impersonal standards, neutral competence, and technical efficiency, and offering to the already privileged holders of a select range of occupations the additional luxury of a clear conscience, professionalism legitimates the existing social order.

To call professionalism an ideology is not, however, to imply that it has always served the interests of the existing social order faithfully and well, or even that those are the only interests it has served. The rhyme in "it's no sin to win," which continues to accent the very moral perspective (winning as sinning) that it also tries to deny, offers one small suggestion that professionalism's replacement of morality with efficiency is not as unalloyed or unambiguous as I have just made it seem. Other suggestions are present in the different meanings of the term "professional" itself. On the one hand, the professional is distinguished from the "amateur" by the fact that she or he earns a livelihood by the given activity. This gives "professional" negative connotations of self-interested, mercenary motive as opposed to the desirable alternative – historically based on and limited to the leisure of certain social classes – of disinterested love of the activity or subject in and for itself. On the other hand, professions are often distinguished from *other* ways of earning one's livelihood – that is, from "occupation" or "trade" or "employment" in general – as possessing a superior degree of learning or skill and/or public utility and also, whether for these reasons or not, a superior social prestige. It is this distinction, and specifically the element of education, that introduces the antithetical sense of professional as, paradoxically, *dis*interested. Education also suggests a close association with "theory," which in fact is where the term comes from. The original sense of "profession" was a declaration of belief made upon entry into holy orders; to enter into membership was to announce shared theory. If what discriminates professions from other crafts and occupations is the necessary possession of theory, associated with a potentiality (even if unrealized) for the overcoming of self-interest – though like all other criteria, this one remains controversial – then a door opens in professionalism for a scrutiny of values and ends.

I will be coming to further ambiguities shortly, and will be returning to them throughout this book. Indeed, there would be no book without them. My aim here is a historical one: to place the recent history of intellectuals, in particular those of my own profession, in the general context of professionalism, exposing and evaluating professionalism's ideological influence in shaping how and why critics and other intellectuals have been doing what we do. But in speaking of its ideological functions, I cannot claim to stand outside those functions. Whatever my own desires, I continue to speak as a professional both in ways that are visible to me (a certain vocabulary, syntax, tone of voice) and in others, I am willing to believe, that are not visible to me. And you, reader, are most probably in the same boat. How many of us are willing to relinquish the use of the adjective "unprofessional" for work or behavior (usually other people's) that doesn't rise to our standards? Few of the people likely to be turning these pages can be confident, I imagine, that the language, values, habits of thought and judgment, and pleasures of their working and even non-working lives – like the pleasures of viewing *The Professionals* – stand entirely or even predominantly apart from professional ideology. Yet I can offer, and you can receive, a critique of professionalism – a critique both offered and received, that is, from *within* professionalism. It is hard to avoid the conclusion that the ideology of professionalism is not single, unitary, and monolithic, but interestingly self-divided and ambiguous.

My own interest in exposing these ambiguities is anything but selfless. It is only if the ideology of professionalism is understood to leave room for self-scrutiny and contestation, or even to produce them, that the enterprise of understanding professionalism from the inside can avoid blatant self-contradiction. But to say this is not of course to prove to anyone's satisfaction that such room actually exists. The demonstration remains to be made.

2. "Code of the profession?"

In 1966, the same year *The Professionals* came out, the American Association of University Professors adopted the following statement on professional ethics:

> The professor, guided by a deep conviction of the worth and dignity of the advancement of knowledge, recognizes the special responsibilities placed upon him. His primary responsibility to his subject is to seek and to state the truth as he sees it.... He accepts his share of faculty responsibilities for the governance of his institution.... He determines the amount and character of the work he does outside his institution with due regard to his paramount responsibilities within it.... As a

member of his community, the professor has the rights and obligations of any citizen. He measures the urgency of these obligations in the light of his responsibilities to his subject, to his students, to his profession, and to his institution.[8]

These sentences offer little evidence of what they seem to assume – that university professors are more capable than mercenaries of standing outside their own profession and observing professionalism from the perspective of society as a whole. The statement acknowledges that professors, like other citizens, have responsibilities to the community, but it works to contain those responsibilities within the bounds of the profession. Obligation to "truth" is effective only as a responsibility to and within one's subject; what work one can do outside is determined by "paramount responsibilities" inside. The urgency of one's responsibilities as a "member of the community" is measured "in the light of" – which is to say, against – responsibilities to subject, students, profession, and academic institution. As an affirmation of ethical principle, this passage defines a stance toward the profession, but it is silent on the ethical stance of the profession itself toward society as a whole.

In maintaining this silence, the statement is no worse than most other codes of professional ethics.[9] It is also no better than the film *The Professionals*. If anything, *The Professionals* seems to take a position that is ethically and politically more desirable. For while the film admires and even idealizes the professional virtues, it also presents professionalism – as the American Association of University Professors does not – as a source of ambiguity, an ethical and political *problem*.

In *The Professionals*, the pleasures offered to the (probably male) spectator – pleasures that are no less gendered, however, than the language of the American Association of University Professors in the same year – extend beyond superhumanly rapid and accurate shooting (for each shot, a body drops) to a whole professional iconography. Much film time, perhaps even more than for the gunplay, is devoted to clichés of insider knowledge (like speaking and understanding Spanish) and symbolic instrumentalities like peering through binoculars (in many shots, associated with the point of view of the camera). Our attention is taken up with the measuring of distances, times, and fuses, the plotting of courses, the synchronizing of watches, the assigning of tasks. Erected on this solid scientific foundation, the spectator's confidence in specialized expertise is repaid with a stupendously high Mexican body count. The abdication of ethical responsibility is clearly presented as a cause or precondition of expertise; the Robert Ryan figure, who is conspicuously ethical, is also the only "professional" to be repeatedly mistaken in his judgments. This means that expert skill can and must be appreciated as a pure good, in and for itself. Mastery over nature (how to get horses across the desert) and over complex social situations (how to kill three bandidos without making any noise) can be enjoyed without any sour admixture of scrupulous afterthought.

We know that it is indeed professionalism that is being enjoyed here, and not merely power, because of at least two distinguishing features. First, there is the importance given to specialization-and-teamwork rather than (or in addition to) individual heroics. Second and most important, there is the visible removal of moral and political legitimation from their work. When the four mercenaries get to the guerrilla stronghold and find Grant's wife, Maria (Claudia Cardinale), they also find that she is not in fact being held prisoner, but is there of her own free will, out of love (for Raza, the leader, played by Jack Palance) and out of belief in the Mexican Revolution. The film's moral plot does not begin at this point – it has already begun, early on, when the Robert Ryan character offers humanitarian objections to the expedient shooting of captured horses – but it takes a decisive turn. At the culmination of lengthy and minute planning, preparation, and well-executed technique, as they are about to "rescue" their object, Maria's evident unwillingness to be rescued deprives their professionalism of its justifying premise.

They go through with it anyway, over the objections of Dolworth/Lancaster. But the question has been posed. What does it mean to act efficiently, to be "successful," when the legitimating framework or end has been removed? To kill others you now know to be blameless, meanwhile risking death for yourself in an enterprise whose (apparently superfluous) moral disguise has slipped off, to insist that the job must and will be done, no reasons given or moral arguments allowed – this is professionalism in its most frightening form. "The contract," Fardan/Marvin says, must be fulfilled. "The goods" must be delivered. The dehumanization of Maria Grant effected by the term "goods" is one sign among many that we no longer have professionalism's permission to suspend or take for granted the question of who the "good guys" and the "bad guys" are, or the question of whether the terms apply. We are asked to look ethically at professionalism itself. The second half of the film thus places the spectator in a double suspense. We want to know whether our heroes will make it, and if so, at what cost. But we also ask ourselves whether we *want* them to make it, or whether we want them to change their minds.

In the end, they do change their minds. Forfeiting their $10,000 fee, they restore Maria to her husband, fulfilling the contract, only in order to release her again and return with her (and the bullet-riddled but apparently indestructible Raza) to Mexico. But some of the suspense persists. In the name of what have they switched loyalty? Have they been converted away from professionalism itself? Have they been converted to the Revolution, for which two of them had once fought alongside Raza? How is the spectator to feel now about the pleasures of professionalism he or perhaps she has been offered throughout the film? As the presumably satisfying emotional climax to a successful popular film, what does this ending say about professional ideology in and since 1966?

The ending looks very much like a simple renunciation of professionalism in favor of ethical or political principles: respect for true love, distaste for lies, perhaps even a rekindling of the revolutionary flame.[10] After all, as Maria tells Fardan, "No man was more loyal to the Revolution than you." In order to supplement Fardan's underdeveloped motivation, a somewhat heavy-handed parallel is introduced between Maria and Fardan's wife, another revolutionary named Maria, who was tortured to death by the Federales. Meanwhile the Burt Lancaster figure, the first to be converted, has answered the question of what Americans were doing in the Mexican Revolution in the first place with the words "Maybe there's only one revolution."

This admirable moral makes a certain sense both in terms of American ideology generally (the revolutionary heritage of 1776) and in terms of the 1960s context especially. There were of course anti-professional counter-tendencies at work in 1966: anxiety that an instrumental concern with technique for its own sake could breed forgetfulness of values, that *how* conceals the ultimate question of *why*, that the public interest is not being served by professional activity, and so on. There was a perception that artisanal wholeness had been lost through specialization and the division of labor, and there were democratic suspicions about professional elitism and mystifications protected by a wall of secrecy and jargon. In the 1960s in particular, explicit protests against professionalism (to be discussed further below) were typically also formulated on behalf of neglected clients and constituencies as well as open access to information.

In addition, work itself was losing some of its ideological luster. Nostalgic voices were already bemoaning the death or degeneration of the work ethic. More radical thinkers like Jean Baudrillard, André Gorz, Jürgen Habermas, and Stanley Aronowitz were beginning to suggest that the left would have to abandon its own version of the work ethic. The critical usefulness of work has faded not just as an ideological tool (how people are motivated to put in their eight hours), according to these thinkers, but also as an analytic concept (the essence of what "man" is or how "history" moves) and as a rallying cry for the forces of change ("workers of the world unite"). Both our social analysis and our political rallying will henceforth have to be done by appeal to social identities formed around other bonds and other activities – formed, for example, around consumption rather than production.[11] Today many voices invite us to think of ourselves as most free, as most truly ourselves, not in the role of producer but in the role of consumer. In this sense at least, consumerist ideology has been replacing productivist ideology. It may be that the critical distance we can now take from professionalism, at least intermittently, owes as much to our new sense of ourselves as consumers as it does to an older, residual sense of ethics or politics. It also owes something to various other collective identities: for example, those of class, gender, sexual orientation, and ethnicity. All of these tendencies have the potential of feeding into an ending in which professional heroes turn their back on professionalism and offer themselves instead to the genuine "cause" of a Third World revolution.

Solidarity with Third World revolution has a special resonance in the 1960s context of decolonization, movements of national liberation, and in particular (though here the allegory may be ambiguous) the US involvement in Vietnam. Beginning with the opening shot (graffiti on a wall: "Viva Villa"), the film repeatedly risks anachronism in order to invoke this context. Discreet references to Jacob Sharp's race and Lieutenant Chiquita's sex evoke the civil rights and (incipient) women's liberation movements of the 1960s. "Peace, brother!" says Burt Lancaster. How does all this inflect the film? The global context of the 1960s, like the domestic context, would seem to oppose politics and professionalism. In walking away from professionalism, our heroes would not only seem to be turning their backs on what has defeated the Mexican/Third World guerrillas, who are brave but technologically and tactically inferior; they would be turning their backs on the ideological image of the West's supposed technical/social superiority.

But do they in fact turn their backs? Could *any* ending compensate for the terrible cost in useless deaths paid before they turn back across the border? Can the ending erase the spectator's intense and varied delectation of the expertise that produced those deaths? Along with these questions, we must also inquire into the political valence of that expertise. Even in the mid-section of the film, the politics of professionalism is not as evident as it first appears. The film actually takes pains *not* to associate the professionals or their professionalism too closely with the icons of Western technology. Where political allegory seems inevitable, as when the guerrillas on horseback chase the Americans on a train, it turns out that the train is empty. The Americans have abandoned the train – for their own horses. Dynamite (the great weapon of anarchism) is prominent in their escape; a captured machine gun is given an ostentatiously muted and insignificant role. Much is said about the situational advantages of arrows over guns ("makes you wonder how we ever beat the Indians"). If the professionals win by being professional, it is strange how little their victory seems to depend on their differences from their enemies.

In later chapters I will have more to say about the cryptic connections between professional ideology at home and the global context of decolonization and neo-colonialism since the 1960s. For the moment, it is enough to notice how, in *The Professionals*, victorious professionalism is not opposed to the guerrillas, as first appears, so much as it tries to include both their technique and, more surprisingly, something of what they stand for. This inclusion might, I suppose, be seen as a formal or tactical preparation for the final reversal in which the professionals join the guerrillas. But even so, it points to an important set of ambiguities within professional ideology.

Does the film turn its back on professionalism in the ending? If so, then it would be hard to explain how very little the professional ethic is discredited, right up to the ending, in the film's scene-by-scene development. The first guerrillas we see conform with precision to the unpleasant "bandido" stereotype of more conventional Westerns, right down to warning the gringos about danger in these hills and marvelling childishly at stolen consumer goods. The film forgets these images of the unprofessional Third World Other but cannot take them back. Moral evidence accumulates in favor of the guerrillas without producing new images of them. Meanwhile, we're still left rooting, minute by minute, for the technical prowess that guns them down.

Consider, moreover, the crucial scene, near the end, when Dolworth/Lancaster decides to stay behind to delay their pursuers so as to allow the rest to make the final dash to the border. Fardan/Marvin wants to be the one to stay for what looks like certain death. No, says Dolworth cheerily. "Let's keep this thing strictly professional." The leader's job is "to make good our contract." His own job is to sacrifice himself for the good of the team – even though, as we have seen, he is the one who least believes in "the contract." Fardan accepts this sacrifice, however reluctantly. It is a difficult moment both for him and for the spectator. Would our usual, unprofessional heroes ever have agreed to allow another to usurp the most dangerous and glorious role? In winning out over what had seemed self-evident emotional common sense, professionalism shades suspiciously toward legalism. *Must* Fardan be the one to hand the woman over to her husband? Isn't this carrying respect for previously unmentioned contractual minutiae a bit far?

The professional ethic continues to assert itself right up through the concluding scene. When Fardan finally hands Maria over to her husband, he insists that Grant pronounce the contract fulfilled. Amused at this legalism, Grant asks, "Code of the profession?" "Something like that," Fardan answers. A moment later, as Maria and Raza are galloping back across the border, Fardan justifies what would appear to be a breaking of the contract by an ingenious, not to say pedantic, twist of the same professional code. We were hired to get your wife back from an evil kidnapper, he tells Grant, and we did – from you. Perhaps professionalism can persist because, within the apparent absurdity of its rule-bound self-enclosure, it also harbors mechanisms that are potentially self-rectifying.[12]

3. Sixguns and Technocracy

Nothing so clear as a renunciation of professionalism has happened. Looking now to the other side of the equation, have the goals and principles of the revolution been adopted, or readopted? Neither Fardan nor Dolworth, the two former revolutionaries, has anything to say about the reasons why a revolution might have begun in the first place. There are no images of misery, exploitation, injustice.

Dolworth's explanation of how he first got involved is conspicuously lacking in principles. The closest thing to a philosophical conversion occurs in the ambush sequence when Dolworth stays behind to win a few hours' lead for the others. But what it suggests is less why the professionals join the guerrillas than why they can both join the guerrillas and at the same time *remain* professionals.

After the first gunfire, the survivors of the ambush lie or crouch, wounded and almost immobile, out of sight of each other yet within earshot, and from behind their respective rocks take part in a stagy yet oddly intimate conversation. What is missing from this conversation is animosity, personal or political. They talk freely, philosophically, cynically, like the old friends that indeed they are, but not like the enemies they also are. It is as if a general disillusionment had made the distinction between friend and enemy both fatal and trivial at the same time – as if there were too much disillusionment for anger, but not enough disillusionment for the struggle to end. Those left alive keep trying to kill each other, but they do so impersonally. At the end, Lieutenant Chiquita, a beautiful and voluptuous member of the Mexican revolutionary band, dying in the friendly but unsentimental arms of Dolworth/Lancaster, who was once her lover, tries one more time to shoot him. The pistol pointed at his head clicks loudly, the chamber empty. Then she expires. Scenes like this have become a cliché of the modern Western and thriller genres because, I think, they capture the elusive tone or feel of the newly dominant professional ethic.[13]

Guerrillas on one side, mercenaries on the other – but the determination to get the job done is no different, nor is the detachment from the merely personal. On both sides, there is commitment that is intense though opposite, absolute though also disillusioned. On both sides, there is an amiable understanding of the other that in no way interferes with the structural antagonism of the work at hand. For emotional purposes, the antagonism almost ceases to exist. It is as if the professional separation of ends and means had progressed so far that opposed ends are now incapable of marking as good or bad the means used to achieve them. Thus the means now seem independent, neutral, indistinguishable from those of the enemy. Thus too, it seems, a new sort of solidarity is born: a solidarity of those who share the pleasures and companionship of technical means and who feel themselves at a shared, perhaps painful distance from the (perhaps banished) realm of more-than-technical ends to which they are nonetheless committed. The atmosphere of this solidarity is too impersonal to be termed friendly. It might be better described as collegial.

At this final confrontation between revolutionaries and professionals, the two sides not only fraternize but also mix and mingle qualities. The professionals, we suspect, are about to join the Revolution. But what is it that they will join? What the Revolution means to the guerrillas, in their leader's account, is something very like a professional affiliation. The Revolution, says Raza/Palance in a moment of monologue, is like a love affair. After the initial excitement, its "terrible enemy" is time. Because of time, Raza says, which brings fading passion, disillusionment, and farewells, we leave. But, he concludes, "we come back because we are lost." Here the Revolution is like the principle that founds the professional group: fictitious, morally arbitrary and imperfect, based on nothing more solid than mutual agreement, yet acquiring and retaining the power to bind, it seems, by its contrast to the still more arbitrary orders and less desirable moral imperfections that await those who try to live without it. One can comprehend Raza's absence of malice toward his enemies. The "terrible enemy" of the Revolution has been displaced from the holders of power and those they hire to defend them, becoming instead that temporally relativizing element *within* the Revolution which undermines commitment to it.[14]

We may want to conclude that the film understands nothing about Mexican revolution and has superimposed upon it, with commonplace provincialism, a characteristically North American professional thematics. But such a conclusion would not take away the film's credit for exposing, within North American professionalism, the ideological potential to undermine the mercenaries' commitment to their contract and to connect them in solidarity – even on messily compromised terms – with their supposed enemies.

In *Sixguns and Society* (1975), Will Wright shows that a certain absence of malice between heroes and villains is in fact to be expected from the Western of the 1960s, which tended to replace the Western's classical plot with what Wright calls a "professional plot."[15] *The Professionals* is one example, for Wright, of a "transformation from the lone hero fighting his way into society to a group of heroes, each with special fighting ability, who combine for the battle.... Each man possesses a special status because of his ability, and their shared status and skill become the basis of mutual respect and affection" (86). "The heroes are now professional fighters, men willing to defend society only as a job they accept for pay or for love of fighting, not from commitment to ideas of law and justice" (85). "Although these men are generally fighting for some social cause, as a group they separate themselves from society and have virtually no contact with it. The fight itself and, more importantly, the comradeship that the fight creates provide sufficient justification for their actions" (86). It follows, in Wright's acute analysis, that "the motivation for the fight is largely irrelevant" (87). "In *The Professionals*," he remarks, the heroes "even fight the wrong people" (168). Thus their enemies need not represent evil or anti-social forces, and often indeed are themselves professionals, like the heroes. So, too, the question of who wins and who loses cannot be decisive to the genre: "the professional heroes can win or lose, and the meaning remains the same; they have formed a group and fought together" (169–70). The emphasis falls on the word "together."

Wright's description of the professionalized Western, the best account we have of films like *The Professionals* and *Butch Cassidy and the Sundance Kid* as well as highly successful examples of other popular genres, seems brilliantly accurate. The question that remains is how to interpret it. For Wright, the interpretive key is the "transition from a market to a managed economy" (174), which requires planning, expertise, and corporate teamwork more than the old-fashioned virtues of individualistic striving and competition. In this stage capitalism legitimates itself by telling the public that the decisions of the managers "involve only technical problems that, as laymen, they are unqualified to understand and evaluate" (176). "The technical approach to social decisions becomes an ideology that legitimates the new political power to the depoliticized population. . . . the public becomes convinced that social values are coincident with the technical needs of the economic system" (177). In short, the values of the professional Western, including solidarity between professional heroes and professional villains, do nothing more than affirm the values of technocracy.

This conclusion is curiously out of sync with Wright's desire to demonstrate the Western's "redeeming social value" (2). From such a perspective, how could it have *any* social value? Applying the "technocracy" reading to *The Professionals*, we would find ourselves with two equally ineligible alternatives. Either (1) the spectator is identifying with a new professional-managerial class which rules precisely by excluding ordinary people from decision-making, now presented as neutral, technical, and none of our business; or (2) we are forced to take the climactic scene of antagonism between the

44

professionals and their wealthy employer as nothing but a horrible deception, since in fact professionals must always represent precisely those, like Grant, who have the capital and pull the strings. Our pleasure, then, would stem from sharing imaginatively in an independence that is totally illusory.

Both interpretations treat the spectator's most likely and powerful responses as deluded and valueless. In effect, they exclude the public from the interpretation of the film. In this respect, they are an instance of professionalism itself as Wright urges us (erroneously, in my view) to understand it: professionalism as the systematic exclusion of the public. The structuralist criticism that Wright brings to bear on *The Professionals* is itself a sort of mimicry of professionalism as he describes it: asocial, amoral, technical, valuing structure for its own sake. As it happens, the advent of structuralism in the US (to be discussed again in a later chapter) is often dated from 1966, the year of the Johns Hopkins "Sciences of Man" conference as well as of *The Professionals*. More to the point, Wright's insistence that, in these same years, the "motivation" of the professional hero ceased to be relevant duplicates structuralism's own insistence (whether in its Proppian or Lévi-Straussian variants) that narrative be interpreted without reference to such vague, psychologistic, and in any case extraneous matters as motivation. In other words, Wright is practicing precisely the "technocratic" criticism he preaches against – to the extent, that is, that he preaches at all.[16] Knee-jerk distrust of professionalism is so automatic, it seems, that it causes even so astute a reader as Wright to mistake what is in front of him, and what he is saying about it.

But there is no need for professional practice to be blind to the motivated presence of "society" and "the public" within itself. Describing the professional collectivity as "independent and elite" (171) and "socially self-contained" (172), Wright sets it in absolute opposition to "society" and "the public." Both terms are of propagandistic use to those who need an object to define their privileged apartness against, whether Western hero riding off into the sunset or structuralist critic seeking legitimacy for a new and esoteric professional vocabulary. But they cannot be permitted to function, as in so much of the professional discourse on professionalism, as vaporous universals that vanish at the moment when any particular group, like professional women, stands up and claims rights of participation in them. As Wright uses the term "society," for example, the presence of women fighting alongside the men in the

45

professional Western, and no longer presented (as in the classical Western) simply as domestic objects to be fought for or over, cannot even register as a "social" fact. Women are simply to be reclassified. Once they counted as "society," now they are professionals. Their historical origins are irrelevant, as is their gender and what it may add to their professional motivation. Yet surely the unprecedented existence of female professionals says something of importance about the category of professionalism itself? When the social composition of its members changes, surely we must at least try to ascertain whether it too has changed. If professionalism represents technocracy as against "public" decision-making, then what about the women in these films who are actually starting to make decisions from which their "private" status once precluded them? In *The Professionals*, they do make decisions; in fact, it is the characteristic act of their (still minimal) screen presence, from Maria Grant's attempt to escape from her rescuers down to Lieutenant Chiquita's decision to lead Raza's final attack herself and even the spirited defense that Dolworth's nameless lover puts up against her husband in the opening sequence.

The inclusion of women may not show up on Wright's structuralist grid, but it amplifies a point that he himself suggests, if somewhat indirectly: that the defining principle of professionalism is not, as he elsewhere implies, exclusion. According to Wright, the real center of the new Western is the construction of professional community.

> In each of the professional films, the demonstration of mutual respect is even more central than the detailing of the fight itself. The major interest becomes the building and maintenance of the unity of the group, and tension arises from the question: Can this unity survive, or will internal conflicts destroy it? (104)

The implication here is that the professional community does not, or need not, define itself either against its (equally professional) enemies or against an unprofessional "society." Like Conrad's ships and Solzhenitsyn's prison, the band of heroes is, rather, a microcosm of conflicting social forces whose inclusiveness can be and often is precisely the issue. In this sense, its struggles are by and large variants of society's struggles. And the special pleasures it holds out, beyond the representation of struggle, include the pleasures of imagined, desired resolution.

Let us take a resonant example: the strange sense of incipient, quasi-technical solidarity between heroes and enemies in *The*

Professionals, based in part on the arbitrariness of their reasons for fighting each other, in part on the respect for professional competence and cooperation that each can recognize in the other, and in part on the extra-professional ideals of the Revolution itself. This solidarity draws up at the text's horizon the plans for ideal, unrealized endings: for example, one in which the struggle between guerrillas and professionals, having revealed its arbitrariness, would be replaced by their *common* struggle, a far less arbitrary one, against Grant and all he stands for, and another ending, perhaps, in which there is an end to any and all fighting.[17] Discovering, displaying, and testing the solidarity which constitutes the professional group in the first place forms the single strongest emotional vector in the professional Western, as Wright points out – weightier for the spectator than victory itself – and this is where such Westerns lead. The forging of professionalism's "common bond of respect and affection that transcends any private desire for personal gain" (104) can and should be seen as an alternative to or management of competition – the social principle figured in the fighting – without becoming for that reason, as it does for Wright, a mere symptom of all-consuming and irreversible technocracy. Technocracy defines professionalism as exclusion. But our pleasure in professionalism is also, and perhaps increasingly – the proportions are continually renegotiated – a pleasure in extending the *inclusions* of professionalism's new or counter-society.

4. Women and Experts

The first evidence in *The Professionals* that there are values within professionalism, however hidden or incipient, that work against professionalism's apparent banishment of value is the Robert Ryan character, Ehrengard. As his name (German for "guard of honor") suggests, Ehrengard serves from the outset as a sort of humanitarian check on the callous technical expediency of the others and as an internal marker of that to which they will finally be converted. At the same time, he is sometimes made to seem a bit extraneous. (It might have been assumed, for instance, that these fellows could attend to their own horses.) Thus he is made to suggest that under these circumstances certain humane values too might be misplaced, or at any rate might require revision. In short, he is there not just to make an ethical case against professionalism, but to qualify that case.

The figure closest to the spectator's ignorance, Ehrengard has to have things explained to him by those in the know. He must learn, specifically, that his immediate moral impressions are likely to be wrong because they are uninformed by expert opinion. When he objects, as the spectator might object, to the execution of government prisoners by the guerrillas, witnessed by the group of four from a hilltop, he is told that these prisoners are the "Colorados," "expert marksmen, also expert at torture," who killed Fardan's wife, among many others. There are two conflicting lessons about expertise here. On the one hand, the Colorados' separation of expertise from morality ought to serve as a cautionary parallel to the same separation in "the professionals" themselves – though the film never explicitly draws it. On the other hand, the episode argues that a certain (professional) disengagement from the confident moral universalism based on experience *without* expertise – here, Ehrengard's spontaneous distaste for the execution, and the viewer's – is not only efficacious, but also a *moral* necessity.[18]

The full weight of professionalism's moral ambivalence does not fall on any of the professionals, however; it falls on the woman whom they both seek and exclude. It will have escaped no one that this is a band of men only. Gender provides a convenient vocabulary for professional exclusion as such – most obviously, the familiar elitist claim that restricted admission means higher standards. But there is nothing arbitrary about the role of woman here. Women are, or rather were, excluded from professionalism as *ends* are excluded from it – but similarly, perhaps, need not be. As in the familiar gendering of production and consumption, men can seem to signify (sordid, technical) means only if women signify the (pure, justificatory, compensatory) end toward which those means tend. Yet what professionalism seeks to exclude, according to this film, is also what defines it. The realm of means is haunted by the realm of ends it tries and fails to exclude. In the person of Maria Grant, woman defines and then redefines the end of professional effort. It is when she manifests her will not to be rescued that the question of ends is first posed, and it is she who gives the plot its symmetrical conclusion. They have come to rescue her, but it is she who rescues them. Her power to do so seems to be the power of the end over the means. It is a power that the film cannot clearly locate, however, because the film cannot decide whether ends belong inside or only outside professionalism.

At times, Maria's power is merely that of a stereotype: woman as beauty, mystery, the helplessly passive object of desire, the pure End in itself. At other times, her lucid political convictions combined with the courage and cleverness to carry them out make her, like Raza, a superior though recognizable version of the professionals themselves: a vision of the possibility that technical means and political end can finally fuse. Or even – when the professionals join the community from which they stole her – that they already have fused.

For feminists, Sandra Gilbert asserted in an interview, "the professional can't be separated from the personal since, to para-phrase a traditional feminist saying, for us the professional *is* the personal."[19] There would be a certain convenience for my argument if feminism could be brought forward at this point so as to exemplify an ideal fusion of the professional and the political that *The Professionals* never quite achieves. In the academy since the late 1960s, the extraordinary success of the new feminist scholarship in transforming the professional order of things should indeed, I think, force a change in the blithe, commonsensical disdain for profession-alism that professionals themselves so often take for granted. Watching and reflecting upon this success has been one of the crucial experiences behind this book, and helping the change along by drawing conclusions from it is one of my motives for writing. But it would be no service to feminism to display it, once again, on a pedestal, as if all struggle and ambivalence were now safely behind it. And there is more to learn about professionalism in general from paying attention to the struggle and ambivalence that continue.

There is something to be learned, for example, from feminism's efforts to tell its own story, a story in which the critique of professionalism has a salient part. In *For Her Own Good: 150 Years of the Experts' Advice to Women* (1978), Barbara Ehrenreich and Deirdre English looked at the rise of expert power over women and saw a narrative that resembles the first half of *The Professionals*: a violent triumph of (all-male) scientists over the supposedly more "primitive" native traditions of women's healing and nurturing.[20] "Women did not learn to look to an external 'science' for guidance until after their old skills had been ripped away, and the 'wise women' who preserved them had been silenced, or killed" (33). The paradigmatic case of this "allegory of science versus superstition" (33) is the de-credentialling and elimination of midwives. "With the elimination of midwifery, all women ... fell under the biological hegemony of the medical profession. In the same stroke, women lost their autonomous role as healers. The only roles left for women in the medical system were as employees, customers, or 'material'" (98).

This is how women's special dependence on professional expertise begins. It ends, unsurprisingly, with the rise of feminism itself, and with the "feminist assault on the experts" (316), from the late 1960s on.

> In consciousness-raising groups, in women's study groups, and in college classrooms women held the scientific theories up to their own experience, and the old "facts" went up in smoke as myths. The immutable maternal instinct ... the sanctity of vaginal orgasms ... the child's need for exclusive mothering ... the theory of female masochism – all the shibboleths of mid-century psycho-medical theory – shriveled in the light of the feminist critique. (315)

> The great romance between women and the experts was over, and it ended because the experts had betrayed the trust that women had put in them.... They turned out not to be scientists – for all their talk of data, laboratory findings, clinical trials – but apologists for the status quo. (316)

Ehrenreich and English never simply reverse the triumphalist professional narrative. They do not present expertise as necessarily a male principle of violent, instrumental, dominating pseudo-science locked in struggle with women's experience and traditional wisdom, which by definition would then have to be militantly anti-professional. Their narrative is nuanced from the outset. "The notion of medicine as a profession," they write, "was in some ways an advance over the unexamined tradition of female healing" (34). And their ending is also nuanced. What has followed the rule of the male experts, in their view, is by no means an obvious improvement. "The monolithic grip of the old romanticist experts has been broken, and the horde of pop psychologists, sex therapists, counselors, liberal gynecologists, etc., who take their place offer no answer – or all answers" (322). By a gospel of self-help that privatizes and de-politicizes the issues, these unregulated free-market alternatives to professionalism's monopoly of credentials make the latter look, by contrast, more public and even, perhaps, more ethical. At any rate, such an ending takes professionalism out of the domain of polarized sexual allegory.[21]

These nuances help to qualify what might otherwise seem, in political terms, the one natural, inevitable narrative of professionalization. According to T.J. Jackson Lears and Richard Wightman

Fox, who (like Will Wright) give eloquent expression to this view, professionals rose to power along with consumerism, and their rise was the decline of democracy. To the extent that they could "generate needs only they could fulfill," their services (including therapeutic advice and advertising images of the good life) undermined the autonomy of the recipients of those services. The result has been "the decline of autonomous selfhood" and a "sense of unreality."[22]

There is much empirical substance to this version. But the narrative by which "reality" is replaced by professionally produced symbols and images and one's own "experience" is exchanged (at a loss) for the "expertise" of others falsely assumes a prior reality that has no need of symbols or images, a prior (self-reliant) selfhood fully in possession of its experience. In so doing, it condemns all intellectual and artistic activity, of which professionalism becomes representative, to the status of more or less redundant, reprehensible, "undemocratic" imposition upon an otherwise "autonomous," self-satisfied public that needs no advice, no images, no art – that *has* no needs it cannot fulfil itself.

If one begins not with an autonomous (implicitly male) individual but with women who, as victims of patriarchal oppression, are not so self-evidently satisfied with the status quo, then the relations between professionals and the public immediately appear more subtle than this absolute opposition implies. Even the midwife example is thus shown to be misleading. Professionalism need not be a sort of zero-sum game in which professional knowledge establishes its authority only by eliminating the knowledge and authority of someone else.[23] The self-interest that did of course motivate professionals – theorists, reformers, therapists, advertisers, muck-rakers, and so on – need not be identical with, but it also need not be opposed to, the self-interest of the recipients of their images and advice. What is happening is less Manichaean: for better and for worse, social customs that had been considered "nature" or "second nature" were opening up to new consciousness of alternatives, to a new possibility of choice. It is true that the professionals who make such matters their business acquire new significance and new authority from the professionalization of society. But must we mourn when matters traditionally kept within the family, like the rearing of children or the household division of labor, are thrown open to public scrutiny – even that of the most exclusive experts – and thus to the possibility of change? Perhaps the only wholehearted mourners will be those, like Christopher Lasch, who would be content to remain under the traditional power of patriarchy. Even in the worst case, as consumers and conduits of expertise produced by men about, say, "scientific motherhood," women might wield a certain power and participate in social changes that could serve their own interests.

But women have of course *not* remained mere consumers and conduits of expertise. Today women are professional producers of expertise, lawyers, doctors, and members of the other professions – not on anything like an equal basis with men, but in sufficient numbers, and with sufficient power to put gender issues on the agenda, so as to demand some inflection of the "romance" that aligns women, experience, ends, and politics against men, expertise, means, and professionalism. And the result, a decade and a half after *For Her Own Good*, is a narrative interweaving of feminism and professionalism that is less like the first half of *The Professionals* and more like the exemplary ambivalence of the film as a whole. In an extraordinary reversal, professionalism now becomes the scene of feminism's most visible triumph – and at the same time a monument to limits not yet broken down "If the recent opening up of the professions has been feminism's greatest victory," Barbara Ehrenreich writes in *Fear of Falling* (1989), "it is a victory whose sweetness the majority of American women will never taste."[24] Feminists "questioned the core assumptions of the professions – their exclusivity, their claims to scientific objectivity and public service." They "wanted to abolish medicine as an elite profession and encourage the skills and participation of more humble health workers, lay practitioners (such as the self-trained midwives . . .) and the 'consumers' of health care." They "attacked it for its sexism, racism, and greed – qualities that seemed to betray any claims to objectivity and public service." However, they also "wanted women to be doctors." "With all the professions, feminists wanted, paradoxically at times, to open them up – and close them down" (215).

Though Ehrenreich's statement is exceptionally forthright, ambivalence like this would seem to be closer to the rule than to the exception. In the interview cited above, shortly after suggesting that for feminists the professional is the personal, Sandra Gilbert acknowledges their non-identity again; "professionalism is both cause and consequence," she says, of the current split between criticism and creativity (121). "Necessarily," Nancy Fraser concludes in *Unruly Practices: Power, Discourse and Gender in Contemporary Social Theory* (1989), "we speak in several voices."[25] For Lisa

Jardine, the rise-and-fall narrative of literary criticism is a simple product of the "residual professionalism of the male Left": "the 'rise to power' version of English Studies has to go. We know by now that in the field of practical and intellectual activity, whatever has been traditionally done by women tends to occupy an inferior position in the socio/sexual division of labour." And if men are so quick to see a decline, can this be unrelated to the fact that women are now a majority of literature students?[26] Seeking a way to narrativize the course of feminist criticism since the 1960s, Jane Gallop hesitates at the suggestion "that feminist critics have betrayed political commitments in pursuit of academic credibility." Rather than a movement from a politicized feminist stage (the late 1960s) to a professionalized literary stage (the late 1980s and early 1990s), she proposes, "we might want to consider this division into stages a simplification of what has been, from the beginning and up to this moment, an ongoing history of divided loyalties."[27]

Since the beginning of the 1990s, professional narratives of decline have become familiar. The generation of the 1960s (feminist, civil rights, anti-war, and so on – Gallop's generation, and my own) has been looking back on its youth, sometimes from more or less comfortable positions in the professions, and thus its autobiographical narratives have often been narratives of professionalization – inescapably embarrassed and ambivalent narratives. By refusing any simplifying nostalgia, Gallop refuses the pastoral idealization of the 1960s – the other side of jeremiads against the professional present – that tempts such narratives, as well as the worse temptation to let ambivalence serve as a sign of redemption in a fallen world. Suggesting that neither the political nor the professional exists in a pure state which excludes the other, Gallop helps extricate us from the narrative paradigm of the Fall. She does not so much cast suspicion on narrative itself as move us toward more complex narratives – narratives that might, for example, acknowledge, as Barbara and John Ehrenreich argued in "The Professional-Managerial Class," that the institutional and ideological structure of the professions was not simply and ironically what the radicals of the 1960s were fighting against, but also a major influence in defining what they were fighting *for*. It would make a difference if we could see that the energies unleashed in that decade have not completely disappeared in being relocated and transformed by professional institutions like the university, however much they may have been problematized.[28]

Some of the ambiguities that tie 1960s radicalism to profession-alism are suggested by Thomas Haskell's account of challenges to the professions in the 1970s and 1980s. "In the Goldfarb decision of 1975," he writes, "the Supreme Court jerked constitutional supports out from under a host of anti-competitive professional practices of ancient vintage." This case came about only because of the inter-secting interests of "the campus radicalism of the early 60s, the entrance into the professions of people willing to challenge the conventions of guild solidarity, and the general resurgence of libertarian values and free enterprise policies that made the decade such an unsettling period for the professions." The cumulative result was a delegitimizing of professionalism: "by the end of the decade [the 1970s] it was clear that a heavy burden of proof rested on anyone who believed that professionals were anything more than profit-seeking businessmen."[29] This result, symbolized by the Gold-farb decision, was equally satisfying to

> three very different constituencies: consumer advocates, who saw in it hope of lower prices; the left, for whom it reaffirmed that expertise is just another device for creating inequality and maintaining capitalist hegemony; and the resurgent right that would soon carry Ronald Reagan into the White House, for whom it was a token of their own increasing assertiveness and refusal to play second fiddle to any non-entrepreneurial elite. (xvi)

Yet this result was thus also a sign of political contradiction and incoherence, like Richard Rorty's agreement with Dan Quayle. It suggested that, at least in some cases, the true heritage of the 1960s left belonged on the side of public, non-entrepreneurial standards of practice, and thus against the resurgent right, rather than on the side of the right's free-market attack on expertise.

Haskell's analysis also makes it clear that much of what looks like anti-professionalism within the professions today is really anger at Reaganism and its profit-oriented subversion of standards that *were* professional. A recent Op-Ed piece in the *New York Times* reported on a survey revealing that 30 percent of US doctors "felt no moral responsibility to treat AIDS patients." Entitled "The Doctor Won't See You Now," it concludes with angry sarcasm:

> I hope no one counters with the tired argument that doctors, because of the place they occupy in society, not to mention their incomes, should treat anybody who is sick. This plea is based on the long-discredited idea that doctoring is a profession, a calling, requiring commitment and

integrity on the part of those who practice it. Really. How dumb can you get?[30]

This writer offers a critique of professionalism in the name of professionalism. Left critics of professionalism who reject the name, along with any version of these (admittedly imperfect) standards, run the risk of being lumped together with Reagan's free-marketeers while they also lose writers like this as potential allies.[31]

"The real contradictions of our lives notwithstanding," Nancy Fraser writes in *Unruly Practices*, "the radical academic is not an oxymoron" (1). The agents of critique are inside the gates as well as outside, and the same holds for the ends to which critique is mobilized. To begin with this premise is to reject the dichotomized narrative that some readers might derive from *The Professionals*: a romance between (strictly male) professional means and the (strictly female) unprofessional end that professionalism would both worship and banish. This romance, with its polarizations between female experience and male expertise, private ends and public means, politics and professionalism, has now lost whatever usefulness it may once have had without, however, losing its honored and accustomed place in our common sense. Changing that common sense is therefore a task of narrative analysis. What I try to expose in the allegories of vocation I examine here are the anticipatory traces of a different common sense, an institutional consciousness no longer enslaved by the line between inside and outside, and thus no longer politically immobilized by its professional status.

One such allegory, I have been suggesting, is *The Professionals* itself. If the first half of the film allegorizes professionalism far too simplistically, the film as a whole is oddly apposite to the demands placed on narrative by a radical professional like the academic feminist. Acknowledging the danger that professionalism may lead us politically astray, it also demonstrates that we need not succeed in getting entirely outside it – if such a thing remains possible, now that professionalism is so bound up with the very conditions of modern action – in order to pivot in place and move toward a different political outcome. Getting outside it is the more frightening dream of Reagan-era films like *Alien* and *Predator*, each of which shows not the composition and triumph of a team, but the *de*composition of an already existing team by serial deaths. In the end, only one survivor is left, the presumed fittest. In each case this decomposition is the work of an alien being with which no kinship is possible. Against this more recent backdrop, *The Professionals* reveals its virtues. It reveals that even our carefully trained skepticism can metamorphose into unsuspected solidarity; and, thanks to the interpenetration of the professional and the public, that there are resources within our imperfect professionalism that radicals can draw on.

Culture and Distance:
On the Professionalizing of
Literary Criticism

After several days of it ... I happened to pass a bonfire of rags and
oil in a village and suddenly, in an overwhelming moment, I was in
a field in Normandy and the next tank, with my friends in it, was
burning and about to explode. I think I then understood the
professional culture of distance. ...
                    Raymond Williams[1]

> Criticism is a matter of the correct distancing.
>   Walter Benjamin[2]

> ... distance, or what we might also call criticism.
>   Edward W. Said[3]

1. "Distance"

The first epigraph is taken from an essay called "Distance," written
during the Falklands/Malvinas war of 1982, in which Raymond
Williams offered a critique of British television's coverage of the
fighting. The reporting had been dangerously sanitized and abstract,
he suggested, because of the "culture of distance" that results from the
management of society by professionals. Television, which comes
"from the Greek for 'afar'" (36), is "professionally understood,
managed and interpreted" (37) in such a way as to distance the reality
of war from the viewer. There is a sort of conspiracy: "The television
professionals," who are "deeply integrated" with "military professionals," join with them to suggest that "war is a profession." In the
"antiseptic presentation of the images of war" by this "professional
culture of distance," emerging from "models and convictions without
experience," the real experience of violent death is disguised, distanced, alienated. "Throughout the crisis, across different opinions, I
have not heard any talk of that distant calculating kind from friends
who had been in actual battles" (40).

Though the Falklands/Malvinas conflict has itself retreated into the distance, much of Williams's commentary seems no less pertinent to the recent war in the Persian Gulf. Here, as so often, Williams seems the exemplary intellectual. He attends with fervor and astuteness to the "popular" culture of television as well as to the "elite" culture of Dickens and Ibsen, to present urgencies as well as to past monuments. Like George Orwell, about whom he writes so well, he speaks in a public, reasonable, jargon-free voice that tries (not without difficulty) to be both independent and representative; he counters the abstraction of professional specialists by calling us back to the commonality of shared experience. He stands up in public, outside his area of competence, and loudly takes an unpopular position on a matter of the national welfare. He is thus a "critic" in a stronger sense than is required by the academic discipline of "literary criticism."

What *is* the relation between the discipline of literary criticism, to which Williams also of course belonged, and the act of raising one's voice in public, as Williams does here? The gist of Williams's critique of the war heightens the sense of a deep antagonism between them. For his target seems in fact to be not so much Margaret Thatcher's imperial policies in themselves, as one might expect, but rather the professionals of the military and the media who implement those policies and veil their consequences. This detour is not merely a rhetorical tactic designed to jolt neutral, depoliticized television spectators out of their passive consent to the war. For in other contexts, Williams speaks in much the same way about the professionals of his own discipline.

In a retirement lecture in 1983, less than a year after "Distance" was published in the *London Review of Books*, Williams presented "distance" as his discipline's inner principle. In modernism, he said, the "estrangement" which was presented as the truth of the "mobile and dislocated" modern world was really more true of the intellectuals themselves. The intellectuals broke away from their homes and became "distanced from, though often still preoccupied by, more local cultures." Their characteristic experiences were "estrangement and exposure."[4] Soon, however, modernism's estranged, extra-territorial intellectuals were grounded – in the academy. "What began in isolation and exposure ended ... in an establishment," an establishment that included "a new way of life – in the universities – for intellectuals" (222–3).

Like so many other accounts, Williams's little narrative ends in disappointment at the intellectuals' unheroic institutional grounding. But there is an important new twist. Unlike the story of the Fall from High Modernism into Sordid Professionalism that we find in Atlas, Ozick, and the New York intellectuals generally, Williams's version insists that the original experience of "estrangement and exposure" is not blunted or cushioned in this grounding. On the contrary, it is preserved, solidified, grounded not in the sense of restriction but of foundation. Rather than tracing a fall from modernism into professionalism, Williams suggests that in its essence modernism already *was* professionalism. And that is what is wrong with it. Without commitment, old or new, to local culture or community, the professionalized intellectual remains estranged, free-floating, cosmopolitan. In Williams's words, criticism is "the profession of a stranger," and those who practice it look upon the world "with the eyes of a stranger." Though Williams is generous, as always, in his willingness to acknowledge how he himself belongs to and respects this history, he forcefully and almost unreservedly condemns its result. "I can feel the bracing cold of their inherent distances and impersonalities and yet have to go on to say that they are indeed ice-cold" (223–4). We are left to understand that literary critics, in the chilly modernism of their "critical distance," belong as a group among the professionals who help make the war, not among those who stand up against it.

Yet if we look again at the terms of Williams's own stand against the war, this distribution of roles becomes less clear-cut. Speaking in the name of "friends who had been in actual battles" (he himself fought in Normandy in the Second World War), Williams obliquely invokes the familiar formula of the one who possesses experience: I know, I was there. This formula gently strongarms its reader into the proposition that, in order to understand, what we need is to be there, and that that is all we need. But nothing could be less evident. Is physical presence in a battle really a sufficient guarantee of pertinent knowledge about that battle? Is it even necessarily superior to a more distanced perspective? Williams himself associates "the professional culture of distance" with new weaponry that kills at distances which once seemed, and perhaps still seem, inhuman, from "beyond the range of normal vision" (38). Could a sailor stationed on a battleship struck by a tele-guided missile know anything useful about the logic of battle, or even about his "experience"? And in a modern society determined by forces as distantly and invisibly deadly as the Exocet missile, how much does "being there" really guarantee the pertinence or reliability of our social knowledge?[5]

Williams contrasts "experience" with "models." However, it is not the intensity of his own individual experience – the whiff of burning rags and oil that turns into a sudden involuntary memory of the burning tank – that he appeals to, but rather a generalization from that moment.[6] "Experience" in his loaded sense – implying that someone engaged in battle fully understands the meaning of the actions in which he or she takes part – presupposes its own model. The experience of combat, an extraordinary collective enterprise, functions in his essay as a radical simplifier, temporarily effacing social differences and divisions and gathering what might ordinarily seem to be a chaos of private actions into a single, publicly intelligible whole. Behind the hypothetical immediacy of the battlefield, that is, lies the model of the natural, rooted wholeness of the "organic community," a bounded and knowable society assumed to be capable, like a battle, of rendering individual experience fully meaningful because it is united against its outside and innerly transparent, harmonious, consensual. Combat is a microcosm of what Williams called, in a famous phrase, "a whole way of life" – that is, a microcosm of "culture."[7]

"Culture" in Williams's sense, which enables and defines his condemnation of the war, is also the ground on which the discipline of literary criticism was founded. We know this because Williams himself has supplied the evidence.[8] Williams's early masterpiece *Culture and Society* (1958) tells the story of how the imaginary wholeness of culture was projected onto the past, in the Romantic response to the Industrial and French Revolutions, and how it came to serve, after elaborations by Arnold, Pater, and their successors, as "a court of appeal" against the all too visible divisions and fragmentations of industrial society, as well as "a mitigating and rallying alternative" to that society (xvi). "Culture was made into an entity, a positive body of achievements and habits, precisely to express a mode of living superior to that being brought about by the 'progress of civilization'" (254). This history marks the founding of the cultural criticism that is the intellectual's stock-in-trade, for it produces a concept of "culture" that is "critical" – set against social actuality – *by its very definition*.

In so doing, it also suggests how "criticism" in the narrow, disciplinary sense – the study of *literary* texts – could base its ascent on the grandiose claim to be a kind of self-appointed conscience of modern society. And it explains how this rise in the pretensions of literary criticism could have taken place during a period when literature itself was being relegated to an increasingly marginal role within the cultures of Britain and the US. How could literary criticism become the staging ground for social critique when literature itself was losing its social influence? It was precisely because literature was not central to society or representative of its dominant trends that it could serve as a condensation and epitome of culture, "an abstraction and an absolute" (xvi), against which society would be judged.

If literary criticism does not owe its very existence to this grounding in culture – there were certainly other reasons for teaching vernacular literature on a large scale – its recent place among the disciplines is probably inexplicable without it. Surveying the social sciences and humanities in Britain in 1968, the historian Perry Anderson found them condemned, by their refusal to think society as a whole, to "a vicious circle of self-reproducing fragmentation and limitation." The exceptions were anthropology ("brilliant and flourishing") and literary criticism, the two disciplines dominated by the concept of "culture." "Suppressed and denied in every other sector of thought," Anderson writes, "totality" – society considered as a whole, and therefore critically – "found refuge in the least expected of studies." The vitality of literary criticism is a direct result, he suggests, of the fundamentally critical slant of its determining premise. Williams himself, who continues as well as revises the tradition he describes, is the best example. "It is no accident that in the fifties, the one serious work of socialist theory in Britain – Raymond Williams's *The Long Revolution* – should have emerged from literary criticism, of all disciplines."[9]

The point here is not to congratulate critics on a job well done. Rather, it is to understand both the force and the limits of this disciplinary grounding. Among the limits of what he calls "culturalism," Richard Johnson lists, for example, its tendency to oppose itself to "political economy," on the one hand, and to "abstraction" or "theory," on the other: each of them a supposed violence done to the seamless wholeness of culture, yet each of them in fact a tool that the cultural critic cannot afford to deny her- or himself.[10] Andrew Ross has written eloquently on the contempt for popular culture, for commerce, and for technology that these same assumptions helped propagate.[11]

In addition, there is the visibly paradoxical logic that leads from oppositionality-via-culture to a routine of uncritical praise. Indeed, in a sense culture made true "criticism" impossible. While the very concept of culture was critical in relation to the "society" it was defined against, by the same token anything that fell *into* the category of culture was protected from all but relatively superficial criticism, and certainly from any dismissive intepretation that threatened its ultimate preservation. In relation to the actual cultural texts under discussion, in other words, critics have been largely forced by their premises into a rhetoric not of criticism but of praise. For the presence of any such text, transported from outside the lived "society" of the student and placed before her or him as an object worth discussing, had to be justified. And since it was, by definition, a mere memory or exhibit from afar, the more distant the better, without social force here and now – for to possess social force in the present would have put it into the category of "society" – it could not be justified by any ostensible social need to criticize it. The need to talk about it in the first place, rather than about some other thing, presumably came from its difference, but could not come from differences that were now considered errors; it could only come from differences that were somehow improvements on present opinion. Culture as such, then, must always be praised.

Doing without "culture" could therefore show us a "criticism," liberated for the first time from the imperative to praise, such as we have never seen. Against an age of resurgent nationalisms and would-be moral majorities, there is much reason to affirm, with Edward Said, that "culture has been used as essentially not a cooperative or communal term but rather as a term of exclusion," and to accept what Said calls "the great modern or, if you like, post-modern fact, the standing outside of cultures."[12]

Williams himself illustrates the limits as well as the force of opposition in culture's name. On his example, culture serves to ground both the professional critic and the independent intellectual, and thereby undermines the usual division between them. But in grounding both, culture also produces the division between them, and then reproduces that division over and over again. For the first and most persistent protest culture arouses is an insatiable complaint against the intellectual's own inevitable dividedness – the contradiction between, on the one hand, an intellectual and political ideal of wholeness which gets called "the intellectual," and on the other hand a real, necessarily partial place within the division of labor, a place which is called "the professional." Literary criticism, though a discipline dedicated to culture, cannot represent culture without inconsistency for the very reason that it *is* a discipline among other disciplines. As a result, critics tend to direct their oppositionality against themselves, often to the exclusion of targets that are more distant and arguably more urgent.

Hence the strange detour that leads Williams's protest against the war down the path toward protest against professionalism. It is as if the television professional's "distances and impersonalities" could properly stand in for imperialism. And as if abstraction from the full experience of battle in a news report, instead of producing an analysis that was enlightening *because* abstract, necessarily constituted a sort of aggression against television spectators that could properly stand in for aggression against the people of Argentina or Iraq. The Third World nation, especially as victim of imperial violence, is one of the most powerfully rejuvenated paradigms of culture. If such a national culture cannot be praised, as in Argentina in 1982 and Iraq in 1991, because the personified wholeness of imperialism's victim wears the face of a military dictator, then the culturalist left is at a loss. It cannot *divide* that nation's wholeness and throw its support to a fragment within it, for fragmentation is just what the culturalist left is trying to escape. Especially its own fragmentation. Obliged to prove their fidelity to culture by expressing their independence from professionalism, intellectuals are also obliged to ignore or condemn culture's cohesive warmth and closeness if such qualities should happen to show themselves in professionalism's own fragmented, imperfect communities. Intellectuals *as* intellectuals cannot belong, or cannot belong without apparent self-betrayal. In their very diatribes against modernist "distance," they fall back on distance for their self-definition.[13]

I will be coming back again and again to this profound paradox of culture as, at the same time, both oppositional cutting edge and professional ground. Modernism in this sense seems to define a predicament from which we have yet to extricate ourselves with any great success – *the* predicament, perhaps, of intellectuals at the present time. Before going on, in the next chapter, to discuss the efforts of postmodern critics to find a grounding for themselves *other* than culture, I want therefore to examine in greater detail Williams's identification of modernism with professionalism – the apparent anomaly of a social formation that coheres around the principle of distance, modernism institutionalized.

2. The Origin of Criticism: Modernist Histories

In June 1915, in a letter to T.S. Eliot's businessman father, Ezra Pound defended Eliot's desire to stay in England and pursue his vocation as a poet rather than return to the US to complete his studies. Pound was unsuccessful in arguing his friend's case; Eliot's father remained unreconciled up to his death in 1919. The irony of this failed instance of literary legitimation, according to Louis Menand's *Discovering Modernism: T.S. Eliot and his Context* (1987), is that there was in fact a case to be made that the father could and should have appreciated. The modernist revolution Eliot was bringing to literature occurred, in Menand's words, along with "the rise of professionalism," and its values are largely those "of what [Eliot] does not scruple to call literary professionalism." Hence "the irony that the manner in which the modern artist tried to keep his ideological distance from the businessman, to guard the autonomy of his work, was also one of the ways in which the artist and the businessman were both, in spite of their self-conceptions, bound together."[14]

By now, connections like this are no longer shocking. Social developments like "modernization" and "professionalization" have become a regular if not an inevitable context in which to discuss the former avant-garde. The phrase "The Institutionalization of Modernism" has appeared in the *Norton Anthology of English Literature*, a textbook that is formidably central to bringing about the condition this phrase describes, thereby suggesting that modernism's witting or unwitting collusion with contemporary institutions has become a comfortable commonplace. Indeed, it is the very commonplace whose recognition defines, by contrast, the postmodernism we take ourselves to inhabit.[15]

Like many commonplaces, this one is largely true. The period in which modernism moves beyond little avant-garde reviews and establishes itself in the security of academic literature departments – roughly speaking, the decades immediately before and (especially) after the Second World War – is also the period in which academic literature departments expand along with it, or so as to accommodate it, matching its powerful case for artistic autonomy with a new sense of institutional autonomy. What this commonplace narrative necessarily obscures, however, is the next step in the story. Indeed, it doesn't leave the sequel many options. What can possibly follow the achievement of autonomy? If postmodernism comes into existence by recognizing and reacting against modernism's institutionalization, then does it – do we – now stand in some sense outside of institutions? Clearly we do not. There have been important changes and stages beyond or inside the "professional autonomy" that seemed to be a decisive endpoint, yet there are no names for these stages within the vocabulary of professionalization. As sociologists themselves have recently come to see, the standard narrative of professionalization is cripplingly end-stopped. It allows for no significant history beyond the ending, beyond the achievement of autonomy, except the possible loss of that autonomy, which is to say chaos, confusion, the deluge.[16]

In order to come to a less apocalyptic understanding of the passage from modernist criticism to the postmodern criticism we now practice – in order to understand, that is, how postmodernism too is embodied in a mode of professional institutionalization and legitimation, distinctive but also overlapping that of its predecessor – it is necessary to take apart the commonplace narrative, allowing for its partial pertinence but also refusing its implacable over-simplifications of our professional present.

To begin with, this means complicating the identification between modernism and the very essence of professionalism. This identification seems compelling and almost inevitable. The two belong to the same period, and almost any description of either term will set off reverberations in the semantic field of the other.[17] By most definitions, modernism is said to found its cataclysmic divide between present and past on a further break with nineteenth-century literature's submission to realism (the standard of ordinary empirical observation) and authorial responsibility (the author's accountability for her or his words to the moral standards of the public). By contrast, modernism proposes an avant-garde or elite literature that is likely to be obscure or shocking to the ordinary reader and that claims independence both from the life of its author and from the standards of ordinary public morality. Each of these commonplaces collates with those of professionalism. A minimal description, stressing the claim to esoteric, specialized knowledge as justification for a privileged local sovereignty, immediately offers several points of contact: autonomy, exclusiveness, anti-empiricism, obscurity to the layman. "In contrast to the empiricist," Burton Bledstein writes in *The Culture of Professionalism* (1976), "the professional person grasped the concept behind a functional activity," "penetrated beyond the rich confusion of ordinary experience" (89–90). It was only by delimiting and controlling a "magic circle of scientific knowledge which only the few, specialized by training and indoctrination, were privileged to enter" that a profession could constitute itself as such and protect its "precious autonomy against all assailants" (90–2). In consequence, the profession became self-selecting and, still more important, self-policing: it could promulgate a code of ethics distinct from and often in conflict with other moral and social responsibilities, and could refuse outsiders the right or competence to judge what was done within it. "The dehumanization of art," Ortega y Gasset's approving phrase for modern art's transcendence of the human-all-too-human concerns of life, seems equally apposite to this description of professionalism. To base professional claims on a structural disengagement from ordinary personal motives and ethics is to define the profession as a social aestheticism, an art-for-art's-sake of the working world that agrees to table questions of ultimate social consequence in return for a free hand within its territory of specialization. It is a short step from the "special grasp of the universe" that a profession demonstrates through "obscure and technical formalisms" to the "technical display" and "specialism" of modern literature, and the special language of poetry declared by the New Critics.[18]

As Edward Said pointed out a decade ago,

> the intellectual hegemony of Eliot, Leavis, Richards, and the New Critics coincides not only with the work of masters like Joyce, Eliot himself, Stevens, and Lawrence, but also with the serious and autonomous development of literary studies in the university, a development that in time became synonymous with "English."[19]

In a sense, then, the profession of literary criticism was born as a modernist institution. The professional standard of scientific rigor came to literary studies earlier, as Gerald Graff observes in *Professing Literature* (1987); the philologists of the nineteenth century professionalized, in effect, without assuming any specialized definition of "literature" as a professional knowledge base, let alone the specific model of *modernist* literature.[20] But in the early and middle years of the twentieth century, there occurred a further stage of professionalization which, perhaps because it happened around a redefinition of "literature," came to seem final, definitive, the one true representative of professionalization as such.

According to another commonplace, the professionalization of literary criticism was largely accomplished by the New Critics, who established the integrity of the discipline by in effect making up an object for it. Notoriously, the New Critics narrowed their definition of "literature" to an organic whole, its parts balanced and self-sufficient. Neither cognitively reliable nor practically useful, "literature" in this Kantian sense referred to nothing outside itself. Thus it stood apart from the cognitive, utilitarian knowledges of other disciplines and could serve as the firm, distinct, autonomous base for an autonomous profession. One characteristic statement was John Crowe Ransom's aptly titled "Criticism, Inc." Ransom, who did not himself possess a degree in English, hammered the theme home:

> Rather than occasional criticism by amateurs, I should think the whole enterprise might be seriously taken in hand by professionals. Perhaps I use a distasteful figure, but I have the idea that what we need is Criticism, Inc., or Criticism, Ltd.

What Ransom wanted for English was a unique identity, securely fenced off from all extraneous (moral, philosophical, and political) considerations:

> It is really atrocious policy for a department to abdicate its own self-respecting identity. The department of English is charged with the understanding and communication of literature, an art, yet it has usually forgotten to inquire into the peculiar constitution and structure of its product. English might almost as well announce that it does not regard itself as entirely autonomous, but as a branch of the department of history, with the option of declaring itself occasionally a branch of the department of ethics.[21]

It is no accident, then, that many of the finest existing histories and anthologies of literary criticism were produced in this period of modernism's hegemony. Classic works like M. H. Abrams's *The Mirror and the Lamp: Romantic Theory and the Critical Tradition* (1953), William Wimsatt and Cleanth Brooks's *Literary Criticism: A Short History* (1957), and Hazard Adams's anthology *Critical Theory Since Plato* (1971) can all be seen as professional creation myths.[22] Each fused together a seemingly unsynthesizable multitude of theoretical materials. Each was inspired to do so by the shared goal of shoring up the new modernist edifice. Each helps consolidate the New Critics' professionalization of criticism by providing more or less fictive, more or less anachronistic antecedents for criticism's newly autonomous object (literature), thus guaranteeing the newly triumphant autonomy of the profession based on that object. The hidden key to these allegories of vocation, it would appear, and the reason why they were written when and as they were, is the rise of the specialist to an ultimate disciplinary autonomy.

In *Literary Criticism: A Short History*, as in Hazard Adams's anthology, for example, literary criticism begins with a specialist's nightmare, a moment of acute professional embarrassment. In Plato's *Ion*, the protagonist is a rhapsode – paid to recite, perform, comment on, and even to some extent compose poetry – who professes to know Homer better than anyone, but is unable to tell Socrates what it is, exactly, that he knows. Socrates, the most nightmarish of extra-professional interlocutors, gets Ion to admit that a charioteer would be better able to judge Homer's rendition of a chariot race, a general would know more about the battle scenes, and so on for fishermen, doctors, and masters of other technical skills. Only the rhapsode, mere interpreter of interpreters, has no area of expertise he can call his own, no unique body of specialized knowledge.

What then does someone know who knows about poetry? Hazard Adams's *Critical Theory Since Plato* delivers the delayed but definitive answer: "Socrates will not allow Ion to argue that he is an expert on the poem itself as an object or an indivisible whole" (11). Adams's answer is also what Wimsatt and Brooks call, in the title of their second chapter, "Aristotle's Answer: Poetry as Structure." For all of them, the poem as structure, object, indivisible whole takes the place of all cognitive claims for poetry which might conflict with the expertise of others, defining that knowledge the possession of which will count as the unique professional expertise of the critic. Thus professional embarrassment at the lack of a distinct object of knowledge is dispelled, and professional autonomy is secured.

The vigor of this will to achieve autonomy is manifest not only in how much the New Critical solution surrenders to Plato – how far the New Critic remains, like Ion, the passive slave of an inspired, cognitively empty experience of magnitude – but also in the extent to which classical antiquity had to be rewritten in order to produce the professional creation myth. As we now know, "literature" in the modern sense ("creative," "imaginative," "non-utilitarian," "self-reflexive," and so on) is a late eighteenth- and early nineteenth-century invention, and "literary" critics and theorists from Plato and Aristotle on were therefore not discussing the same concept as Coleridge and Arnold. What these early figures were discussing, more often than not, was rhetoric. This has been common knowledge to classicists for some time. According to the *Oxford*

Classical Dictionary, the dominant mode of literary theory in antiquity was rhetorical. The Greek rhetoricians, as Eric Havelock pointed out in his *Preface to Plato* (1963), did not see "poetry" as "aesthetic, impractical, non-informative." Poetry and a good deal else were covered by Aristotle's description of rhetoric: "the faculty of saying what is possible and pertinent in given circumstances." It is no surprise that Aristotle's *Poetics* was largely neglected in antiquity, and that his influence with regard to those subjects now recognized as "literary" came almost entirely through his *Rhetoric.*[23] The surprise is that it is Aristotle's *Poetics* rather than his *Rhetoric* that has begun our collective professional self-justification.

What is most interesting here, for my purposes, is not the scandal that an invented ahistorical constant could be imposed retrospectively upon centuries of writing to which it is wholly or partially alien. At least one reason for the (Romantic and modernist) cover-up is relatively obvious: the fact that rhetoric, with its implication in the messy worldliness of legal and political decision-making, could not so easily serve as the basis of a pure, autonomous (modernist) disciplinary identity. (The related fact that, from Kant and the Romantics on, literature could accuse rhetoric of "manipulation," thereby outflanking it to the left, will be discussed below.) It is precisely because of this worldliness that rhetoric has now returned, and – like narrative – has made a place within our new sense or senses of disciplinary identity. As I will argue in the next chapter, it is rhetoric's implication in public matters of politics, property, and power that gives it such power in criticism's current discourse of public legitimation. In the context of the modernist identification of artistic autonomy with professional autonomy, however, the crucial point is how rhetoric surfaces, as an instance or operator of legitimation, *even here*, in a modernist narrative where there would seem to be no room or need for legitimation.

Many of the reservations expressed about the New Critics, during as well as after the period of their hegemony, seem in retrospect to express an anxiety that, with their emphasis on autonomy based on skill exercised upon a distinct object, the New Critics were giving up on the opposition of culture to commerce that had been something of a legitimizing fundamental, and thereby leaving criticism without legitimation. At the risk of seeming to quibble, I want to stress the distinction between absence of legitimation and the weakness of a particular legitimation.

M.H. Abrams's *The Mirror and the Lamp* aims in the same direction as the two other modernist assemblages of critical tradition. It is less a collection of esteemed but anachronistic ancestors than they, however, and more a genuine history, in at least two senses: it is in collusion and continuity with the writers of the decisive period it treats, the period when literature in the modern sense finally does come into being; and it is committed to the resolution of contradiction. Thus it puts revealing pressure on the achievement-of-autonomy narrative that the three share, bringing its implicit legitimizing logic closer to the surface.

Abrams conveniently divides criticism into four orientations: mimetic, expressive, pragmatic/affective, and objective. Only two of these appear in Abrams's title – the expressive (the lamp), and the mimetic (the mirror). The chronology as he presents it is from the mirror to the lamp. But what about the two terms that don't get any catchy titular metaphors – especially the pragmatic, the domain of moral utility and rhetorical effect on the reader? The historical passage from the mirror to the lamp that Abrams wants to demonstrate appears to leave out the pragmatic and objective orientations. How do they fit into the chronology? Each of these two repressed terms in fact surfaces in a surprising way. First of all, the actual history Abrams tells – unlike the mirror-to-lamp progression declared by the title – fits the rise of the expressive into the larger but less visible rise of the *objective*: that is, of the text "in isolation from all ... external points of reference," "as a self-sufficient entity constituted by its parts in their internal relations" (26).[24] At one level of analysis, then, objectivism, the doctrine of the New Critics, would seem to be the absence that pulls the book forward, resolving the titular contradiction between mimetic and expressive and providing, once again, an autonomous base for literary study.

But both the resolution and the autonomy are jeopardized by the other unrepresented term. In telling the covert story of objectivism's rise, Abrams acknowledges another story. By his own account, the "pragmatic/affective" or rhetorical orientation had already taken over from the mimetic in ancient Greece itself, and it lasted from "the Hellenistic and Roman era almost through the eighteenth century." Not only was the pragmatic in fact far more powerful and pervasive than the mimetic at the outset, but it remained so for most of Western history – and then, in a surprise ending, it steals the climax even from seemingly hegemonic objectivism.

In order to end his book, Abrams must, it seems, have recourse to just that pragmatic or rhetorical orientation which his entire history has suppressed. The final section of the final chapter of *The Mirror and the Lamp* is entitled "The Use of Romantic Poetry." It begins: "The need to justify the existence of poets and the reading of poetry becomes acute in times of social strain." Here what has been suppressed throughout reasserts its rights. Instead of poetry as a "self-contained universe of discourse" of which we can demand "only that it be true to itself" (272), here is poetry as something of which we can and apparently must demand the "use," the value by an external, pragmatic criterion. And it comes in answer to Abrams's own need, in addition to and via that of the Romantics, to respond to a time of "social strain" with a myth – specifically, a professional creation myth – that will assert something more than art's autonomy. In order to reconcile, in his own description of the Romantics, "aesthetic detachment" with "social responsibility," he argues that "poetry as a moral instrument" (332) was *always* what the "imagination" had been about. The proposition that "poetic value" should be judged in the light of "effects on the reader" "had been held, with few exceptions, by critics from the Greeks through the eighteenth century. In England . . . it continued to be affirmed right through the romantic period" (328). The carefully constructed chronology that led to a non-mimetic (expressive or objective) orientation crumbles, revealing in its place an uncharted, unperiodized expanse of literature's "non-cognitive moral efficacy" (330), its social uses and social effects. The pragmatic, that is, is everywhere. Earlier, Abrams has suggested that, paramount among the four orientations, objectivism is central, "all-inclusive" (27); it "lay[s] claim to unlimited scope in the province of aesthetics" (284). Now, all of a sudden, everything is rhetoric, and has been all along.

This appeal to the *concept* of rhetoric is also of course a *use* of rhetoric. As the rhetoric manuals recommend, Abrams turns in the peroration – even at some risk of logical inconsistency – to the feelings and values of the audience, the ultimate ground of the rhetorical performance. And this turn tells us something about what audience is thereby intended for it. Whether it is "specialist" or "general," this audience clearly has a general, unspecialized interest in judging the moral, social, or political *value* of the "critical tradition" that the argument constructs. For it is this interest which must finally be satisfied, or whose satisfaction will give the argument its finality. In other words, even in what one imagines as an address to literary specialists, and even in an argument which seems so clearly

71

to prepare or corroborate the rise of a specialist who is value-free and autonomous, autonomy declares itself dependent, in the end, on the value judgment of a promiscuous public, dependent on appeal to a circle of values that are shared by specialist and non-specialist alike. (The question of what specific values these are, which is to say of how to evaluate the legitimation itself, will be raised later.) The internal disturbance within *The Mirror and the Lamp* is also perhaps what has made it so successful a narrative of legitimation: it argues for professional autonomy by means of a reaching out to the ears and values of others on whom it depends, thus demonstrating that the professional is not in fact autonomous. The idea of an autonomous artwork is not good enough to win Ion's argument and protect his profession. Unable to leave the public *agora*, the critic remains locked in risky dialogue with Socrates. Socrates is thus a figure both of extra-professional interlocutors and of professionals themselves.

3. The Rise of the Specialist, the Fall from the Public

In the other modernist classics I've been discussing, the most striking evidence of internal dialogue which undermines the illusion of autonomous, bounded professional identity is what Stanley Fish has called "anti-professionalism."[25] Take, for example, the first chapter of *Literary Criticism: A Short History*, entitled "Socrates and the Rhapsode." With genial self-deprecating humor, Wimsatt and Brooks note that the rhapsode, who dresses unlike other people and for a fee makes a spectacle of himself over poetry, comes uncannily close to their own professional activity; they describe him as "a sort of combined actor and college teacher of literature" (5). There is in fact a lot of professional language surrounding Ion: they speak of his "professional secrets," of "the rhapsode's type of actual professional discourse" (9), and so on. Given that Wimsatt and Brooks are defending their own "professional discourse," however, it is strange that they seem to identify so easily and so completely with Socrates' universalizing irony, which pokes gentle fun at Ion's professional deformation from a point of view that one can only assume is located outside the degrading specificities of any particular craft or trade.[26] It is as if only the universal Socrates, and not the narrowly professional Ion, could be the true voice of the profession.

John Crowe Ransom in "Criticism, Inc." reveals something of the same disloyalty to professionalism even as he champions it. If professionalism in his view is the cure for what ails criticism, it is also a kind of poison. While calling for poets and critics to develop "their own appropriate kind of specialization," Ransom supports the view

> that business as a self-contained profession has created business men who are defective in their humanity; that the conduct of business has made us callous to personal relations and social justice; and that many of the occupations which business has devised are, in the absence of aesthetic standards, servile. All these exclusions and specializations, and many more, have been making modern life what it is. (68–9)

This is somewhat noncommittal, but it still leaves us wondering why "specialization" will not produce critics, like businessmen, who are "defective in their humanity." To be a professional would seem to *mean* being defective in one's humanity.

Finally, consider a representative selection of the views on literary professionalism culled from Hazard Adams's *Critical Theory Since Plato*. (I pass over Plato's *Ion*, which has already been mentioned.) The selection from Sidney frames the discussion of "my unelected vocation" of poetry with a self-deprecating parable in which a horseman declares "soldiers were the noblest estate of mankind, and horsemen the noblest of soldiers" (155).[27] The selection from Schiller aims poetry at healing the wound imposed on modern man by the "rigorous separation of ranks and occupations," a situation in which man "becomes nothing more than the imprint of his occupation or of his specialized knowledge" (419). The selection from Wordsworth's "Preface" contains the "one restriction only" on the poet, that of giving pleasure to "a human being possessed of that information which may be expected from him, not as a lawyer, a physician, a mariner, an astronomer, or a natural philosopher, but as a man" (438). If the "question of belief or disbelief" comes up, according to the selection from I.A. Richards, "we have for the moment ceased to be reading poetry and have become astronomers, or theologians, or moralists, persons engaged in quite a different type of activity" (854). Among those theorists whom Adams might conceivably *not* have chosen, and who can therefore be taken to represent most forcefully his own preferences, we have the following: R.P. Blackmur: "Criticism, I take it, is the formal discourse of the amateur" (892); Kenneth Burke, who attacks professional specialization and proposes his categories as an "outrage" to "those persons who take the division of faculties in our universities to be an exact replica of the way in which God himself divided up the universe" (947); and Jean-Paul Sartre: "A blacksmith can be affected by

73

fascism in his life as a man, but not necessarily in his craft; a writer will be affected in both, and even more in his craft than in his life" (1067).

Why is it that the assumption of superiority to the (also assumed) restrictions, deformations, and inhumanity of professional specialization should run so markedly through the very middle of a critical tradition which is being constructed, in these very modernist texts, as the foundation of a new specialization? Why is it that modernist critics are urged, in effect, to take the viewpoint of the non-professional? There is one general and one specific answer. The general answer is that a defensive case for autonomy, which marks off literature's purity from contamination by other discourses without explaining why anyone should care about it in the first place, is no substitute for professional legitimation. On the contrary, the supposed self-containment of the literary artwork begets in critics a terrible anxiety that their profession, too, is self-contained, hence – since no profession can stand in fact on its own feet – vulnerable to society's misunderstanding and eventual withdrawal of support. In rites of propitiation or self-protection, therefore, critics impersonate and ventriloquize outsiders – and not any outsiders, but precisely those who are most critical of professions and their pretensions to self-sufficiency. They adopt the very point of view that interrogates most stringently the social usefulness of their activity, an anti-professional point of view which seems capable of representing and bestowing the legitimacy they fear they lack. Among other things, anti-professionalism is a ritual of professional legitimation – a ritual which cannot be assumed to be ineffectual.

The specific explanation for modernism's professional anti-professionalism goes back to the Romantic origins of modernist assertions of artistic autonomy: that is, to culture. In the *Aesthetic Education of Man*, Friedrich Schiller made the central Romantic critique of the "division of labour and specialization of function." [28]

> When the community makes his office the measure of the man, when in one of its citizens it prizes nothing but memory, in another a mere tabularizing intelligence, in a third only mechanical skill ... when, moreover, it insists on special skills being developed with a degree of intensity which is only commensurate with its readiness to absolve the individual citizen from developing himself in extensity – can we wonder that the remaining aptitudes of the psyche are neglected in order to give undivided attention to the one which will bring honour and profit? (35–7)

74

Thus (in the passage already cited from the Adams anthology) the human being "becomes nothing more than the imprint of his occupation or of his specialized knowledge." It is against this horrified vision of specialized work that Schiller and the other Romantics define the wholeness of art, culture, literature. As M.H. Abrams writes in *Natural Supernaturalism*, the "fragmentary specialization of human powers" can be reconciled and healed, on a higher level, by culture. Set against the division of labor, which creates specialized, deforming professions, culture is defined by the synthetic, formative imagination, by redemptive wholeness and harmony.[29] Given this definition, however, the labor of academic literary criticism can hardly be anything but self-contradictory and self-hating, for it is dedicated to an end it can never achieve. From the instant criticism itself enters the division of labor by becoming an individual discipline differentiated from other disciplines, it can only be seen as the very wound it was intended to heal, a fragment rather than a whole, a falling away from the unity that founds it.

The rise of the critic specializing in literature, according to this definition of literature, is thus necessarily the rise of an *anti-professional* specialist. In a sense, then, it is a fall. But this is not a contradiction that can easily be resolved. For there is some question as to whether that rise could have happened *without* the "decline" narrative, or without some other version of anti-professionalism's general logic – the logic, as I've suggested, of professional legitimation.

Wimsatt and Brooks, Adams, and – negatively – Abrams all tell the story of criticism's rise as an internal, relatively autonomous history culminating in the achieved autonomy of the New Criticism. The texts that have done most to consolidate our more recent professional common sense have tended to look at criticism more from the outside, as a social institution – a fact that is rarely factored into the resulting history. Yet this external perspective shares with its internal predecessor (associated with a time when the political could be casually ruled out-of-bounds) a common view of the endpoint of critical history: the achievement of a specialized autonomy that is seen as not requiring, or indeed as refusing, social legitimation. And, with extraordinary symmetry, they thus offer in effect the same narrative – in the first case, valued positively (the rise of the specialist), in the second negatively (a fall from the public).

Histories like John Gross's *The Rise and Fall of the Man of Letters* (1969) and Terry Eagleton's *The Function of Criticism: From "The Spectator" to Poststructuralism* (1984) are mirror images of their New

75

Critical predecessors.[30] They interpret criticism's rise as a fall: a fall into specialization, which is to be lamented, from a formerly higher, broader, more public and more adversarial estate. Both narratives are shaped around a supposedly decisive move from an oppositional public "before," conveniently located elsewhere, and a complicitous professional "after," right before our eyes. What is so remarkable is that neither Gross nor Eagleton in fact succeeds in narrating this transition. The terminal void that each ascribes to the "decline" narrative keeps filling up and having to be re-emptied. In his "Epilogue," Gross announces the sad fall of the man of letters into professionalization – triviality, specialization, false originality, and so on (294) – as both already having occurred and as imminent, hence not quite complete. Though the critic "may take a certain pride in being the last amateur in a world of professionals" (287), the reality is that "Most English literary critics and scholars are already academics by profession, and in the nature of things the proportion is going to grow" (292). But reading backwards from the present, one sees that professionalization has in fact always already occurred. "By the 1920s, a mood of sombre professionalism had set in, best exemplified by the founding of the *Review of English Studies* in 1925. The academic *apparatchiks* were in full command" (189). Professionalism has also already triumphed in the 1860s and finally, at the very beginning of the book, in the eighteenth century. On the very first page, Gross finds in Goldsmith "the professional critic" already arisen.

The same multiplication of falls structures Eagleton's narrative. By the twentieth century, Eagleton says, a "socially marginal professionalism" (69) has resulted from "the founding of English as a university 'discipline.'" "The academicization of criticism provided it with an institutional basis and professional structure; but by the same token it signalled its final sequestration from the public realm" (65). In fact, the book describes a *series* of sequestrations from the public realm. Within the fall from the exemplary public sphere of Addison and Steele into the narrow professional specialization of our century, each chapter represents another fall from another Golden Age: from Samuel Johnson, then from the Victorian man of letters, and then from Leavis and *Scrutiny*. This cyclic sub-narrative permits Eagleton to praise each of the figures he discusses – praise being an essential constituent of our professional rhetoric of legitimation – for a public responsibility that the overarching narrative would otherwise deny them. But there are other reasons for believing that praiseworthy public responsibility is distributed more generously than that master narrative suggests. The *repetition* of these sequestrations from the public realm indicates that criticism successfully withdrew from the public realm neither in the first act nor, more importantly, in the last. In fact, the point when English criticism supposedly touches bottom, its entrance into the university – that is, the moment of *Scrutiny* – is also, in Eagleton's own account, the moment of the strongest critique of professionalism and the strongest assertion of public responsibility. Public responsibility, it would seem, belongs within rather than outside professionalism. The moral of these stories is that there is no clear opposition between the public and the professional. The narratives go up as well as down because their principle of buoyancy, the public, inheres in their very substance and thus cannot be jettisoned.

This principle also suggests why Marxists like Eagleton do not necessarily sink to the nethermost depths of their profession, as Eagleton's account would lead one to predict, and why Eagleton himself could write a Marxist introduction to theory viewed by most of the profession as required reading – one of theory's more devious political consequences. In so doing, it sends us back as well for a second look at the commonplace of the-New-Criticism-as-modernist-professionalization. Eagleton's *Literary Theory: An Introduction* (1983), a work which has done a great deal to define the common-sense view of our recent revolutionary theoretical changes, suggests that the organic self-sufficiency of the New Criticism's post-Romantic artwork, disentangled from social or historical context, "had its roots in the economically backward South – in the region of blood and breeding where the young T.S. Eliot had gained an early glimpse of the organic society" – and that it transferred into aesthetics "the right-wing Agrarian politics of the 1930s," with its revolt against the South's "rapid industrialization" and "the sterile scientific rationalism of the industrial North."[31] The New Critics, Eagleton writes, "reinvented in literature what they could not locate in reality. Poetry was the new religion, a nostalgic haven from the alienations of industrial capitalism" (47). "Poetry was to be the new organic society itself" (49).

In Eagleton's account, it is deeply ironic that the New Criticism should have begun in this oppositional way, since its fate was to abet professionalization, based on a model of scientific rigor ("the toughest, most hard-headed techniques of critical dissection" [49]) and – this goes without saying – signifying the end of all opposition. New Criticism, Eagleton concludes, evolved in the years when literary criticism in North America was struggling to become "professionalized," acceptable as a respectable academic discipline. Its battery of critical instruments was a way of competing with the hard sciences on their own terms, in a society where such science was the dominant criterion of knowledge. Having begun life as a humanistic supplement or alternative to technocratic society, the movement thus found itself reproducing such technocracy in its own methods. The rebel merged into the image of his master. . . . The long trek from Nashville, Tennessee, home of the Fugitives, to the East Coast Ivy League universities had been accomplished. (49–50)

This narrative of professionalization makes the same highly problematic assumption as the modernist classics discussed above (and, for that matter, as Will Wright's *Sixguns and Society*). It takes for granted that professionalization is a single pre-established terminus – in a weightily comprehensive word, technocracy – which is reached by a single path, the path leading to autonomy via scientific rigor. Thus the organic text as microcosm of the organic society can be no more than an ironic backdrop to the achieving of professional status; it cannot be seen as a causal factor in that achievement, nor as part of the specific ideological substance achieved. According to this view, technocracy permits no discrimination of specifics; empty of any public representations that might try to fill the same space and thus collide with one another, it can only be unarticulated, a void, the end of narrative.

Eagleton is thus obliged to introduce into his narrative the awkward fiction of temporal succession – *first* there came organicism, as "humanistic supplement or alternative," and *then* there came rigorous methodology and professionalization – in order to camouflage their simultaneous coexistence, which is to say the scandalous fact that *both* figured in New Criticism's new legitimation. The vision of a pre-capitalist world embodied in the New Critical version of the poetic text, which is another version of culture as described in *Culture and Society*, is an indispensable part of the New Criticism's argument to society-at-large about why it deserves its hegemony, and about why the profession where it claims that hegemony deserves to exist at all. In the New Critical narrative, the narrowing of literature as autonomous professional object is simultaneously the clearing of an exemplary oppositional space, a kind of anti-capitalist microcosm, which criticism sets itself the task of propagating. The boundaries of the poetic text, which seem to cut it off from the world outside, are also the means by which the discipline reaches out to make a place for itself in that world.

This is the argument implied by the other narratives about why society should care whether or not literary criticism exists as a discipline – an ultimately political question that is irreducible to Socrates' epistemological question of whether the discipline possesses a distinct object that it knows better than anyone else. It is the argument from culture. There is no escape from the blurring of political lines that is here revealed. What is more or less glancingly touched on in Abrams's final chapter and in the helpless anti-professionalism of the other texts mentioned is fulsome and explicit in, of all places, Williams's *Culture and Society*, whose political differences from them seem overwhelming. *Culture and Society* is so powerful and moving a case for professional legitimation not despite but because of its fundamental commitment to political opposition. And its commitment to political opposition does not make it any less of a case for professional legitimation.[32]

4. Theory

It should come as no surprise to find oppositionality and professionalism together. Barbara and John Ehrenreich make the point that while most professionals may not be leftists, a great many American leftists have been professionals. This coexistence surely says as much about the professions as about the leftists. After all, the pronounced if minoritarian tendency of professions to attract, produce, and value political progressives can be explained entirely without idealism. Most service professions have come into existence within the past hundred years. In order to do so, they had to convince the state, which controls licensing, that there was a problem they and only they could properly treat. No problem, no profession. In this basic sense, service professions feed off the social miseries they are called in to remedy. Social conscience is not only in their interest, but in many cases their *sine qua non*.

But neither criticism's self-interest nor its homology with con-sumer capitalism, which is also committed to the definition of new needs, says anything one way or the other about the value of the need addressed. John Ehrenreich makes just this point in his history of the professionalization of social work, *The Altruistic Imagination* (1985). If the task of

> mitigat[ing] the worst features of industrial capitalism ... also corre-sponded to the psychological, occupational, and social needs of the

newly emerging class of professionals and managers, it is neither coincidental nor damning. During the Progressive Era, in the context of working-class unrest, the moral vision of the young professionals, their occupational needs, and the desperate need of the poor for social amelioration and reform more or less coincided with, and could be incorporated into, the needs of the capitalists for political-economic rationalization.[33]

Just because you're looking for trouble doesn't mean there isn't trouble there to be found.

Professionalization is not a zero-sum game in which every gain is someone's loss. There are of course instances of professional independence won by reducing non-professionals to dependence. Taylorite Scientific Management and the suppression of midwives by physicians, for example, demonstrate how some monopolies of expertise are achieved only by expropriating knowledge that already exists. It is true, as Sherry Gorelick shows, that public education (which enabled teachers to professionalize) was attractive to capitalists because it "substitut[ed] publicly taught skill for union-controlled apprenticeship." But it is also true that "Workers *demanded* compulsory schooling" (my italics).[34] Worker demand was as constitutive of the profession as teacher demand, and it remains operative within the profession as we have it.

Like other "therapeutic" professions, then, literary criticism tries to convince people both that they're sick and that our profession has a cure. The fact that it is in criticism's interest to make this case does not mean that the case is wrong. Criticism's interest and society's interest are neither necessarily harmonious nor necessarily opposed. The question comes down to particulars.

The sense that criticism's interests and society's interests had begun to clash became acute in the 1960s. With the rising interest in structuralism, poststructuralism, Lacanian psychoanalysis, Althusserian Marxism, and other less classifiable currents of thought – the phenomenon known colloquially as "literary theory" – that followed the Johns Hopkins conference of 1966, it was suddenly unclear to many critics that the concept of culture, in particular, could continue to mediate successfully between professional routine, on the one hand, and social value, on the other. Culture became a contested object.

This same period also witnessed the general crisis of American professionalism which one historian of engineering has labeled the "revolt of the client." Across the whole spectrum of professions from law and medicine to engineering, social work, and university teaching, agitation on behalf of "relevance" and "responsiveness" in fact engaged both clients and professionals themselves and probed into the theoretical grounds as well as the practical effects of professional expertise and authority. It seems plausible that literary theory, coming in the same years, was criticism's version of the general phenomenon. While some of its clients – especially women and minority students – were making their dissatisfactions heard, literary theory was expressing parallel dissatisfactions. It threw open the definition of "the work," of "the canon," of "literature," of "culture" itself. It undermined authorial intention, historical reference, and textual coherence, thus compromising the claim to objectivity in interpretation and with it the sanction of the professional interpreter. As theory's antagonists complained, criticism no longer seemed to possess any unique expertise to call its own, any basis or grounding as a discipline.

I will be suggesting below that this fear was unfounded. Much as some champions of the new theory might like to see its increasing dominance as a refusal of disciplinarity or professionalism as such, what was happening was, rather, a shifting of disciplinary grounds, a renegotiation of the profession's legitimation. New terms like "ideology" and "rhetoric" and "narrative" and "discourse" that were suddenly in the air, taking up discursive space that had been filled by the vocabulary of culture, were in many ways alternatives to culture, but they tried to serve the same function: like culture, they mediated between a routine of professional activity and a set of social values to which it held that activity accountable. They redefined the professional object, *but it was a professional object they redefined.* They promised the profession an alternative expertise, an alternative grounding.

This sketch of literary criticism's recent history is itself an alternative to the dominant narratives offered on the one hand by theory itself, on the other by its enemies, who often speak in the name of culture. The first group tends (or perhaps tended, until the more recent rise of "cultural studies") to see their own ascent as an unprecedented, revolutionary rupture with institutional forms and continuities. The champions of culture have tended to see theory as still another fall into professionalism. According to David Bromwich's version of one popular narrative, for example, theory itself represents professionalization's highest, which is to say most sterile and most unfortunate, stage.[35] The once genuinely subversive literary and political avant-garde, he says, "has taken up residence in the academy," and, in becoming "identified with literary study in the universities" (35), it has lost any pretension to political significance. "The consequential debates in our culture," Bromwich adds, "have always taken place somewhere else" (36).

If culture is a matter of "experience" rather than distanced abstraction, and a matter of "wholeness" rather than fragmented disciplinarity, then a specialized academic discipline that devotes itself to the posing of theoretical questions (however much it thereby shifts the alignment of the disciplines amongst themselves) can have little claim to truly cultural significance. With culture as center, literary theory becomes a pre-eminent case of that experiential poverty Williams describes as "the professional culture of distance." And this is more or less the judgment that Williams himself passed on it. What Williams says about television in "Distance" is also what he says about the rise of literary theory. In "The Future of Cultural Studies," he gives a standard narrative of lament: "having got into the university, English studies had within twenty years converted itself into a fairly normal academic course, marginalizing those members of itself who were sustaining the original project.... It became ... a professional discipline." Then, in the 1960s, "a body of theory came through which rationalized the situation of this formation on its way to becoming bureaucratized and the home of specialist intellectuals."[36]

Culture and Society renewed the rationale for criticism as a specialized profession within the division of labor – the same division of labor that criticism also (as in Williams's own critique of military and media professionalism) constituted itself by standing apart from. It is a measure of Williams's own greatness, but perhaps also of the resilience of the tradition he represents, that he could also glimpse, in both television and theory, how "culture" and "society" might be something other than opposing terms. Given the narrative of descent implicit in culture, he had trouble believing television contained any redeeming virtues whatsoever. Yet with horrified fascination he returned to it again and again, searching for the emergence of emancipatory potential. And what he found radically revalued his judgment of the "distance" shared by television, theory, and professionalism.

Television, Williams says, is "an authority without rivals and beyond effective challenge, imposing itself professionally" (114); its "outraged professionalism" responds to calls for interrogation from the outside with the argument that only professionals can understand, or judge, each other. Thus "there is no normal space in which news reports can be examined and interrogated" (117). What Williams actually calls for, however, is an explicitness about assumptions – a version of this "normal space," both inside and apart, at a distance – that he explicitly locates within rather than outside professionalism:

> there is no profession which can fail to learn from someone making explicit just the training, the usage, the taking for granted, that underlie all practice. These can then be consciously affirmed, or consciously amended. This is how all rigorous professions work. (118)

Here television breaks out of the narrative of decline, displaying a potential, at least in theory, to function as a transfiguration of culture, a new democratic public sphere. At the same time, this passage also offers a positive description of what theory itself has represented within literary criticism in particular and the humanities in general: a "normal space" for self-examination about "the training, the usage, the taking for granted, that underlie all practice." A "space" that defies all catastrophic narratives of decline by virtue of its recent birth, by declaring itself to be both professional and public at once, and by being "normal."

3

The Insistence of the Public in Postmodern Criticism

1. Scenes of Legitimation

In the fall of 1972, when I was starting graduate school, the professor in charge of the first-year colloquium asked us all what we would say if a businessman held a gun to our heads and demanded to know why society should pay for us to study literature – what we would say, that is, that Matthew Arnold had not already said. Nobody had the confidence to take up this challenge. Our painfully prolonged and embarrassed silence seemed to make, among other points, the point our instructor desired to make: that there hasn't *been* a better case for criticism since Arnold talked about poetry taking the place of religion, about "culture" as "the best that is known and thought" and "the free play of the mind," and so on.

We did not seriously expect to have our brains blown out, but we were, I think, more nervous than usual. It may have been the general fearfulness of the first year of graduate school, or the respect we all had for the professor, Walter Jackson Bate, who had conjured up the gun-toting businessman and was probably somewhat confused with him in our minds. Or it may have been, at least for me, the fact that my father had good reason to be mystified by what critics do, since he was a businessman who had not been to college. Whatever the reason, there was something intimidating about this forceful bit of pedagogy, and at the same time also something exhilarating. The moment stuck in my memory. But I didn't begin to reflect on the imaginary scene of self-justification before a menacing outsider, or ask what it might have to do with my own or anyone else's sense of vocation, until the scene was repeated.

Almost two decades had gone by. I was now a member of the profession to which I had then been starting my apprenticeship. Along with two other faculty members from other literature departments, I was asked to speak to a large group of Rutgers University undergraduates, most of them not English majors, about what I did and why I did it – specifically, about what it meant to do Marxist literary criticism.[1] The audience was hostile and bored – correctly, as it turned out: we discovered later that the students were forced to attend a certain number of panel discussions like ours in exchange for the privilege of not living several miles from campus. Under the pressure of their visible hostility, I dropped my prepared but manifestly insufficient remarks about such things as Marx's preference for the royalist Balzac over the socialist Zola. Instead, I found myself blurting out that I certainly hadn't gotten into this line of work, as they might think, because I dreamed of spending my life in the analysis of sonnet structure or digging up unknown manuscripts. I had gotten into it because what it studied was "narrative," and "narratives," whether they realized it or not, were what they themselves were living by. Ethics or religion or science or politics – it was all narrative.

My fellow panelists had been chosen so as to represent different approaches to literary study, but they rallied behind my impromptu bit of disciplinary rationale with surprising enthusiasm, and they held to it even after the most articulate students had reacted with anger and outrage ("Are you saying that my religion is like Sidney Sheldon?").[2] I was thus permitted the fantasy that, rather than simply embarrassing myself, I had successfully if inadvertently ventriloquized the discipline of literary criticism itself. It suddenly seemed that after and perhaps because of two decades of "literary theory" – the same two decades, roughly, since my fellow graduate students and I failed to respond to the "gun-to-the-head" ultimatum – a new answer had indeed emerged to supersede Matthew Arnold's famous formulas: something like the phrase "everything is narrative."

There is much more to say about the peculiarities of "narrative" as the predicate of a sentence whose subject is "everything," as well as its hypothetical claims (versus those of other candidates) as a rationale for literary studies.[3] For the moment, I am more interested in articulating what my fantasy of speaking for the profession has to say about the profession. "Everything is narrative" may not be the truth that most literary critics would present to themselves, in quiet moments of scrupulous self-consciousness, as an adequate account of the discipline's philosophical foundation. But if my experience is any indication, this phrase is indeed one truth about the discipline, or one example of a kind of truth, that critics present *to others* – and thus to some extent also to themselves – in those unquiet moments when offensively indifferent, inquisitively public-minded, or maliciously budget-conscious non-critics oblige them to attempt a satisfactory public portrayal of what they do. It is the pressured, embarrassed utterances produced by such moments that I want to explore here: the strange, alienated genre or mode of professional truth that tries, at whatever cost and with whatever success, to render some account of the activities inside a profession in answer to an explicit or implicit interrogation by the society outside it.

To identify the existence of such a mode of professional rhetoric is to begin looking at professionalism from an unaccustomed and disorienting angle. The reason why it is unaccustomed is also the reason why this mode or genre has not been more visible. Given the assumption that professions are inherently exclusive, elitist, and self-enclosed, there is something counter-intuitive in the notion that a professional discourse aimed at outsiders indeed exists, or exists on a scale substantial enough to warrant further discussion. The two scenes that I've taken to exemplify such a discourse seem quite exceptional. They are memorable in part because we do not think of their intimidating quality as common in academic conversation, even in lectures. We tend to assume that professional discourse is ordinarily calm and unruffled, that its conflicts and controversies are channeled and contained by professional boundaries, by premises agreed upon in advance. We (professionals and non-professionals alike) may therefore look upon the self-legitimating responses shaken loose from professional speakers under the impact of this intimidation as false testimony extracted under extraordinary and uncharacteristic duress. We also tend to assume that professional discourse possesses, even to a fault, a technical, relatively autonomous vocabulary, a jargon. But in order to make or maintain contact with external interlocutors, responses like "everything is narrative" are able to translate out of the profession's technical vocabulary and into the putative imprecisions of common speech – to compromise, that is, the rigorous internal standards of professional discourse. Such responses will therefore seem, as my own crude credo seemed even to me, embarrassingly unprofessional.

In sum, the two scenes will seem exceptional because we do not typically think of our professional work as forced to pay heed to outsiders at all, at least in the usual sense of "work" as criticism or scholarship. We know that much of what is said and written in the profession works its way back or out to the public via our students, who remain to some extent professional outsiders whether they are undergraduate non-majors or first-year graduate students in a doctoral program. We know that letters of recommendation and grades most often have an extra-professional readership. We know that teaching evaluations, tenure reports, and proposed changes in the curriculum are interpreted by university administrators, who may not share the assumptions of our discipline or department and who must in turn answer to their funders, whether corporate or governmental.[4] But the distribution of power and the channeling of tasks within courses are such that faculty are not often conscious of being threatened by any of these versions of the public. How could anyone be threatened inside a course? Most often we do not consciously look back over our shoulders at any of these publics, let alone at other members of the unprofessional public farther afield, as we attend to the bread-and-butter of our craft: analyzing a given line or text or career, refining a theoretical category, framing a historical context, teaching a course.

Indeed, this is one of the most frequent criticisms that critics level at themselves. Louis Menand, reviewing Roger Kimball's *Tenured Radicals: How Politics Has Corrupted Our Higher Education* (*New Republic*, July 9/16, 1990), offers a representative formulation. It is not surprising, Menand writes,

> that so little of what gets passed around bears much useful relation to life as people outside the profession know it ... as humanistic study has become increasingly professionalized, its practitioners have become less and less disposed to respond to any intellectual challenges except those presented by the work of their colleagues within the discipline (39)

If one thinks about these words for a moment, however, the notion of professional address to outsiders may suddenly stop looking quite so strange. Menand's argument goes down easily; we have heard a great many arguments that closely resemble it. Yet on second thought there is something paradoxical in this familiarity. For if what Menand says is true, then how is it that he himself and so very, very many others (whether or not they have access to non-specialized journals like the *New Republic*) seem willing and able to observe "their colleagues within the discipline" from a position outside it? How is it that so much discursive space inside the profession is devoted to such observations, that is, to criticizing the profession from the perspective of a "useful relation to life as people outside the profession know it"? How is it, in short, that criticism of the discipline in the name of *outsiders* can be so characteristic an act of the disciplinary *insider*?[5] The answer would seem to be that Menand is wrong, after all, to rely on the familiar assumption that professional means private, exclusive, esoteric, inaccessible. For the easy, habitual antithesis between the professional and the public excludes just what Menand himself exemplifies: the professional's own will, *as* professional, to test out the discipline's "useful relation to life," to take over and mobilize the point of view of "people outside the profession," to enter into some sort of dialogue with the extra-professional public.

Menand's well-worn charges also exemplify the plentiful, entirely unexceptional texts in which professional confrontation with the public can be shown to take place. Scenes in which professional rationale issues directly from traumatic confrontation with extra-professionals may be rare – though there are certainly many other everyday situations that on reflection might be placed in this category – but discourse which invites some representative of the public to participate in a moment of professional inventory and self-evaluation is not restricted to overt dramatic confrontations. It is also to be found concealed in the most ordinary critical prose – readings, reviews, theoretical arguments, and (as we saw in the previous chapter) literary and critical histories. Menand's argument itself offers a striking analogue to the scene in which Walter Jackson Bate invented the businessman with the gun. In both, the speaker imagines and momentarily joins or identifies with a figure of the professional outside in order to expose or verify or shift the profession's internal alignment. This is to say that the profession's self-legitimating dialogue with outsiders is not a rare genre marked off by some set of uniquely distinctive traits, like violence and embarrassment. It is a mode in which many different genres can and do operate on a routine basis. The characteristic scenario is a relatively widespread one: beneath the surface of writing that has some other declared intention, most likely a design of immediate interest solely or primarily to insiders, some figure or agent of "the public" can be detected which introduces into that prose another agenda, a second, hidden logic linking well-defined business *in* the profession to the larger if vaguer purposes *of* the profession.

To argue that there is confrontation with the public beneath the surface of what appear to be very different sorts of literary commentary and argument is to suggest that the public is something like a professional unconscious. This phrase might be misleading,[6] but it teaches at least two useful lessons about how to read the discourse of vocation. First, it steers us beyond an exclusive, paralyzing attention to actual, empirically measurable publics – though of course attention must be paid to them – and to the empirically verifiable communication that passes between us and them. Applied to our profession, the psychoanalytic model broadens the meaning of the term, suggesting that versions of "the public" have been *internalized* by critics and that these internalizations act with real force upon the profession's psychic economy, whether or not they correspond faithfully to extra-professional collectivities. There can be no clear border, therefore, between speaking to ourselves and speaking to others. Even at our most private, even in what we hope or fear may be professional soliloquy, we are to some extent looking over our shoulders, listening for other voices and adapting our own to what we think we hear. Like the Dostoevskian characters analyzed by Bakhtin, we match our fragile, dependent condition of social being with a condition of discursive being marked by inescapable, indeterminate polyphony. We listen "for" the public in two equivocal senses of the preposition: we listen so as to hear what the public may be saying, and we listen *to ourselves, on behalf of* the public, which is of course us too. Both senses invite us to surrender the illusion of a professional identity that is hermetically sealed and to recognize instead the social reality of an identity that is looser, less autonomous, more diversely populated.

By the same token, the notion of a professional unconscious also suggests that public address is not a simple rationalization or self-deception. (Hence the exhilaration, even if accompanied by embarrassment, that goes with touching base, reconnecting with the grounding premises of professional activity.) An alternative model comes from social science, where the work of mediating between "the public" as a rhetorical figure of professional discourse, on the one hand, and actual social collectivities and interests, on the other, bears the recognized name of "legitimation."[7] If discourse that does this work cannot be taken at face value, it nevertheless performs, as the name suggests, a real and necessary social function. According to theorists like Hayden White and Jean-François Lyotard, legitimation is the special province of narrative. A publicly accessible form, narrative is uniquely suited to the task of integrating any given ideas or practices into the public's judgment of what is right and proper, making them seem rightful and legitimate.[8] (The traditional intimacy between narrative and legitimation may help to explain the spontaneous force of the phrase "everything is narrative" in a moment of desperately defensive rationale.) Thus there was special reason, as in the last chapter, to search the narratives that critics produce – literary histories, histories of criticism, narratives shaping a text or a career – for evidence of legitimating functions, double agency, a discourse of vocation that takes the hidden form of an allegory.

Just because professional insiders invent publics for themselves, therefore, it does not follow that the outside is imaginary or that there is no real connection between what is invented inside and the forces outside that must be managed, assuaged, responded to, negotiated or compromised with. We know, or should know, that the autonomy the profession seems to abandon momentarily when faced with the demand for a generally accessible account of itself is never more than relative and provisional. It is granted by social bodies outside the profession, whether the state (as often in Europe) or "public opinion" or some mixture thereof. And it can be sustained only for as long as its support continues – as long as the profession's authority in a given area is judged, by enough of those people who have the power to withdraw that authority, to be not only legitimate, but more legitimate than that of other contenders. In this sense, the businessman holding a gun to the head of a humanist is not an entirely inappropriate scenario for professional speech, though it may be a "worst case" among other interlocutors. A professional edifice can be shaken and even toppled by challenges from rival versions of expertise as well as from corporate funders. General ideological shifts, too, can allot the area of professional jurisdiction to others or drastically shrink it.

A number of recent historians have insisted, in this vein, that the professions are inexplicable if one does not factor in public demand and public opinion. The guiding principle of their research, according to Gerald Geison in *Professions and Professional Ideologies in America* (1983), is "that the public (or the laity) also plays a crucial role in the success of professional market strategies," and that historians must therefore "take account of the demand for professional services as well as the willingness of the public (or at least their elected representatives) to grant special status and privileges to specific occupational groups."[9] For those groups, this means that – as Magali Larson writes – "Persuasion tends to be typically directed to the outside – that is, to the relevant elites, the potential public or publics, and the political authorities." For "[p]rofessional indifference may be broken from the outside." Administrators too can evoke the public welfare, and "privileges can always be lost." With

90

regard to knowledge bases that are excessively esoteric, Larson finds it "doubtful . . . that specialties whose functions are not really understood by any significant sector of the public" can survive as professions.[10]

Historically, failure to professionalize often depended on the inability to mobilize public support, in the form of state licensing or market demand. And success, for example in the case of lawyers discussed by Stephen Botein in the Geison collection cited above, depended as much on "the 'claim' . . . to be oriented toward the public good" as on the " 'claim' to 'esoteric knowledge' " (121). Jan Goldstein, in the same volume, gives the example of French medicine in the early nineteenth century. Again, it was the intervention of the state rather than doctors' own expertise that won them their professional monopoly: "In terms of the therapies they offered, 'official' accredited medical practitioners were . . . virtually indistinguishable from their competitors, the mass of unaccredited healers whom they typically called 'charlatans' " (184). Doctors obtained the state's support partly by promoting the concept of "moral contagion," which linked their efforts to government policy against other sorts of disturbance.

What I'm offering is empirical evidence of the real if uneven historical power of persuasion, and the real accountability of professions to the public. This evidence suggests that professions are not, in Shaw's phrase, conspiracies against the laity. If the laity, in the form of state and/or market, is not a party to the conspiracy, if the conspiracy is not *leaked*, as it were, then it cannot achieve its desired effects. Professions are not hermetically sealed, but porous. To associate professional language with jargon incomprehensible to outsiders is thus a serious historical error. Address to outsiders, according to these histories, is indispensable to professional speech. A good illustration is Thomas Haskell's book *The Emergence of Professional Social Science* (1977).[11] Haskell accepts the older narrative that professions tend to tell about themselves. On his account the replacement of the amateur by the professional in social science is required by the specialization of expertise, which is required in turn by the facts themselves: the increasing complexity of modern society. Haskell calls this complexity "interdependence," meaning an interdependence of social groups, institutions, and interests so complex that no individual or amateur view can encompass it. But this term for the objective social facts that supposedly necessitate and justify professionalization shoots beyond those facts. It compromises the explanation by introducing the counter-principle of persuasion. For Haskell also speaks of *professional* interdependence, meaning the cooperation of an "ongoing, disciplined community of inquiry," and he implies that professionalism is thus a desirable alternative to the selfish individualism of amateurs. Throughout the book, he insinuates that to accept interdependence is a *moral* and *social*, rather than simply an epistemological, imperative. This doubling of cool objectivity with warm virtue exemplifies the sort of rhetorical turn, a turn to the public, which finds no place in Haskell's narrative of how the profession was established, but by which, as that narrative inadvertently shows, professions are in fact established and maintained. Haskell answers a challenge from the public that he declares he doesn't hear.

The intimidation of such challenges goes with the territory. And so, therefore, does the discourse which answers intimidation, adapts to changing values, defends areas of expertise: the discourse of professional legitimation. In *The System of Professions: An Essay on the Division of Expert Labor* (1988), Andrew Abbott offers further illustrations of the principle that "Societies have little time for experts who lack cultural legitimacy." "The ability of a profession to sustain its jurisdictions," he argues, depends in large part on its ability to link its activities to "major cultural values." As an example of how professional jurisdiction depends on appeal to cultural values, Abbott cites "the attempt of psychiatry to take over criminality in the twenties," an effort to extend the territory of psychiatrists at the expense of lawyers by means of "a largely academic assault on the concept of responsibility." "The psychiatrists actually won a number of intellectual battles in this conflict, but ultimately lost the jurisdictional war, partly because . . . the public believed too deeply in the lawyers' version of personal responsibility" (53–5). But professions defending their jurisdiction cannot always rest content, like the criminal lawyers of the 1920s, with such support from public values as they already enjoy. For "values change," and such changes "can sharply change demand for professional services." "As a consequence," Abbott goes on, "professions continually revise their legitimation systems" (184–7). The most obvious example (an example of special pertinence to a discipline still indebted to Matthew Arnold) is secularization, the decline in "concern for salvation" in the industrialized nations (186), and its effect on the profession of the clergy. From the nineteenth century on, those clergy least protected from the force of diminishing public interest in being saved have undertaken a major revision of their "legitimation system," their language for recruiting new members, their discourse of vocation. Giving up to a large extent on salvation, they have gone in the direction of mass education, and more recently toward "social melioration" (186–7).

The example is worth pausing over. It illustrates the strict social logic that can make meaningful a discourse which might otherwise appear to be mere window-dressing, ideology in the negative sense, an emptily sonorous claim to "public service." And it also undoes an uncomfortable implication of the term "legitimation." To identify "legitimation" with "mass education" and "social melioration" is to dissociate it from any necessary connection with the defense of a fixed professional status quo or of the dominant, ruling-class values of the society around it. On the contrary, it appears, legitimation can and often does mean the sort of wholesale refashioning of professional mission and daily practice that has given us, say, the (highly successful) "sanctuary" movement of churches in defense of Central American refugees. In order for professional autonomy to be defended, professional expertise must frequently be transformed and hegemonic social values must frequently be affronted. In the academy, this characteristically means a refashioning of the object of study – for example, the rise of the more democratic social history, or history "from below," in response to the social ferment of the 1960s. In literary criticism, one thinks of the literary theory phenomenon of the same years, and more recently of the move toward some form of cultural studies.

It is just this dynamic of professional self-fashioning in response to shifts in public value (or even in anticipation of such shifts) that we can see, I think, in the contrast between the two scenes of legitimation, nearly twenty years apart, where real or imagined hostility from the outside precipitates awkward avowals of what literary critics are collectively up to. "Poetry" or "literature," as described by Arnold and Bate, defines one version of the professional object of knowledge and establishes one sort of relationship to society-at-large. "Narrative," "rhetoric," "textuality," and "discourse," to name some of the recent candidates to replace it as criticism's object, must also be seen as more or less successful candidates to establish new discourses of legitimation, new allegories of vocation, new alignments between society and the profession. The breaks and the continuities between the two scenes, the two sets of objects, the two modes of legitimacy offer a framework in which the criticism's recent history can be re-evaluated.

This is not to assume, as the examples above may seem to hint, that new alignments with the public must inevitably take us toward a more responsible professionalism – toward more democratic subject matter and more oppositional practices of scholarship. It is not clear that *different* alignments mean *closer* alignments, an increased responsiveness of the profession to the public, let alone that the unpremeditated, makeshift phrase "everything is narrative" describes with any accuracy even the most revisionist forms of *Marxist* criticism, my supposed subject before the Rutgers non-majors. The point of insisting that public alignments are perpetually at stake in criticism's discourses of legitimation, as they are at stake in the legitimating discourse of other professions, is to ensure that the theme of professionalism can be brought up as a real political *question*, rather than a presumably complete political judgment – brought up, that is, without professionalization serving as the endpoint of a teleological narrative of either triumphalism or degeneration.

It is these schematic and misleading alternatives – triumph or collapse – that I am trying to move the discussion away from. Many observers have attributed the questioning of criticism's founding premises over the past quarter century to a theoretical frenzy of sterile, esoteric professionalization. Others, consciously or unconsciously clinging to a positive assessment of professional status, have interpreted what René Wellek calls "the attack on literature" as a step toward the collapse of all standards of value and expertise and thus toward the loss of criticism's professional autonomy. Meanwhile, partisans of "theory" have sometimes been happy enough to reverse this valuation, priding themselves on achieving the same departure from professionalism's hierarchies of value and social legitimacy that the others deplore. These three versions of our recent professional history share two common and disabling errors. First, that getting outside professionalism is at present a feasible choice. And second, that public, social values are only to be found outside it.[12] The professional history proposed here, on the other hand, assumes that work done in institutions like the university will necessarily fall within the horizon of professionalism. But it also assumes that to be professional is not to be cut off from the realm of public value. It asserts therefore that "theory" is indeed a professional formation. But it also asserts that for this very reason "theory" cannot be entirely private, empty, esoteric. As a professional formation, it can only survive if it finds for itself some form of public legitimacy.

In rethinking criticism's history over the past decades, then, we cannot make a political choice for or against professionalism, between fullness and emptiness, public and private. We can only distinguish between different versions of legitimacy, different alignments of public and profession. We must recognize that the discourse of legitimation brings the social world outside into the act of constituting the professional object, into the very heart of that object, hence into what insiders actually do as well as what they say they do. And we must recognize that this implicit debate over professional objects and the choices of professional direction they embody remains unfinished, open to change. Otherwise we have little chance of understanding why "politics," including political judgments of the profession itself, has come to enjoy the immense prestige within the profession that it so recently and notoriously has, or why so many critics, like so many members of the clergy, have become so committed to "social melioration." Nor can we assess what, if anything, critics can contribute to that purpose.

2. Rhetoric in Public

In *The Trial of Socrates* (1988), the late I.F. Stone addressed a chapter to "Socrates and Rhetoric."[13] Speaking on behalf of the Athenian public, he took sides against Socrates and for rhetoric. Rhetoric, he said, was a skill enabling citizens "to protect their interests in the assembly and in the law courts" (90), hence an essential tool of Athenian democracy, and that was what the anti-democratic Socrates most mistrusted about it. "The unspoken premise of the Socratic assault on oratory was disdain for the common people of Athens" (92).[14]

In academic departments in the humanities and social sciences, the defense of rhetoric against a universalizing Platonic or scientific reason is not news. Among the many who have lately been trying to move rhetoric, in Stanley Fish's words, "from the disreputable periphery to the necessary center," one can cite the historians Hayden White and Dominick LaCapra, the economist Donald McCloskey, the sociologist Jean Baudrillard, and literary critics as otherwise diverse as Mikhail Bakhtin, Paul de Man, Wayne Booth, Terry Eagleton, and Fish himself.[15] In anthropology, communications, philosophy, political science, law, and even medicine, and especially in interdisciplinary projects that connect them, the revival of rhetoric has been proceeding for some time.

What does it mean when an exemplary intellectual like I.F. Stone, whose bold independence from the large institutions of American journalism was an inspiration to so many, agrees with the supposedly esoteric, jargon-ridden dogmas of literary theory, which presumably is incomprehensible to all but the bedazzled inhabitants of elite educational institutions? Is it possible that theory is after all translatable into a common language? And a common language that is also a *critical* language?

One cannot quite conclude from Stone's eloquent non-specialist defense that there has been a sudden conjunction of academic high theory with the common sense of the general or extra-academic reading public. Most often, the public has taken the term rhetoric as a slur, a synonym for deceit, manipulation, and propaganda, for the tyranny of words unchecked by the truth of things, and there is little evidence of widespread change.[16] Nevertheless, this encounter marks a patch of common ground that will bear cultivation. My argument here, then, will be that Stone's grounding of rhetoric in the democratic *polis* or public offers a significant but also troubling analogy to the rehabilitation of rhetoric in the university, which much contemporary opinion, both left and right, *opposes* to the public as specialized, professionalized, private. I will suggest that the interdisciplinary move toward rhetoric moves scholarship in the direction of the public, and as such is politically desirable.[17] But I will also suggest that the phrase "the public," which I and others plug into our politico-disciplinary arguments at value-laden points like this, is itself a piece of rhetoric, and as such to be examined carefully for its multiple, devious, and perhaps even unintended persuasive effects.

Let me confess at the outset the specific disciplinary situation that has provoked this line of thinking. If rhetoric's return seems on the whole desirable to me, it's probably not unconnected to the fact that thus far the results have been rather beneficial to my own discipline. In literary criticism, the current rhetorical reawakening should, I think, be seen as the advocacy of one candidate – not the only one, but certainly one of the strongest – for the replacement of "literariness" as the discipline's cognitive object or knowledge base, as how we name what we are doing both to ourselves and, equally important, to those outside the discipline. When criticism embraced a self-conception founded on the aesthetic as non-pragmatic, non-instrumental – in short, as anti-rhetoric – it imposed a certain marginality upon itself. Today, with new self-conceptions in play that share, to varying degrees, an impatience with this anti-rhetorical posture, this marginality has to some extent been fought off; criticism has been able to claim a more public role. For example, it has offered its tools of analysis to other, more authoritative disciplines beginning to problematize their own rhetoric. And it has claimed a central place in politically charged interdisciplinary projects like cultural studies, whose collapsing of the elite/popular divide and democratizing of subject-matter give it another claim to public responsiveness.[18]

Readers who do not have the good fortune to be literary critics will perhaps catch the "public" doing double duty here. That is, the word stands in for the general welfare, while it also protects and promotes the imperial ambitions of a single discipline at the expense of other disciplines. When Richard Rorty celebrates literary "textualism" for taking over the "public" role of philosophy, it is precisely this ambiguity that surfaces in the word "public." Rorty's two senses of the word correspond to two high points or Golden Ages from which philosophy has supposedly fallen into privacy and profession-alization: the age of Kant and the age of Dewey. In Rorty's essay "Professionalized Philosophy and Transcendentalist Culture," the public role of Dewey's pragmatism is seen in *national* terms: "The period between the World Wars was one of prophecy and moral leadership – the heroic period of Deweyan pragmatism, during which philosophy played the sort of role in the country's life which Santayana could admire."[19] Kant, on the other hand, stands for a Golden Age defined by philosophy's role not in the nation, but vis-à-vis *other disciplines*, which it put in their places. This is the adversarial, non-altruistic sense – one might say, the rhetorical sense – in which "textualism" is public.

> The claims of a usurping discipline to preside over the rest of culture can only be defended by an exhibition of its ability to put the other disciplines in their places. This is what the literary culture has been doing lately, with great success. It is what science did when it displaced religion and what idealist philosophy did when it briefly displaced science. (155)

One should not be too quick to judge the obvious disciplinary self-interest behind such claims. As Andrew Ross suggests in *No Respect*, all appeals by intellectuals to "the public" are self-serving in that "the public service model makes provision for cultural standards set by intellectuals and also accommodates interventions by intellectuals."

Identifying public welfare with the *market*, on the other hand, makes no obvious place for their "standards and interventions" (106). This is undoubtedly a reason why, from Matthew Arnold through today's interdisciplinary advocates for rhetoric and cultural studies, intellectuals aligned themselves with the public and – in one way or another – against the market. And it gives intellectuals a strong motive, as Ross indicates, to reconsider their aboriginal, self-defining disrespect for the market and its cultural products. But to do so is not to give up on "the public," or even on the would-be identification of intellectuals with it. On the contrary. Ross intimates, in effect, that while we have been looking for "the public" in all the wrong places – for example, in a single collective will rather than in irreducibly plural fragments – we were never wrong to look for it. Indeed, it is precisely in order to find it and represent it better that we must start going to the market, among other places. Rhetorically speaking, it is this implicit *invocation* of "the public," and not some purist avoidance of all legitimizing appeals or representativeness, that gives his argument against elite anti-consumerism its persuasive force. Though one can, of course, advocate that we rethink ourselves as Foucauldian "specific" intellectuals who would forsake all efforts at public legitimation and instead cultivate a homely "private" oppositionality, it seems significant that the case for such a shift itself appeals, and perhaps must appeal, to "the public."[20]

In capitalist society, appeals to "the public" have often been appeals for decision-making by visible, accountable representatives rather than, as would otherwise be the case, by the market's invisible hand. Perhaps the market's invisibility and unaccountability are in part our self-serving myths. Has a truly "free" market ever existed? It may be that we have needlessly or selfishly made ourselves blind to the complex, mediated ways in which the market can express elements of popular will and desire. (It may be helpful to remember that in Greek *agora* meant "market" as well as "public forum.") On the other hand, the current crisis of representation that subjects all "representatives" as such to the immediate charge of abusing/ inventing the "public" from which they claim to derive legitimacy might be seen as a phenomenon produced *by* the market, and as serving the capitalist status quo rather better than it serves the public interest. At any rate, if we reflect for a moment on the efforts of the Israeli government to discredit the PLO as legitimate representatives of the Palestinian people, we will be encouraged to inquire into the motives of our apparently insatiable urge to deconstruct all putative objects of representation, like the public, along with the circuits of legitimation they found.

The claims of the Chicago school of economics that the market should be allowed to decide social and moral issues which have as yet been protected by law from market forces (for example, that the free sale of babies should be permitted) are also claims, we sometimes forget, that free-market economics can explain the subject-matter of other disciplines.[21] They are a reminder, in other words, that interdisciplinarity as such need not be, as it has often seemed, a motto of the left. They are thus also a reason for inquiring into the interdisciplinarity that makes its "public" claim by putting forward such implicitly totalizing assertions as "*everything* is rhetoric" – or "discourse," or "narrative," or "textuality."[22] There is already something paradoxical about taking rhetoric, defined by its local, conjunctural situatedness, and thus universalizing it to cover "everything." But more innocuous expressions of the form "the rhetoric of x" also produce a multitude of indirect effects, options, agendas, principles, and values whose diversity is deviously or sophistically camouflaged by the all-embracing label rhetoric. This deviousness in the ways "rhetoric" is currently functioning in our discourse might be called "the rhetoric of rhetoric."

In literary studies, there is no longer much disagreement about the limits of "literature" as an organizing concept and the need to expand or replace it with some more inclusive one, like rhetoric. When René Wellek entitled a collection of his essays *The Attack on Literature* (1982), he put in a single phrase a widely shared worry that the upshot of two decades or so of literary theory and other iconoclasms, from the undermining of the canon in the name of greater inclusiveness to the anti-art of the avant-garde, has been a threat to the value and definition of the object we purport to study, and thus to the very existence of literary criticism as a discipline.[23] What is so remarkable about the title essay, however, is that the greatest historian of criticism of our century more or less concedes the main point. Wellek in effect admits the arguments of Raymond Williams and Michel Foucault that for most of its history the term "literature" has not meant what the discipline usually takes it to mean, a source of distinctively aesthetic enjoyment – that is, "imaginative" literature (15). All that such arguments fail to recognize, he says, is that, since the classics, "quality" or value has always been a criterion of literature. In conceding that literature is a historically shifting object without distinctive aesthetic properties,

Wellek opens the door to the new champions of rhetoric as a traditionally sanctioned but more inclusive or otherwise attractive alternative. (He also saddles them with the question of "value," to which I will return.)

What are the effects of subsuming so much diversity under a single banner? One minor effect is a "distortion" of history very much like the distortion involved in gathering the history of criticism around the false constant of literature. We who purport to believe, as good pre-Socratics or post-Foucauldians, that "everything flows," find ourselves describing the "quarrel between philosophy and rhetoric" as – again in Stanley Fish's words in *Doing What Comes Naturally* – "one thing that does not change" (476–8): "the debate continues to this day and ... its terms are exactly those one finds in the dialogues of Plato and the orations of the sophists" (485).[24] (Many other histories hold the rhetoric/ philosophy opposition constant in much the same way.) Historical logic says that this *is* a distortion, at least in the sense that it eliminates the changing circumstances which have changed in turn what rhetoric meant at any given time and place. Rhetoric has a reply: namely, that this view of rhetoric is itself rhetorical in that it encourages us to praise and blame, to take sides. But the reply of history or, more precisely, of politics in the imaginary dialogue I find myself constructing is that, yes, history conceived as a rhetorical form does aim at the taking of sides, but this historical simplification drastically cuts down the range of sides it is possible to take, for it suppresses the diversity of meanings *within* rhetoric. For example, the notion of an eternal battle between rhetoric and philosophy suppresses the difference between hermeneutics (say, Habermas) and poststructuralism (say, Foucault), two quite different versions of the European "linguistic turn," as it also suppresses the differences between both and American pragmatism, whose "consensus" theory of truth-as-persuasion rhetoric prefigures. It demotes or assimilates other, perhaps rival candidates for the "everything is x" position, like "narrative," without permitting an open contest in which each could show its merits. And it discourages questions about the monism of the "everything is x" formula itself.

There is also deviousness within the work of rhetoric's individual champions. In Hayden White, for example, rhetoric sometimes means the fixed framework of four tropes – metaphor, metonymy, synecdoche, and irony – which define the neo-Kantian "base" or "deep structure" of the historical imagination. At other moments, however, rhetoric refers to the creative poetic *freedom* of the historical imagination, its irreducibility to any prior base or structure.[25] In the first case, rhetoric is determination; in the second, it is indeterminacy. In literary criticism as well as history, the promiscuous mingling of these two senses in the one term enables the discipline to postpone hard questions about the sort and value of the knowledge it is teaching.

The issue here, as Wellek indicated, is one of "quality" or "value." White's sense of rhetoric as "deep structure" is both universalizing (it refers to everybody) and value-neutral. On the other hand, his restricted, indeterminate sense of rhetoric permits him to single out free, creative *individuals* for *praise* of their creativity and achievement. In other words, it adds the dimension of value to a scheme that seemed to preclude value. I would like to propose as a working hypothesis, not having the time to argue it through but hoping it might serve to stimulate further reflection, that if there is at present a rhetoric common to the disciplines of the humanities, it is the epideictic rhetoric of praise and blame, a rhetorical mode appropriate to raising questions of value (in our case, the value of the monuments of the cultural heritage) before a general public (rather than, say, judicial bodies or legislative assemblies).[26] Without suggesting that praise-and-blame is a necessary foundation of all or even just of scholarly discourse, one can, I think, see it as provisionally determined by the professional pact that the humanities have concluded with "society at large" – a pact to transmit values from the past to a commercialized or dehumanized present seen as acutely in need of them – and therefore as invested with considerable social force. The fact that Hayden White is forced into something resembling a self-contradiction indicates how intense is the disciplinary pressure to produce praise-and-blame, however little one may desire to do so. The point is an impersonal one. Thus, though that same pressure is undoubtedly working right now on my own discourse, it does not require any special blaming or praising of Hayden White. Mapping the prevalence of "praise-and-blame" in scholarly discourse, and the swerves and slippages it effects, opens up a line of research into the rhetoric of the humanities that I think can yield interesting results throughout the disciplines – and notably, for our purposes, in regard to all the major figures associated with the recent theoretical rehabilitation of rhetoric.

Anyone who begins from the widespread premise that "there is no metalanguage" would seem to be asserting that "everything" is language, or literariness, or textuality, or rhetoric. But this generalizing of, let's say, rhetoric to cover "everything" – I ignore for now the specific implications of choosing rhetoric over, say, textuality – leaves the differential issue of value totally uncovered. Hence the problem in disciplinary rhetoric of how to make, or what will count as, a scholarly argument – since closure in an argument, as in a narrative, has thus far seemed almost unthinkable without some terminal gesture of axiological grounding. Hence also, what is more pertinent for us, the drive to break up the universality of language, literariness, text, or rhetoric into an inside and an outside, theory's secondary impulse to elaborate boundary lines and establish limits, however awkwardly. The awkwardness of some of these efforts is notorious. I'm thinking of periodizing distinctions like Roland Barthes's line between the valued "writerly" and the devalued "readerly," no sooner drawn than (in S/Z) seen as untenable, as well as generic distinctions like the line Bakhtin draws between prose, supposedly dialogical, and poetry, supposedly monological, an absurdity for which Bakhtin's appreciative readers seem silently to have forgiven him.[27] My point here is that, no matter how awkward such oppositions may be, they embody an urge to generate differential value, to generate praise and blame, that appears for the moment to be a disciplinary necessity. If we recognize this necessity (whether it will or must *remain* a necessity can, I think, be left open), we can also recognize in it a certain freedom: the freedom to deal directly with the values smuggled into our discourse, and in particular to see to it that specific values we thought had been shamed away during the past twenty years do not make a surreptitious comeback under cover of the organized discursive blindness to value as such.

It would, I think, be possible to show that criticism in the postmodern age is traversed from end to end by an unacknowledged distinction between a *weak* sense of literariness and a *strong* sense of literariness. The weak, or "value-neutral," sense indicates merely that passive submission to language that characterizes *all* discourse. The strong, or "value-laden," sense indicates a willed, conscious acknowledgement or cultivation of that which other texts only exhibit unconsciously or reluctantly. Everything is literary, in other words, but some things are more literary than others. The maintenance of this unsupervised border has allowed critics to smuggle in and reinstitute extra-linguistic, extra-textual qualities of "self-consciousness" and "creativity" and "independence" that were considered to be, before the "linguistic turn," special if not exclusive privileges of "Literature," and that now once again are being unjustly denied to human activities on the other side of the border. Put another way, the monist rhetoric of "everything is x," including the phrase "everything is rhetoric," first results in a general erasure of lines. This erasure or general levelling immediately gives way, however, under the pressure to produce differential value, to a multitude of hierarchical *re*inscriptions. The difference between the first and second inscriptions is that the new lines are less visible as such, and hence render the values they produce more difficult to recognize or adjudicate. Examples might include the deconstructive critics of the Yale School, and the argument might go back to Nietzsche. Nietzsche's identification of all truth with metaphor is often taken to initiate the deconstructive universalizing of rhetoric – that is, the "weak," value-free, expansive sense of rhetoric. But in addition and in contradiction to this sense of rhetoric as unavoidable tropological swerving, you can also find in Nietzsche the stronger, restricted sense of rhetoric or art as a mode of action, more specifically something that some people (not all people) do to or for other people. Nietzsche never abandons value-terms like "greatness," but he asserts them only about rhetoric in this second, non-universal, interpersonal sense: rhetoric as public project.

3. Poststructuralist Populism

In suggesting that the issue of rhetoric's limits belongs to the domain of social theory, I have been not too subtly taking sides between the two most obvious rival leaders within the rhetoric camp: the de Manian insistence on rhetoric as perpetually destabilizing figuration and the Greek tradition of public project, political persuasion, civic prudence.[28] I have already suggested my own preference for the practical, public speech of oratory and education, which links its indeterminacy not to language or literariness per se but to the contingencies of action, of historical audience, and of politics. But waving the banner of persuasion is no guarantee that literary studies will be any more public in its self-conception or social practices than it was under the New Criticism.

Consider the example of Stanley Fish. In his essay "Anti-Professionalism," to which my own project is visibly indebted, Fish defends both persuasion and professionalism together. Rhetoric, he says, is identified as the art of illegitimate appeal, as a repertoire of tricks or manipulative techniques by means of which some special interest, or point of view, or temporary fashion, passes itself off as the truth. The rhetorical, then, is that which stands between us and the truth, obscuring it, preventing us from allying ourselves with it, and tying us instead to some false or partial god. These are exactly the charges that are levelled against professionalism, and it seems clear that anti-professionalism is basically an up-to-date, twentieth-century form of the traditional hostility to rhetoric. (219)

So far so good: in fact, so far *very* good, in that Fish steps outside what might otherwise seem a consensus, as we shall see, coupling the defense of rhetoric to an *attack* on professionalism and disciplines as such.

But what precisely does Fish himself defend when, like so many others, he takes the side of rhetoric? When the subject of rhetoric comes up again a few pages later, he stops to insist that he's not falling into a dichotomy of praise and blame. It is a strange moment to parody the anti-rhetoric position, and it brings into sudden relief how closely that position in fact fits Fish. The gesture of refusing to take sides, which creates for itself the illusion of a position above all sides, is of a piece with Fish's most characteristic rhetoric, the rhetoric of neither/nor. It is also of a piece with his most notorious conclusion: the paradox that his own argument, like theory in general, has "no consequences." Now the reductive urgencies of praise-and-blame involve, precisely, taking sides and urging consequences, at least ideological ones. The persuasive goal of rhetoric was to have a decisive effect upon one's hearers – what Paul de Man called, with audible displeasure, "actual action upon others." But this is precisely the goal Fish disavows when he affirms that his own words have not praised or blamed, have not taken sides, will not or should not have consequences. In the very act of championing rhetoric, he takes a position outside its principles of public consequence and responsibility to constituency.[29]

The power of the rhetorical transgression is breathtaking. To transgress the convention that speaking is an action addressed to a relatively free listener and intended to change things is to announce in effect that "I" (the subject doing the talking) am, or rather – to let grammar reproduce the transgressive effect – "I" *is* really only a symptom, a subject being talked about. Within the rhetorical mode of persuasion, and in the very midst of a defense of rhetoric, Fish denies the rhetorical nature of his own words. In other words, he opts theoretically not for rhetoric, but for a traditional and self-marginalizing literariness. This might be thought of as rhetorical aestheticism: rhetoric for rhetoric's sake.

It also might be thought of as an aestheticizing of professionalism. "Anti-Professionalism" explicitly addresses my theme here, the existence of opposition within professions. Opposition, Fish argues, is central to professionalism. "Far from being a stance taken at the margins or the periphery, anti-professionalism is the very center of the professional ethos, constituting by the very vigor of its opposition the true form of that which it opposes" (106). In brief, the argument is that professions work by denying that they *are* professions. The professional wants to believe in his or her own merit, which requires freedom. But since self and merit are in fact constructed and determined by the profession (this is the strong, foundational sense of the term), you have to attack the profession in order to assert your own freedom vis-à-vis the profession. And in so doing, you are asserting the ideology of professionalism: freedom, merit, etc. The thrust of the argument is to take any merit away from opposition. In being oppositional, Fish says, you are just following the profession's orders.

Fish's own rhetoric protects this argument by first invoking clients and constituents (so as to gain public credit for the speaker). Then, when these extra-professional figures become inconvenient to his case for monadic professional self-sufficiency, he silently drops them, thus allowing the merit-seeking self to efface collective considerations of justice, the general welfare, and the interests of clients, considerations which might seem to account for anti-professionalism better. Fish's point is precisely that these considerations are external and irrelevant. Constituting itself by attacking itself, the profession becomes invulnerable to attack from outside. Indeed, it has trouble recognizing that there *is* an outside. The profession becomes a sort of literary text in the Romantic sense, an autonomous organic whole.

Fish has in fact been caught in this backsliding toward aestheticism by Gerald Graff, who was responding to the original article in *New Literary History*.[30] The point at issue is the professional pressures that force a small college in Joplin, Missouri, to fill a gap in the department by hiring a specialist in Renaissance literature, however little the students likely to attend the college may need such a specialist. Fish accuses Richard Ohmann of attacking "the internal requirements of the profession," which have led to this over-specialized situation, in the name of an illusory non-institutional freedom. To which Graff responds:

> Take Fish's remarks on Richard Ohmann, who questioned "the presence of a Renaissance specialist in a small college in Joplin, Missouri" as an instance of parochial professional interests having been placed above larger community interests. Fish charges that Ohmann has sought to invoke "a noninstitutional standard", something "outside" institutions in general. But has he? So far as I can see, what Ohmann has invoked is not a *non*institutional standard but the standard of "the needs of Joplin," which, whatever we take those needs to be, are as "institutional" as any other standard we could name. In fact in this case, the Joplin standard is not even external to the professional standard, insofar as professional literary study claims to hold itself accountable to the larger values of the nonprofessional community. Ohmann has not attacked literary studies from outside the profession, but has held it responsible to its own declared values. (116)

In response to this, Fish concedes, somewhat grudgingly, that

> No intepretive community exists in a hermetically sealed or monolithic state; the activities of any interpretive community are legitimized not only by the interests and goals it explicitly proclaims, but by the more general interests of the larger society, interests that provide a rationale when the activities of the community are interrogated by those who are not members of it. (126)

But there is no *conceptual* place for "the people of Joplin" in his account either of professionalism or of rhetoric.

For all the ingenious originality of his arguments, Fish should, I think, be seen as a representative figure: representative of a postmodern or poststructuralist professionalism which is deeply suspicious of all legitimizing claims to representation. For this reason or for others, such professionalism tries to imagine intellectuals both as grounded in their own individual circumstances and, at the same time, as "free-floating" in a new sense, no longer symbolically or analytically localizable within society at large. So-called "New Class" theories would seem to offer a parallel, except that for them the concept of "class" itself continues to bind intellectuals to the means of production, and thus to society as a whole. A closer parallel is Michel Foucault's concept of the "specific" intellectual (discussed in Chapter Six), which has no use for class. In effect, Fish's critique of what he calls "anti-professionalism" draws out the consequences of Foucault's critique of the pretension of "universal" intellectuals to represent any constituency other than themselves. Fish's professionals, like Foucault's specific intellectuals, are properly seen as "local."

If the "decline" narrative, left and right, looks upon the Fall from public concern into professionalization and despairs, the postmodern narrative retains the "decline" plot but reverses the moral emphasis. It looks upon this unprecedented separation from public concerns and finds it good, exhorting intellectuals to sever their remaining ties. Claiming to be socially responsible is a vain way of claiming to be socially representative, hence socially important. It would be better for intellectuals to cultivate their own gardens.

Again, this covers both left and right. For Fish, cultivating their own gardens means doing what professionals always already know how to do. In the left-Foucauldian variant of Paul Bové, whose *Intellectuals in Power: A Genealogy of Critical Humanism* (1986), on the contrary, is extremely critical of the professional status quo, it means giving up all pretension to speak for or lead anyone else.[31] Recourse to the public has never been anything but a self-aggrandizing illusion, comparable to claiming the illicit authority of other universals. Local isolation, at a safe distance from the public, is a fate both we and they should be grateful for.

But what are the boundaries of the local? The attempt to build a wall around it characterizes Fish's two most prominent arguments, the argument against theory and the argument in favor of professionalism. They are really the same argument: an argument *for* the inviolable independence of professional skill from any authoritative public scrutiny, which (the scrutiny) is what one might take theory to be. Fish makes this combined argument in an article in the *Yale Law Journal* called "Dennis Martinez and the Uses of Theory."[32] Dennis Martinez, then a pitcher for the Baltimore Orioles, figures as an illustration of the futility of coaching. All his coach can tell him about pitching is what he already knows, namely, "Throw strikes and keep 'em off the bases." The point of all this is that theory is like coaching: a redundant if not offensive advising of those who can by those who can't. And professional practice is like pitching: something that every professional always already knows how to do. Hence the proper indifference of the profession to any public advice or accountability.

This argument raises a variety of doubts. Among other things, one is struck once again by the appeal by a supposed anti-foundationalist to professional skill or expertise as an unquestioned and unquestionable foundation. But what seems most pertinent here is the rhetorical return of the repressed public. According to Fish, professions are monads, entirely distinct unto themselves, hence invulnerable to outside critique. As in the stirring conclusion to the "Dennis Martinez" essay. Theorists, he says, like philosophers,

> want us to believe that the only good king is a philosopher-king, and that the only good judge is a philosopher-judge, and that the only good baseball player is a philosopher baseball player. Well, I don't know about you, but I hope that my kings, if I should ever have any, are good at being kings, and that my judges are good at being judges, and that the players on my team throw strikes and keep 'em off the bases. (1798)

Self-enclosed specialization cannot celebrate itself, it seems, without ceasing to be itself. By talking baseball, Fish undoes his argument. It's exactly the point where his professional audience is *not* specialized or self-enclosed, the point where professionals overlap with the general public, that Fish the rhetorician specializes in appealing to: the (supposed) baseball-fan-in-all-of-us. In order to make an essentially anti-democratic case for the professions (note that his king, if he ever has one, will not be taking advice from anyone about how to rule) Fish must, it seems, make a public, democratic appeal. That is what competent professional discourse seems to require.

Unlike Fish, Paul Bové agrees in his book *Intellectuals in Power* that opposition within the profession does involve rhetorical appeal to the public. The problem, in his view, is that our best and brightest appeal to the public all too successfully. Figures like Edward Said, he says, offer an attack on "narrow professionalism" which seems "politically radical" but is actually "conservative," for it does "more to sustain the professional institution's structure and affiliations than to subvert or challenge them" (298). It does this, exactly as I have argued, by adopting a moral language aimed implicitly at those *outside* the profession. The "influential work" of "leading intellectuals" like Said "represents and, in part, legitimates the profession in the eyes of the state and the public" (110). This is true even of our most agonistic self-images, as restless controversialists and embattled critics of the status quo, proving our combativeness in jousts with other intellectuals. Agonism hides but also supports competition "for social power and authority" (222); it is efficacious. The agony is the efficacy.

Bové's condemnation of "leading intellectuals" who set themselves up as defenders of such universals as truth, justice, and "the people" is particularly violent with regard to "arrogant imaginings

108

and affirmations of other people's struggles." It is interesting, therefore, that he cannot seem to make his own eloquent critique of such intellectuals without doing the same thing. By a sort of inverse populism, the proposition that we should never speak for or to the people, just let them speak for themselves, becomes the claim that "I speak for the people better than you do." On the last page of the book, Bové offers a concluding tableau of professional malevolence: "Forceps in the hands of male medical experts" (310). The figure works as well as it does because it is rhetoric of just the moral, legitimating sort Bové has been attacking. Having broken down the false unity of "the people" into various local fragments and factions, in order to stop intellectuals from borrowing its authority, Bové now borrows that populist authority himself, reshaping his factions and fragments back into the singleness of a body that can be vulnerable, victimized, allegorized. A *female* body, moreover – again the part offered for the whole – with moral credit thus accruing to the male speaker for his championing of the Other. The Other as Mother: for all its Foucauldian trappings, the move to motherhood belongs with politicians kissing babies. If you add Bové's use of motherhood to Stanley Fish's numerous references to baseball, the only thing missing from this poststructuralist populism is apple pie.

At a moment when Bové concedes that his argument "might seem amoral or immoral" – he has just listed "the temptations to build a better world" among those that specific intellectuals have to renounce – it's not hard to see why he needs so widespread and popular an appeal. What *is* hard to see is why the principle of such rhetoric, articulating linkages to feminism and other political move-ments, shouldn't be embraced as a legitimately professional mode of oppositional discourse.

It is hard to see why, finally, we must take as the new, inevitable common sense, Geoff Bennington's characteristic sarcasm at the expense of Marxist invocations of "the people": "Here 'we' are again, outside the scene, all-seeing and all-knowing. We try to tell the lion that it is strong, that it should leap, roar, bite and devour: it opens one eye and yawns, recognizing another tamer when it sees one."[33] The skepticism about legitimizing appeals to "the public" or "the people" which Bennington expresses so eloquently is more entangled in such appeals than it lets on. Bennington accuses the Marxist critic (Terry Eagleton) of locating himself "outside the scene." But with the phrase "another tamer," he puts Eagleton very much inside the scene. He places himself, on the other hand, just as visibly outside it. Even a paying spectator at this circus would presumably want to see the lion do *something*, if only growl at his new tamer. But Bennington's response to the spectacle, if any, is left unrecorded. It would seem, then, that he views the circus of legitimation with a disabused technico-existential indifference. And once again this supposed indifference does not stop him from repeating his own performance. If poststructuralism has often affected a technocratic coolness, it has also tended to ground its sarcasm in its own oblique, concealed populism. Here, too, the rhetoric cannot entirely disavow appeal to "the people." For if Bennington's persona is anywhere present in the scene he imagines – as we must conclude it is, given the slap at Eagleton for being "outside" – it is present as a claim of solidarity with the lion against all tamers, especially those who pretend to set lions free. And even, therefore, as the claim to speak for the lion (the people) *better* than Eagleton does.

Populism of this unacknowledged, apparently skeptical sort avoids the embarrassments that pursue a vocabulary of "legitimation," "constituency," "mission," and "vocation." But in avoiding the embarrassments, it also avoids self-knowledge. It does not want to know its own tricks of lion taming, or how it depends on the bars of the lion's cage. It disingenuously shirks the responsibility to think through the issue of its own vocation, its own authorities, its own grounding. For all its postmodern trappings, it is continuous, that is, with a long modernist tradition which conceives the intellectual as outcast and exile, autonomous and critical: in short, as free-floating *Luftmensh*.

4. The Rhetoric of Rhetoric

If rhetoric can forget its own existence, thus allowing intellectuals to imagine themselves secure in an inconsequential privacy or traditional literariness, there is also a symmetrical danger, on the other side, in rhetoric's very claims to publicness. Terry Eagleton, in the "Small History of Rhetoric" included in his book on Walter Benjamin, makes a representative claim:

> A political literary criticism is not the invention of Marxists. On the contrary, it is one of the oldest, most venerable forms of literary criticism we know. The most widespread early criticism on historical record was not "aesthetic": it was a mode of what we would now call "discourse theory," devoted to analysing the material effects of particular uses of

language in particular social conjunctures. . . . The name of this form of criticism was rhetoric.[34]

In the history that follows, much of the attractiveness of rhetoric stems from its role in "the market-place and public forum" (105); rhetoric's fall begins with "the dwindling of the public sphere" (106).

Now Eagleton is perfectly aware that this "public" was anything but universal. Handbooks of rhetoric, he says, were "handbooks of ruling-class power" (101). But in arguments like his, the powerfully ingenuous association between rhetoric and the public seems to lead a devious career independent of any or all of the particular historical publics and ruling classes rhetoric actually served. Another case in point is Gerald Graff's history of English studies, *Professing Literature* (1987), which, in Chapter Three, both bemoans the fall of professionalized criticism from an earlier, more public "oratorical culture" and, almost in the same breath, acknowledges that the publicness of "oratorical culture" meant "class restrictions," "conservatism," "unredeemed drudgery carried on in the name of archaic social ideals." We must think of rhetoric's publicness, in other words, as an abstract construct, a potent emptiness abstracted from any actual ideological content, not so much a norm as a figure for normativeness, for the absence of normative value.

This figurative deviousness extends further when we bring the publicness of rhetoric together once again with professionalism. Rhetoric refers us to a past time when something like "criticism" (though the extent to which rhetoric's analysis of language was truly "critical" remains one of the more important questions about it) played a large public role. But "the public" also figures as the recipient of a professional discourse *about* rhetoric in the present. The profession of criticism has been presenting itself *to* the public as if it were a renewed rhetoric, thus as if it were as respectful *of* the public today, respectful of its present constituency, as Athenian rhetoric was of Athenian democracy. At a time when critics see themselves, or fear that they're seen, as over-specialized, jargon-ridden, vulnerable to the outsider skepticism of commonsensical public and private funders, this rhetorical doubling of the public clearly serves the purposes of professional legitimation rather well. For example, it takes for granted and thus directs attention away from the question of what equivalents criticism today might have to offer for rhetoric's active role in the Athenian *agora*.

111

This professional functionality is not in itself an argument against such double articulations. It does suggest, however, some additional deviousness in the attitude of rhetoric's champions toward professionalism itself. In classical Athens, the sophists and rhetoricians offered a positive alternative to that contempt for professional work and specialization that, via Plato and Aristotle, we have come to think of as quintessentially Greek. What G.B. Kerferd calls the "professionalism" of the sophists has been as clear as it has been unpopular. Today, however, the most obvious connection between rhetoric and professionalism is an antagonistic one. Rhetoric is largely celebrated as part of an attack on professionalism. In addition to Eagleton, who opposes rhetoric to the "highly specialist division of discursive labor" (103) that followed it, I take two politically very diverse cases in point. In Renato Barilli's recently translated short history of rhetoric, rhetoric is opposed to the undemocratic exclusiveness of (philosophical) expertise.[35] Philosophy "takes the right to judge from the demos and gives it over to the experts" (ix). On the other hand, "rhetoric embraces all human concerns" (x), and thus becomes a unifying, totalizing discourse that tries to undo the deformations of professional specialization. In the same vein, *The Rhetoric of the Human Sciences: Language and Argument in Scholarship and Public Affairs*, a collection of essays edited by John Nelson, Allan Megill, and Donald McCloskey in 1987, repeatedly sets itself on the side of "ordinary folk" and against "the experts" who wall themselves off from the public in isolated, specialized jargons.[36] Richard Harvey Brown speaks, representatively, of an "unmasking of economistic rationality as a rhetoric intended to legitimate professional prestige" (197n21). Richard Rorty looks forward to the day when professionals would no longer think "of themselves as a member of a quasi-priestly order, nor would the public think of themselves as in the care of such an order" (51). Rhetoric appears as a kind of antidote to expertise, or at least (since the general tone of that volume is less threatening) to disciplinary specialization. It names a common discourse that, as the art of rhetoric itself prescribes, will speak the language of its hearers. Thus it will bridge the double gap between separate disciplines and between all disciplinary expertises and the educated public.

One cause for suspicion about this otherwise politically appealing defense of rhetoric is that it is just the sort of argument that has often been used against rhetoric. The familiar charge is of course that rhetoric is merely technical, pure instrumentality prostituting itself in the service of any user, without any critical oppositionality (such as might have influenced, for example, the debates that led Athens to decide, democratically, to massacre the Mytilinians and Melians), without any normative anchoring in the common good: in short, a version of amoral professionalism. This is in fact the argument made by literature itself against rhetoric. As I suggested above, the invention of literature in the modern sense, roughly in the Romantic period, is inseparable from the Romantic literary critique of the industrial division of labor – in other words, the critique of the deformations of professionalism. The new concept of literature could win the sort of oppositional authority it did, at the expense of rhetoric, in part by associating rhetoric with mere professional partiality and technicity while it itself claimed to represent the absent organic wholeness of the public. In the post-Romantic period, the argument goes on, it was this claim that helped found literary criticism as a modern discipline. In short, rhetoric now seems to be trying to do precisely what literature did then: setting itself against the fracturing of the division of labor. And in both cases this claim to public wholeness can be interpreted as a professional strategy, *within* the division of labor, that helps renegotiate upward the fortunes of a particular discipline.

The problem with this joint strategy is that it helps sustain that opposition between particular disciplines or professional specialities, on the one hand, and the general public, on the other hand, that it also shows to be illusory. Given the (apparently irreversible) fragmentation of disciplines, any appeal to the public as principled opposition to professionalism can only be a *permanent* opposition, always there to be appealed to because it never *can* be present, by definition, within *any* individual discipline. This is one source of rhetoric's enormous rhetorical power: it invokes a missing public that all members of all disciplines must respect because, or to the extent that, to enter into a discipline at all seems to mean, by definition, entering into *exile* from that public.

But must we condemn our professional lives to exile and privacy? The subtitle of the *Rhetoric of the Human Sciences* volume, *Language and Argument in Scholarship and Public Affairs*, firmly maintains the assumption that "scholarship" does not, or not yet, belong to "public affairs." Yet the book also maintains a more promising ambiguity. In aiming its revival of rhetoric against "the fragmentation of academic fields" (4), it opens up the question of whether it is trying to construct a "public sphere" for or *within* the supposedly private domain of scholarship – in other words, whether a bridge *between fields* might itself *be* public.

This suggestion would clearly be a departure from rhetorical tradition. Objecting to the modernization program of *The Rhetoric of the Human Sciences*, Michael C. Leff argues in his contribution to it that while rhetoric "could retain vitality only if the orator played a significant role in civic life" (26), rhetoric's return is occurring in a domain which the ancients explicitly excluded from civic life, namely "the technical and theoretical sciences" (21), each of them generating "a technical language alien to the discourse of the generally educated public" (29). But can one, today, oppose the disciplines to "civic life" and the "generally educated public"? To do so, as I suggested a moment ago, is to turn the public into a mythic plenitude from which the disciplines must then ceaselessly and vainly lament their impoverished exile. And it is to make this fictional public so monstrously totalizing that, as Leff himself suggests, even striving toward it smacks of totalitarianism. The effort to "generate a normative rhetoric that would regulate work across the human sciences," he writes, "is doomed to failure, and a good thing too. If it succeeded, we would push the foundationalist bully off the academic block at the cost of permitting an even less disciplined rhetorical bully to terrorize our work" (29).

I believe the current interdisciplinary impulse is both more public and less totalitarian than this characteristic statement suggests. As a slogan of curricular reform, it is supported by public funders of education who share a concern that over-specialized departments have abused their territorial monopoly over the definition of knowledge. Some see this abuse occurring at the expense of vocational training for industry, others at the expense of the monuments of traditional learning, or humane wisdom, or critical thinking. Each of these is a competing candidate representing a competing set of interests, a competing version of the public. And each has its measurable, competing effects on the definition of knowledge *within* as well as *between* disciplines. In other words, "civic life" penetrates the disciplines with its own conflicts, and the disciplines are thus one site or level where public conflicts are fought out.[37]

Fears of bullying might be appeased if the contemporary public sphere were thus reconceived as a plural, provisional, and multi-layered concept, a concept that includes rather than excludes the disciplines and that disperses its debts and obligations rather than concentrating them in a single totalizing instance.[38] According to this reconception, pushing the interests of a specific discipline or trying to rearrange the hierarchy of the disciplines into a new constellation, as in Rorty's description of German idealist philosophy, would be very much a public activity. The public could no longer serve as a potent because non-specific abstraction, always at a convenient distance from where one already is.

Rorty is clearly wrong in exempting criticism from the general professionalization. To critics, at least, it seems obvious that literary theory was not after all the ultimate challenge to professionalism, but a power play in which certain professional values and structures (say, culture) were traded in for others (say, rhetoric or narrative). But Rorty is right to insist that theory has effected a realignment among disciplines, and in so doing he exposes the insistent place of the public in theory's new professionalism. Whether or not one accepts the simplicity of a narrative in which criticism wins out over other disciplines, criticism's influence over other disciplines is undeniable. Criticism has exerted that influence by exporting its highly developed qualifications of interpretive authority to fields like law and anthropology, whose interpretive procedures and authority had remained largely unqualified. In other words, qualifications which within criticism itself seemed to sap professional authority were in fact extending it – as long as one understands that professionalism in any one discipline is inseparable from, and indeed defined by, the relations *among* disciplines. The foundation of professional authority is not unchanging control over one's own exclusive expertise, but rather an ever-shifting relation to other, competing disciplines and professions. From this perspective, theory represents a questioning of criticism's professional "knowledge base" but it simultaneously expands that base. (The fact that there is nothing shockingly unprofessional about comparing professionalization narratives from various disciplines, as I've been doing, is a sign of that expansion.) Criticism loosens its grip over its own territory in order to seize *more* territory, thus indulging its (higher) professional self-interest.

But this does not mean that it is either publicly inconsequential or reducible to mean-spirited territoriality. If Rorty is unjustified in concluding, on the contrary, that success in interdisciplinary competition is *necessarily* in the public interest – the model here is Adam Smith's invisible hand – his idea that the constellation of disciplines at a given moment will both reflect and help constitute the social order of that moment, and that a shift in the first will therefore constitute a shift in the second, deserves to be rescued from his free-market assumptions. For this idea also rescues the concept of the public from the realm of ideal constructs and historical elsewheres to which our narratives so often relegate it. In order to touch the public, on this reading, one would not have to reach *down*, as to a base or foundation; lateral movement on the same plane, as for example between disciplines, would already be movement within the public domain. This is precisely what happened, I would argue, when literary theory spread a militant interpretive anti-authoritarianism to disciplines whose authority visibly matters, such as the law.

Inadequate as it is, this argument will have to stand in for the new theory of the changing public sphere that the subject of rhetoric clearly deserves and requires. Without it, at any rate, rhetoric risks falling back once again into mere literariness. The editors of *The Rhetoric of the Human Sciences* – none of them, I think, a literary critic – describe their interdisciplinary version of rhetoric as follows: "The literary criticism of a field requires showing how it departs from its official norms of research" (16). Like the project of making rhetoric an agent of interdisciplinary unification, this statement can be taken in at least two directions. On the one hand, it extends to "fields" a traditional definition of literature, in Derrida as in Cleanth Brooks's "Heresy of Paraphrase," as that which always departs from official, paraphrasable meaning. In this sense it merely preserves a traditional literariness that puts a safe distance between itself and officialdom, or the public. If the aim is for rhetoric to play a public role, this self-understanding is clearly self-destructive. On the other hand, showing how fields depart from their norms of research might also be understood as revealing not a formal, content-less, "literary" incongruity, but rather the historically specific lack or incompleteness opened up within any given field by its relations with other fields and – though the two are really one – with the public.[39]

I am proposing, more as a concluding gesture than a complete argument, that what produces an incongruity within any field, the presence of the Other in it that keeps it from being entirely and complacently itself, is precisely the public, that is, the discipline's need to legitimate its existence vis-à-vis other disciplines and society at large. The interdisciplinary role of rhetoric, then, would approximate the role some have ascribed to theory: an opening of what appears private in disciplines to public scrutiny and to public accountability. This task could be described as "public-making": making public or visible, opening to a variety of perspectives and

116

judgments, but also the interdisciplinary *fashioning* of new publics, new instances of judgment, new collective viewpoints. It is within such a framework, for example, that one might profitably study "praise-and-blame" in the rhetoric of the humanities.

This is by no means the end of the public's problems, which after all fill shelf after shelf of political theory. If it is to be so enfeebled, why hold onto the term "public" at all – especially when, as feminists have pointed out, the public/private opposition comes loaded down with such heavy and apparently unjettisonable ideological baggage? What are the consequences of saying that "everything" is public, as some claim that "everything" is rhetoric? Mustn't some differentiation, some scale of public and private, be retained in order for the concept to designate significant targets, for it not to lose its oppositional cutting edge against the status quo? After all, the order we confront is occupied with other activities besides denying self-expression. In trying to describe the point at which the self-evident good of self-expression or identity politics passes over into some higher good, some level of confrontational demand more difficult to satisfy, do we need some other terms than private and public?

From the moment we ask the public to refer both to here and to elsewhere, to be both adversarial, on the one hand, and (the presumed goal of our efforts) central, dominant, hegemonic, on the other, some paradox is not to be avoided. The public may be no more or less paradoxical than the radical changes we ask it to support. Perhaps we would do well, for the moment, to read it as a figure for such changes.

4

Enchanted Enclaves, Family Romance

What kind of hell must that be, she wondered, to be tormented by your own creations? To know that the absolute best you can do in your career is the absolute worst for mankind?

John Le Carré[1]

1. "A contradiction of which he himself is the resolution": Fredric Jameson on Max Weber

In the course of narrating Conrad's *Heart of Darkness*, Marlow is interrupted by his listeners only once. He has been talking about how he saved his sanity, in the Congo, by focussing attention on his work – repairing the hull and navigating the ship. But at the same time, he says, he felt a "mysterious stillness watching me at my monkey-tricks, just as it watches you fellows performing on your respective tight-ropes for – what is it? half a crown a tumble – " At this point he is interrupted by the words, "Try to be civil, Marlow." And he resumes:

> I beg your pardon. I forgot the heartache which makes up the rest of the price. And indeed what does the heartache matter, if the trick be well done? You do your tricks very well. And I didn't do badly either, since I managed not to sink that steamboat on my first trip.[2]

I take this passage to illustrate late Victorian professionalism as it most closely resembles our own. Marlow is both invested in the Victorian work ethic and edging toward divestment. Not unwilling to see work as monkey-tricks lacking any meaningful goal or value, he reveals what Karl Löwith calls the "hidden nihilism" of the work ethic.[3] And to judge from the interruption, his nihilism is not utterly eccentric. The interruption does not so much deny the nihilism as acknowledge it and try to keep it hidden. The interrupting listener, earlier identified only by profession, becomes the voice of that "mysterious stillness" Marlow felt watching him as he worked, a voice that urges Marlow to be "civil," or civilized, by being silent about the ultimate meaninglessness of work, which is the presumed content of that silence. The subsequent unbroken silence of *all* the listeners looks much like assent to the modified version of professionalism that Marlow then provides. In this version, doing your monkey-tricks competently, without inquiring overmuch into their meaning or consequences, becomes the ironic, self-conscious version of "civilization" that post-Kurtz Europe will set against Africa, civilization's fall-back position after the damage Kurtz has done to the earlier professional language of civilizing "mission."

Victorians who are devoted to the skilled accomplishment of their work while recognizing, or trying not to recognize, the ultimate groundlessness or unthinkable purposes and consequences of that work are the contemporaries, I think, of today's professionals, ancestors of an ambivalence that has not yet been resolved. In his chapter on *Heart of Darkness* in *Reading for the Plot* (1984), Peter Brooks speaks of "the fiction of the mission, which upon inspection is seen to cover up the most rapacious and vicious of imperialisms."[4] The sentence sums up an acute and historically justified suspicion of missions and missionaries that, by the last decade of the twentieth century, has become second nature. Yet at the same time it remains possible for late twentieth-century critics to speak, with all the marks of admiration and no apparent sense of contradiction, of a writer's or a thinker's or even a critic's "sense of mission." We habitually say "sense of mission" rather than "mission" itself so as to protect ourselves from the nakedness of what may seem an impossible assertion. A "mission" must have a sender; a "vocation" must have a caller. Are we prepared to fill in these blanks? After all, we imply defensively, this may only be a "fiction," a *sense* of "mission"; the "mission" may only be in the writer's head.

And yet we continue to use terms like "mission" and "vocation." For we believe, or want to believe, in the meaning of our own work – especially if that meaning is defined, as it often is these days, by its opposition to the "horror" of what Kurtz meant by civilization. Inverting but also remaining dependent on the horror and the "imperialism," the modest civility of professional criticism remains structurally blind to its own sorts of "civilizing mission." Amid the general anti-missionary skepticism, newer and less obvious senses of mission pass uncriticized. In particular, Conrad's own solution. Today we continue to see professionalism as empty technical competence, chosen in existential privacy against a backdrop of ultimate public or global meaninglessness – a privacy protected from scrutiny by the rules of "civility." This is a nightmare left to us, I think, by the intensities of the earlier and continuing sense of divinely inspired "vocation," much as Marlow's existential sense of therapeutic work is produced in reaction to the catastrophic results of Kurtz's sense of "vocation" in Africa. But it is a nightmare from which it is time to awaken. Our Conradian technico-existential ambivalence – what Fredric Jameson calls, in his essay on Max Weber, "heroic cynicism"[5] – is a mistake, I will argue, a mistake we have preserved in part because, though painful, it is also professionally self-serving, but a mistake that should now be rectified.

In *The Way of the World: The Bildungsroman in European Culture* (1987), Franco Moretti describes the demise of the novel of vocation as a retreat from the public to a privacy that has all the earmarks of professionalism itself as we are used to viewing it. Although his book is about the *Bildungsroman* genre in general, Moretti chooses to end it with the subgenre of the novel of vocation and its end. The part offers closure to the whole, it seems, because it is only the subgenre which stands for the *social* whole, for the public. The goal of the *Bildungsroman* is the synthesis of "free individual development and happy social integration." Integration is something an individual can hope to achieve. Not so, however, for the protagonist of the novel of vocation. For this subgenre is more "ambitious." Vocation demands not just "integration," but *"collective* benefit." The synthesis of individual self-interest and general welfare that we call vocation "can occur," Moretti says, "only if history moves forward: only through progress, and as progress" (215). Progress, the magic ingredient in vocation, demands not just a rise in the fortunes of a private individual, but a successful engagement in raising the fortunes of the community as a whole.

According to Moretti, who here follows the lead of Lukács and Jameson, the achievement of true vocation is thus an impossibility. The novel of vocation must end in failure because vocation – what he calls the "homeland" of meaningful work – is possible "only in the pre-capitalist [or, I suppose, post-revolutionary] world" (27). But the protagonist's failure, which keeps the sense of struggle alive, is the success of the genre. And the reverse is also true. As Moretti argues in his final chapter, the novel of vocation genre fails and dies, specifically in George Eliot's *Felix Holt* and *Daniel Deronda*, when its protagonists successfully achieve a vocation. They can only do so by renouncing the grand public ambitions that vocation had formerly signified and accepting a lesser, more private substitute. "To suggest that [vocation] can be fulfilled within everyday personal relationships suggests a perversion of its meaning" (218). "With Daniel and Felix vocation no longer has anything universalistic about it: it originates from an ethnic or social partiality which it tries to *preserve and even accentuate as such*.... Daniel and Felix are not interested in the public sphere, with its polyphony and its conflicts, but in the erection of barriers." "They entrench themselves within *sub-cultures*," Moretti says, or – in a telling phrase – "enchanted enclaves" (226).

I present this bit of Victorian literary history not for its own sake, but because it is clearly an allegory of our *present* professionalism. It is no coincidence that the narrative by which a Victorian "public sphere" declines into subsequent professional privacy should be so widespread among professional humanists.[6] For if it seems to depict professional humanists as, at least by unconscious implication, poor and diminished things who, like Felix and Daniel, have retreated into enclaves after the grandeur of public vocation is past, this humble self-abasement of the professional critic is not as humble as it seems. Like Matthew Arnold's 1853 preface, one of our more potent professional creation myths, this narrative allows literature to die only in order to be reborn as criticism. The novel of vocation vanishes, and what takes its place is the successful professional – not just Felix Holt and Daniel Deronda, but the professional critic who is now forced, or authorized, to represent a public-ness which can no longer represent itself.

Paradoxically, this takeover can happen only because the professional critic is *not* simply private, but the preserver and transmitter of the lost public moment. In tacitly accepting the common view that professionalism is merely private and technical, Moretti ignores the question of where the enchantment of professionalism's "enchanted enclaves," where the vocation or authority of his own profession, might come from. He ignores, in other words, his and our dependence, as professionals and intellectuals, on the publicly legitimating values we read into and out of our objects of study.

Yet the professional logic is clear. Vocation, as Moretti says, demands public-ness and progress. Professionalization, in his view, means privacy and regress. How then can a professional have a sense – or, more usefully, the legitimacy – of vocation? One answer, at least for literary critics, is vocation *as literature*, as a literary genre that has died. This is how it works. You take a genre like the novel of vocation, which captures a moment of public striving for collective progress, and you ever so regretfully announce its death, thus freezing it as a henceforth unapproachable golden age which can and must be endlessly congratulated. Then you substitute the genre, which has now taken the form of an authoritative cultural tradition, for a culture of the present that might otherwise have seemed public and even progressive but that, by the standards you have now erected, cannot be perceived to exist – can seem to exist only if it duplicates the earlier form. And, finally, you lament the passing of public-ness out of the present, your own profession included – thus, however, establishing your own professional rights, as transmitter of knowledge about the novel of vocation, to represent what the present is missing. Thus progress is preserved, but in or as the past, as culture; and our vocation obtains the progress it requires – at least, the *memory* of progress, now safely surrounded by a narrative of remorseless decline.[7]

The disadvantage of this particular professional logic is that while it inescapably lays claim to the public, it cannot be public enough. To ensure professional autonomy by clinging to culture-as-failure is to adopt an unconsciously negative attitude toward cultural *success*. We will be professionally encouraged by this logic to see only the commodification of culture, for example, in phenomena where one might otherwise see the democratization of culture.[8] Suspicious of all cultural progress, since it unsettles the praise of the past on which we rest our professional authority, we limit and thwart our own relations to the culture of our present public, and thus our own sense of vocation as well.

As we saw in previous chapters, Moretti's is only one of many narratives which present professionalization as a withdrawal from the public, from meaning and value. But the figure who most famously associates professionalization with a withdrawal from value is of course Max Weber, who lays out the doctrine of *Wertfreiheit*, or value-free scholarship, in his classic lecture, "Wissenschaft als Beruf," "Scholarship as a Vocation" (1919). It will come as no surprise by now if I try to contest this view of professional scholarship. Taking a shortcut, therefore, I'd like to bypass such arguments and instead draw from this presumptive lack of surprise an immediate conclusion about the professional context in which we are all operating.

The phrase that I've taken for the title of this section, "a contradiction of which he himself is the resolution," comes from Fredric Jameson's attempt, in "The Vanishing Mediator" (32), to narrativize Weber's value-free ideal, thus restoring to it the values that went into its making. Jameson's reading sees in Weber a miniature novel of vocation centering on Weber's "unusual parental conflict" and "four year period of virtual intellectual paralysis at the very height of an active career" (5). In this reading, Weber's nervous breakdown comes to resemble Conrad's Congo, a period of spleen or ennui caused by the collapse of an older sense of "vocation." "To know spleen," Jameson writes, "the sufferer must be able to see any activity as pure technical performance without intrinsic purpose or value" (10). Yet, as for Conrad, work without intrinsic purpose or value, embraced existentially or protected by the "civility" of a professional community, is also the *resolution* to this crisis. We might even see this parallel as doubled, with Jameson himself playing Marlow to Weber's absolute, Kurtzian rejection of all value. If so, and if *The Protestant Ethic and the Spirit of Capitalism* (1920), a history of the origins of "vocation" in Protestant theology and its secularization in capitalist society, is, as Jameson says, charged with Weber's agonizing over his own sense of vocation, then there is also a double target in Jameson's comment: "Such a vision of history is doubtless what lends these dry pages, interlarded with dead theology and the most unbearable scholarly apparatus, their emotional impact: de te fabula narratur!" About *you* is the story told. Jameson too is wrestling here with the problematic of *his* vocation.[9]

Jameson has little trouble "containing" the transgressive danger of *Wertfreiheit*, just as Marlow's discourse contains Kurtz's lack of restraint by accepted values. He shows it to be, in historical context, not an escape from all value but a "passionate value judgement" aimed at particular political enemies (on the right). And he shows that, in personal context, it is a synthesis of the values of father and mother, whose clash had precipitated the nervous breakdown. In making this demonstration, Jameson, again like Marlow, is acting within and along with a professional community of listeners. One of the major occupations of Weber's numerous and ingenious commentators has in fact been to demonstrate the impossibility or self-contradiction or stubborn misunderstanding by others of what seems to be but in fact is not Weber's flight from value. The entire scholarly community, so far as I can see, is united in Jameson's effort to restore Weberian scholarship, however diversely, to the common realm of value. This can't be a coincidence.[10] I take it, rather, as strong evidence of its own collective proposition: that professional scholarship *is* a realm of value – a public domain which cannot afford *not* to seek legitimation for itself in and among the values that surround it.

If this seems excessively uncontroversial – I'm not sure it does – then so much the better. What is not obvious, at least, is how one translates the perception that "value" and "the public" lie within rather than outside professional scholarship into narratives of professionalization that are different from those we have.

Some elements of such a narrative can perhaps be glimpsed in Jameson's essay on Weber. Readers of Jameson will probably be aware that his vision of history as ever-expanding, ever-worsening capitalist "reification" comes to him, via Lukács, from Weber's "rationalization." More neo-romantic than properly Marxist, this narrative of inexorable, undialectical decline might be thought of as Marxism's compromise with Matthew Arnold. For those of us in the humanities, it provides a useful professional myth that, spurning dialectic, accepts a dichotomy of past plenitude and present emptiness in order to ensure that the past's cultural artifacts, and thus those who preserve and transmit them, will retain their present exchange value.[11] It is in contrast to this professional narrative that Jameson's commentary on Weber should be appreciated. The "vision of history" that he refers to in the "de te fabula" passage is the one referred to in the title of his essay, "The Vanishing Mediator": a non-linear history in which there is *not*, as he and Weber both may be accused of suggesting, a linear movement of rationalization, disenchantment, and devaluation. Instead of a steady seeping away of value out of the world, he unexpectedly detects in Weber's history of vocation, and in Weber's personal history, a series of *rising* moments in which "the means now [become] more rather than less religious, even while the ends grow ever more secularized" (22). The world does not simply grow more and more disenchanted for Weber, Jameson says. There are mediators which, in more dialectical fashion, interrupt the linearity of disenchantment by producing, at least temporarily, new enchantments, new areas of the sacred.

Each of these is associated in some way with the profane ordinariness of scholarship. As biographical source for the vocational energy Weber invested in scholarship, for example, the central mediator, Jameson says, is Weber's mother. The father's secularism, with its cheery acceptance of an archaic status quo, is not the endpoint of a narrative of disenchantment, but rather the obstacle Weber had to overcome in order to forge his sense of scholarly vocation – what he needed to overcome, ironically, in order to become the scholar who would then produce a narrative of disenchantment. Weber overcame this obstacle by means of his mother's old-fashioned but also rationalizing religion.

> Weber used his maternal heritage to transform that of the father, subsequently discarding the mother's values in their turn when their mediatory function had been fulfilled. The mother's values permitted Weber to achieve at length a scholarly existence of backbreaking and compulsive labor, but only when they themselves had been liquidated: this was accomplished by their thematization as an object of study in their own right. (31)[12]

In this narrative of professionalization, the origin of scholarship lies in the professional (critical, aesthetic) distance that Weber takes, as sociologist of religion, from his mother's values – but also, and equally, in the ties that continue to bind him and his discipline to her values, which are preserved even in their renunciation. To renounce the world while living inside it – one of Weber's descriptions of "scholarship as a vocation" – is not, as we might like to believe, the Conradian motto of a virile professional autonomy earned by unique existential tough-mindedness. It is a lesson taught by his mother's religiosity. Which is to say that the world continues to live inside our apparent scholarly renunciation of it.

Without pausing to savor this resolution, let us think immediately of the contradictions it continues to entail. To associate Weber's mother with the flickers of re-enchantment that warm a chill narrative of disenchantment and lend their support, at least momentarily, to the vocational purpose of scholarship's "enchanted enclaves" is once again to place a woman where a male discourse of vocation had already located her. As Nancy Armstrong and Mary Poovey have pointed out, there is a long tradition of modeling the protected space of culture, as professional knowledge base, on the feminine private sphere.[13] This tradition speaks through Jameson's own attempt to break out of the linear narrative of professionalization-as-disenchantment.

Jameson's rewriting of the history of nineteenth-century fiction in *The Political Unconscious* (1981) can be read allegorically in much the way Jameson himself reads Weber's career.[14] His protagonist, like that of Moretti and of course Lukács, is the realist novel as exemplary bearer of freedom and social progress. Again as in *The Way of the World*, the end of this tale of upward mobility is constrained freedom, blocked progress – the dissolution of realism in modernism, then the glittery apocalypse of postmodernism. And again we can read both the early rise and the final blockage as elements of a professional myth, a myth which allows the critic both to be ferried upward by realism as "vanishing mediator" and to kick loose from it when it vanishes. This is a version of the story which, as I have suggested above, has allowed criticism both right and left the luxurious anomaly of being both established and oppositional. What is more interesting in Jameson's version, however, is precisely what Jameson discovers in Weber: the moment at which this rise-and-fall narrative is interrupted. His history, which proceeds linearly from Balzac's realism to Gissing's naturalism and on to Conrad and high modernism, revises Lukács's realism/naturalism/modernism sequence at only one point: the brief rise that Jameson sketches between Gissing and Conrad. Instead of falling into modernism, that is, it suddenly, unexpectedly *rises* to Conrad's *early* modernism, thus allowing the book an upbeat ending before the final fall. Jameson's equivalent for the mother-mediated ascent to scholarship in Weber is Joseph Conrad, or more precisely Joseph-Conrad-in-the-"Third-World": the point where Lord Jim briefly and provisionally finds a vocation in Patusan.

It is no coincidence that both the aesthetic redemption in *The Political Unconscious* and the redeeming realism that Jameson's more recent work contrasts with a degenerate Western postmodernism should be located in the elsewhere of the Third World. For if the basis of his narrative is "reification," which is seen as steadily and uninterruptedly permeating more and more of social life, then alternatives can only come from the margins – which will thus be in danger of labeling by the same idealizations which have always been imposed upon the marginal. Given the linearity of reification at home, vocation seems possible only in a not-yet-reified "Third World."

Yet it would be too simple to cry "idealization" and drop the matter there. "Third World" intellectuals like Aijaz Ahmad have rightly complained that, through Jameson or through other practitioners of "colonial discourse," metropolitan criticism seems tempted to find a vocation in a supposed "Third World" "difference" which is nothing more than an inversion of all that the metropolis hates in itself, and which displaces the actual differences and similarities between the various societies.[15] Indeed, Jameson himself, in "Third-World Literature in the Era of Multinational Capitalism," suggests the fragility of such idealizations. One page after suggesting that intellectuals are "extinct" in the West yet survive intact, in their full political function, in the Third World, Jameson speaks (apropos of Lu Xun) of

> the seemingly hopeless situation of the third-world intellectual in this historical period (shortly after the founding of the Chinese Communist Party, but also after the bankruptcy of the middle-class revolution had become apparent) – in which no solutions, no forms of praxis or change, seem conceivable.

And he adds that

> this situation will find its parallel ... in the situation of African intellectuals after the achievement of independence, when once again no political solutions seem present or visible on the historical horizon.[16]

Under closer examination, "Third World" intellectuals seem after all to have a great deal in common with "First World" intellectuals.

Yet this does not mean that invocations of the "Third World" are necessarily out of place. First, because the place that the "Third World" is abusively asked to occupy here is too interesting in its own right to dismiss so easily. It is an uninhabitable, an impossible place. Humbly provisional – a *vanishing* mediator – it nevertheless stands for the most elevated figure, the Caller behind the Calling, the parental authority which is capable of authorizing vocation. Since no individual or collectivity can rightfully assume this responsibility, delegating such an authority can only be an abuse of its recipient. Yet there is no meaning to "mission" or "vocation" without authority and accountability of some sort. We must, it seems, use each other and be used in such varieties of family romance. If "mission" and "vocation" cannot be done without, the least onerous solution is perhaps a multiplication and distribution of authorities, diluting the abuse and dispersing the injustice.[17] Instead of God the Father as origin of vocation or the earthly father who bestows worldly occupation, better a father *and a mother*. Instead of the call that leads the protagonist from the provinces to the metropolis, better a call that shows the provinces to be, also, a metropolis.

2. Espionage as Vocation: Raymond Williams's *Loyalties*

> It was plain that in certain important fields of their experience my British colleagues and their Russian opposite numbers felt more community with each other than either felt with his next-door neighbour in a British or a Russian street.
>
> Donald Davie[18]

The secret revealed at the end of Raymond Williams's fifth novel, *Loyalties*, published in 1985, is espionage on behalf of the Soviet Union. The topic is not exotic. Williams was writing the novel in the period just after the revelations about Sir Anthony Blunt, the Cambridge colleague who was the "fourth man" in the spy group of Burgess, Maclean, and Philby; to some extent *Loyalties* may be a *roman à clef*. The topic may also have appealed to Williams for less topical reasons. There are significant parallels between Blunt and Williams himself. Both were leftist students at Cambridge during the 1930s, both later became Cambridge dons, both were professionally concerned with the criticism of art, and for both there was some question about the fit between politics and profession. These parallels suggest a sense in which the spy comes still closer to home for Williams: as a figure for the political-intellectual-as-academic. From the beginning of his writing career, Williams's novels and criticism were troubled by the problematic of his working life and how it fitted into the larger politics of society – his moral, political, ideological "take" on his role as an intellectual, his career as an academic. Through the spy, which has become an especially important figure of political imagination in the post-war period, and through the political thriller, with its formulaic distance from the semi-autobiographical realism of Williams's Welsh trilogy, Williams seems to have found a new and liberating way of speaking about that problematic.

In brief, my thesis is that the figure of the "intelligence agent" belongs to the problematics of post-war professionalism. I can introduce this idea by quoting the essay on Blunt written by George Steiner, entitled "The Cleric of Treason," which came out in the *New Yorker* in 1980.[19] Steiner writes:

> I would like to think for a moment about a man who in the morning teaches his students that a false attribution of a Watteau drawing or an inaccurate transcription of a fourteenth-century epigraph is a sin against the spirit and in the afternoon or evening transmits to the agents of Soviet intelligence classified, perhaps vital information given to him in sworn trust by his countrymen and intimate colleagues. What are the sources of such a scission? (191)

To pose the issue in terms of the working day, setting an evening of treason against a morning of scholarship, is to suggest that its hidden referent is the problematic of work. In fact Steiner goes on to offer the scholarship as the *cause* of the treason, which thus becomes a sort of professional deformation. "Obsessive scholarship," he says, "breeds a nostalgia for action" (199). The nostalgia for action and utility which leads to espionage stems from the absolute uselessness of the "absolute scholar," or of research as a vocation.

This view of *Wissenschaft als Beruf* becomes more interesting when one recalls that the portrait of Blunt is a retake of the figure that first made Steiner's reputation, the concentration-camp-tor-turer-who-goes-home-and-reads-Goethe, a figure we can call the *cultured Kommandant*. This figure should be familiar; Steiner has been playing variations on the theme since the late 1950s. "We know now that a man can read Goethe or Rilke in the evening, that he can play Bach and Schubert, and go to his day's work at Auschwitz in the morning." The names change, along with the times of day, but the "scission" remains the same. In 1986, Steiner wrote in the *New York Times Book Review*: "Too many are the butchers and clerks of totalitarian rule who, in their personal and private lives, respond with cultured delight to the claims to fiction and the arts. We know now that a man can torture in the afternoon and be moved to truthful tears by Schubert or Pushkin at nightfall."[20] The cultured Kommandant clearly represents a major chapter in our recent moral history – but perhaps, as with the Holocaust itself, we've been too close to it to see *which* chapter. The juxtaposition of this figure with Steiner's portrait of Blunt suggests that the former was not simply, or perhaps even primarily, a representative of the moral burden of the Holocaust, as we tend to think. More precisely, it translated that burden into a domestic American dilemma of public life versus private life – that is, the problematic of post-war *work*.

This problematic results from one of the same developments that help privilege espionage as a post-war theme. The Second World War was characterized by an extension of hostilities into the domain of civil society: civilian bombings, Occupation, Resistance movements, and so on. The Resistance, for example, politicized, or rather polemicized, the routine of everyday life. This is why, as James Wilkinson writes, there was a "general tendency among Resistance intellectuals to reduce political questions to the level of personal conduct" and why "the distinction between public and private spheres of action became blurred."[21] This invasion of the everyday (extending the penetration of capital into previously protected areas of life) certainly has something to do with post-war spy paranoia. In the same way, it has to do with a new consciousness of the shifting relations between work and non-work. Many of the major figures of the post-war imagination can only be understood in these terms. Steiner's cultured Kommandant belongs together with Sartre's café waiter in *Being and Nothingness* who is playing a café waiter, a figure of professional identification offered as a paradigm of inauthenticity. It also belongs with Camus's Sisyphus and the hero of *The Plague*, a functionary who "asked only to make himself useful in small tasks." On the level of popular sensibility, one thinks of the Alec Guinness/Colonel Nicholson character in the film of Pierre Boulle's *Bridge Over the River Kwai* (1954), a British colonel so intent on being "happy in his work" that he betrays his country in the interest of organized, efficient bridge-building. If work already served as the hinge between the immanent and the transcendent, as Franco Moretti puts it, the point at which the dialectic of history stooped to illuminate everyday reality, the trials of the Nazi war criminals, who were "just doing their job," touched the same point with a transcendent horror.[22]

I call this motif a problematic because a clear or unproblematic response to it was beyond the post-war range of ideological possibilities. The result of the trials could not be a consensus of humanistic or humanitarian anti-professionalism, as one might expect, for the simple reason that the *excuse* given by the executioners, "I was just doing my job," was also the ideological *solution* offered by post-war "end of ideology" thinking. The "just" in "just doing my job" meant not being personally involved in any political program, but extracting oneself from politics by simply fulfilling one's duties in a given area of specialization or competence. Work was outside of ideology. To speak of war criminals, so the defense went, would be like speaking of *work* criminals. In effect, post-war ideology conceded that such a notion was absurd. At the same moment when professionalism was being labeled collaboration with the enemy, in other words, neutral technical expertise was also being celebrated as the replacement for any political taking of sides. The ideology of privatization, which removed morality and politics from the workplace and consigned them to the home, shrugged off accountability for the meaning and consequences of one's work. It positively welcomed the split between home and work on which the defense of the war criminals rested.

The best example of this contradiction in the post-war problematic of work is the lesson Steiner himself drew from his cultured Kommandant. He offered this figure as a challenge to the belief "that culture is a humanizing force," and thus that the work of scholars

and humanists is socially meaningful. Contemplating his Kommandant, Steiner said he could no longer believe, with Matthew Arnold
and F.R. Leavis, that the humanities humanize. And yet Steiner
almost immediately backs down from his challenge (perhaps under
pressure from the "engagement" of Sartre, the post-war voice who
took the same challenge in the opposite direction), retreating to the
Arnoldian humanist position, with its immense nostalgia for
Europe's lost cultural splendors. The logic of his retreat is as clear as
it is paradoxical. What he wants is culture in privacy – or, rather,
culture *as* privacy. Since public life has proved a nightmare, let us
withdraw into the patient, self-sacrificing, apolitical work of cultural
transmission – even if (here is the paradox) the *capacity* of culture to
remain apolitical, its *in*capacity to prevent or even resist the horrors
of the war, is what has thrown what we mean by culture into
question, and even if the contiguous but separate coexistence of high
culture with the horror of the camps has been (for the cultured) the
greatest horror of all. In short, the solution repeats the problem. This
explains why Steiner's fascination with the cultured Kommandant
has been capable of reproducing itself over and over for thirty years:
the figure represents at the same time what most horrifies Steiner in
the Nazi period and what Steiner now urges intellectual work to
become.

On this point one would expect a clear contrast between Steiner
and Raymond Williams. But that is not what one finds. Like
Steiner, Williams establishes a hidden equation between intellectual
work and treason. Throughout his trilogy of semi-autobiographical
Welsh novels – which are all about the choice and the politics
of vocation – intellectual work is what makes the protagonist leave
Wales and what keeps him from coming back to it, and is thus
a betrayal of his most fundamental loyalty. As the Welsh
protagonist of *Second Generation* (1964) says of his presence in
Cambridge, "a people had conceived its own liberation as training
its sons for the enemy service."[23] In his own eyes, he is *in* the
enemy service. (Later, when he is offered a chance to go to the
US for reasons of work, he frames his refusal as agreement with
an African statesman's discourse of national liberation.) Doing
intellectual work means being a traitor to his nation in much the
same way that Blunt is a traitor to his.

Hence, as the interviewers of *Politics and Letters* (1979) remark,
academics – and especially leftist academics – replace capitalists as
the villains of *Second Generation*, and are treated with barely

concealed fury, although (or perhaps because) they represent nothing more or less than Williams's own vocation.[24] Williams's painful unease with this logic makes itself felt in his treatment of the materials of family romance. The academics of *Second Generation* are surrogate fathers of higher station, produced in order to legitimate the young man's independence or "upward mobility."[25] But identification with these surrogates is experienced as an unendurable, sexually doubled betrayal of the original, Welsh, working-class father. In *Second Generation*, as in *Loyalties*, the *Adam Bede* motif of an upper-class man who seduces and abandons a working-class woman is transmuted into the still more charged tableau of the Other Man as Leftist Academic who takes or tries to take the working-class Mother away from the working-class Father. *Loyalties* (1985) conceals this structure somewhat by spreading the story out over more than one generation, so that mother, son, and academic interloper do not occupy the narrative stage at the same time.[26] In *Second Generation*, on the other hand – which is, as one critic says, a "deeply vocational" novel – the structure is openly visible.[27] The married working-class mother of an already-grown student son has an affair with a (personally unappetizing) leftist academic on the son's faculty. The structure brings out Williams's intention to condemn and reject this intellectual, but it also highlights his failure to carry that intention through. Williams doesn't know quite what to convict the academic *of*, beyond his upper-class accent and (like Norman in *Loyalties*) his poor performance in bed. The disparity between the thinness of the character and the intense desire to repudiate the position he occupies leads the novel to fill up that position with a second academic villain. This second villain, the protagonist's academic advisor, is also the professional model whom he will finally and rather harshly reject ("you're the enemy"), just as his mother rejects her lover. But here too the case against the academic is strangely insufficient. When the advisor reappears in the later novel *The Fight for Manod* (1979), this time working for the government and unquestionably one of "them," it is as if Williams were trying to blacken the earlier portrait, realizing it was not as critical as he had wanted it to be.[28]

The structural problem is of course that Williams cannot repudiate the erotic interloper without repudiating the mentor, since they are the same figure. Which is to say that he can neither accept nor repudiate himself as he has been constituted by the vocational aspirations that lead away from Wales and from the working class.

Work is the locus of equal and irreconcilable loyalties; family romance is thus transmuted into vocational tragedy.

Williams does not accept this vocational tragedy as inevitable. If the Welsh trilogy condemns intellectual work as treason, it also tries to *redefine* that work so as to resolve the conflict of loyalties. In *Second Generation*, the hero concludes, "What I shall try to do, here, is a new kind of inquiry, with ourselves involved in it. And for our own understanding, not just for report . . . not a survey. That's just what's been wrong" (344). Yet even reconceptualized, his work still looks to his father like the enemy's hostile observation: "from what I can see he's in the same trade. And it makes no difference, that he happens to be born here. He wants the same, just to measure and see what we're good for" (344–5).

More or less the same conclusion is reached in *Border Country*, Williams's first published novel (before it came out in 1960 he had written three unpublished novels).[29] On its first page, we find the lecturer-hero's "anxiety about his work," which is research "on population movements into the Welsh mining valleys in the middle decades of the nineteenth century. But I have moved myself, he objected, and what is it really that I must measure?" (9). This turn of the content of his research toward himself puts a great deal of weight on his work. It's in the name of his work that he refuses the offer of a lucrative job that would allow him to return to Wales, so his work bears the burden of not being mere money-making, while it is also not solidarity with his people. The role assigned to work is to resolve the personal contradictions between going and staying, family and militancy, upward mobility and local solidarity. He leaves the community, then seeks to come back on the level of his work: " 'He's studying Wales,' Eira said, 'and he goes to London to do it' " (271).

In short, work is required to function as a synthesis. But this is not to say, as the ending indicates, that synthesis is or can be achieved on that level. What the protagonist has really wanted, it seems, is for his father to tell him he's doing the right work (rather than work like his own, as a railway signalman, which the father has dramatically refused to leave for a chance to go into business), or that it is acceptable for him to be doing it. Just before dying, the father does accept the son's work, but only in unacceptable terms: "You're working for your boys" (279). The real "structure of feeling" here is total intransigence, and that is expressed over and over: in the association of the son's work with the father's death, and again in two key scenes. In the first, news of the father's fatal attack is given to his son on a railway platform as he is about to return to Cambridge. He is "hailed" by a colleague of his father's who recognizes him by resemblance – a classic scene of ideological interpellation in which he is recognized as his father's son and becomes the subject who returns to Wales. The second is at the father's death bed, when the father, in delirium, denies in effect the separate pressure of work over love. "Only the one trade to get into and that's a wife to love you." The father remains an unbending ideal, condemning his son's work, and work thus remains betrayal, treason. It is a vocational form of modern tragedy: he is "Blamed for something that is quite inevitable" (279).

This vocational impasse is also what defines the concept of "tragedy" that Williams develops in his first major piece of criticism. The first chapter of his first published book, *Drama from Ibsen to Eliot* (1952), offers a revisionary reading of Ibsen's career in terms of "vocation," described as "the most persistent single theme in Ibsen's whole work."[30] What is this "vocation" that Williams substitutes for the usual reading of Ibsen in terms of "the destruction of an idealist"? It is more than an ideal in that it is a specifically *individual* call to idealism – that is, a call to a *feasible mode of individual activity*, to a *career* – and at the same time its idealism is *more* than individual: he speaks of vocation as aimed at "the restoration of wholeness" (29) and at "liberation" (34). This is why, as Williams insists, vocations cannot be, as Ibsen's idealists appeared to Shaw, objects of satire. Yet if Williams takes a more sympathetic view than Shaw, his view is sympathetic to both sides in what we quickly see is a tragic sense of vocation. Perhaps "the fundamental statement . . . in the whole work of Ibsen," Williams writes, is the absolute impossibility of answering the call to vocation. "The call is absolute; so are the barriers" (29).

What creates the vocational impasse of Ibsenite tragedy, and how does Williams find himself sympathizing with both sides of it? He summarizes the conclusion of *Brand* as "the impossibility of fulfilling the vocation of the ideal under the load of 'inherited spiritual debt'" (28), and he defines "debt" (still according to *Brand*) as the taking over of parental sins and responsibilities. In other words, in his first piece of sustained critical writing Williams frames the theme of vocational tragedy in Ibsen so as to reproduce, or rather anticipate, the generational conflict and vocational impasse of his first two Welsh novels. Like those novels, it attempts to resolve this impasse by allowing vocation to be brought into synthesis with the world of the parents. Invocation of the parents can sacralize even ordinary, politically quiescent work: "Brand's mission can no longer be the reform of the world, but the actual, limited sphere of 'daily duty, daily labour, hallowed to a Sabbath deed'" (31). Again as in the novels, this solution is judged impossible. The claims of vocation and inheritance are equally peremptory: this is "the essential tragedy of the human situation" (32). Moreover, here Williams adds an ironic twist that is not in the novels. The real vocational tragedy, he suggests, is less the impossibility of fulfilling one's vocation than how *the ideal itself comes to be changed*, under pressure from other loyalties. In particular, how vocation comes to be redefined "not as social reform, but as the realization of the actual self" – how "social reform" is diminished to "self-fulfilment" (30).

In responding to the interviewers of *Politics and Letters*, Williams makes it clear that vocational tragedy is his description of the post-war situation, both for himself as a would-be militant/ academic and in general. He can only assent to their question: "You felt that the hope of a kind of fusion of your personal work as a writer with the general activities of a political militant in the thirties had been frustrated – hence you were in a situation like that which is at the centre of Ibsen's work?" (63). Yet in devoting the post-war years to the (academic) work of laying out this dilemma in Ibsen, he had done something more than define the tragic need for an impossible fusion between large political goals and daily vocational routine; he had done more than displace and contain the impasse within his academic work (as one might say I am here trying to contain my own). His account of tragedy already points beyond the impasse. What is opposed to vocation, what produces tragedy, is "inheritance," in other words the father's intransigence. But the father's intransigence has to be understood generously here: not as private psychological materials that have not been worked through, but as an insistence that redefinition *within* the work, the effort to displace the conflict *into* his work and to present work, reconceived, as the synthesis between leaving Wales and staying, as a way of returning to Wales on a higher level, cannot take him very far. The reason is that it is still self-regarding, in two senses: it sacrifices Wales both to self-interest and to self-reflexivity. Thinking about himself in relation to his subject is good, but it is no more effective than doing the usual sort of "objective" survey. Neither sort of work produces action in and on the world. What is needed is a new relation *between* work and the world: specifically, some mode of acting on the distant forces that have been working against Wales.

It is precisely an emphasis on action that permits Williams to keep the concept of tragedy alive. Here contrast with George Steiner is again useful. Steiner's position inheres in the title of his book *The Death of Tragedy* (1961): for Steiner, there is no modern tragedy. Williams disagrees, above all because he refuses Steiner's Arnoldian premise that significant action is impossible in the post-war world. There *is* significant action, Williams insists in *Modern Tragedy* (1966).[31] (In fact, Williams sees the denial that tragedy exists as a professional deformation of academics influenced by their training to value the past over the present, and to neglect present action [46]). And since there is significant action, there is also tragedy, as he had already shown in Ibsen. But in order to support the belief that tragedy is ordinary, just as "culture is ordinary," Williams must be willing to discover and acknowledge new, post-war genres and resources of action, especially collective, collaborative action, at points where others will see nothing happening. Again as he had showed in Ibsen, one such point was the vocation, which has its own tragedy, at least the tragedy of not being the collective revolutionary action it wants to be. Through his work, if not in full consciousness, Williams could be said to have assumed the task of making moral room for action that our professional deformation would invite us to condemn out of hand: including, or perhaps especially, our own.

One unusual place Williams is willing to countenance professional action is in the political thriller, and in espionage. Williams's first political thriller, *The Volunteers* (1978), introduces the spy as something approaching a positive professional model. Narrated by a journalist, once a leftist militant, who is assigned to cover an act of "terrorism" carried out by people like his pre-professional self, the novel pivots on the question of his commitment. On the most obvious level, this means his eventual refusal of the role of "the watching devil, the staring professional intruder" and his volunteering for extra-professional action.[32] But what is more interesting than this conventional moral frame is the other sense of the title term "volunteers." The "Volunteers" are a group of Fabian-style professionals whose political program is infiltration of the bureaucratic system, using the usual weapons of careerism. Instead of entry only into leftist organizations, or entry anywhere but always identified as leftists, they attempt a hidden permeation of the modern state apparatus, a very "long term" gambit. "To work normally, to attend to their careers, to show no traceable interest in anything else.... But still they've made their commitment." This gambit is subjected to scrutiny: "a commitment to nothing. A commitment that will never be called," the narrator says when he uncovers their secret. By the time it is called, he goes on, "they'll have become their offices.... Haven't you watched your friends growing up? Haven't you seen what happens to people?" But this belittlement cannot overbalance the weight of the thriller's form, which goes with rather than against their politicized professionalism. The head of the "volunteers," Mark Evans, is presented to us as another figure of the successful, hateful careerist, despised by "the committed" (67). Moreover, he is despised as a Welshman who has sold out. And yet he is the figure the reader will be taught, if not to admire, at least to see, against first and second temptations, as a principled radical. A radical who has the power to threaten real damage – "the system will lose its confidence. Who can we trust, they'll all ask . . ." – and who has in fact accomplished something: "not much perhaps but enough" (179).

In *Loyalties*, Williams doesn't much like his upper-class Cambridge spy. The spy's name, Norman, already says enough about which side he's taken to be on. In fact Williams concludes the novel with a rather grand denunciation of Norman and his espionage, put for greater effect in the mouth of Norman's natural son, whom he abandoned (family romance at its most insistent) and who was raised in the Welsh working class. Yet the thriller form again works in the spy's favor. Norman's transformation into a spy is located at a very strange point: it coincides with his jilting of the Welsh working-class girl he has seduced, and who is pregnant. For most of the novel the reader is encouraged to take this as the usual pattern of male upper-class behavior – the *Adam Bede* motif of the gentleman who uses class privilege to seduce and then abandon a working woman, as in the family romance of *Second Generation*. Williams saves until quite late the news that Norman in fact had a *principled* motive all along, but one that had to *remain secret*: his intelligence work. Thus, as in *The Volunteers*, Williams makes the spy's principled motives look very much like the "point" the novel has been building up to. More generally, this is the effect of working within the pre-Le Carré conventions of the political thriller, and allowing Norman's spying to function less as a moral issue than as the novel's mystery, obliquely hinted at but only revealed relatively late in the novel. The reader follows what seems to be both Norman's abandonment of his Welsh

137

lover and his abandonment of his political commitment, a slow turn to the right that coincides with his rising professional career in the government bureaucracy, and develops a bad opinion of him – so bad that it can only change for the better. Thus the revelation of his spying, coinciding with the revelation that he never *did* abandon his radical ideas, makes the point that, whatever else has happened to him, pursuing his professional career was not in fact selling out.

Loyalties clearly locates espionage as a sub-set of the general category of professionalism. Norman is first and foremost a "serious professional" (133). He speaks of others as amateurs (193); he himself deals with matters "too complicated for any amateurs to touch" (373–4). He has only contempt for his sister's "amateur" spying (133). His sister chides him for leaning his politics too heavily on his profession: "You think your professional *couche* is a viable political alternative. But it isn't and it can't be" (168–9). In the view of a Cambridge friend, "He had become used to living in a consensual professional world." But neither the friend nor the sister knows his secret. In fact Norman's professionalism takes him far outside consensus, and in terms of the novel, at least, his mode of action would seem to be the most efficacious, if not the most acceptable "political alternative" around. Williams seems to be asking us to consider whether this isn't what action has come to require. "It's a skilled professional world," Norman tells his sister, "and becoming more so every year, every day" (176). This is what another old friend and fellow Cambridge spy explains to his son, Gwyn, who has accused his father: "why do you not act as you believe? ... Did you fight in Normandie? Did you fight the fascists anywhere?" (268). As opposed to those working openly in the Party, on the one hand, and those fighting in the trenches, on the other, he says, "ours was a different choice, neither political nor military. What we were doing, indispensably, was operational" (318). It was "a special case: one in which others, however brave, could not volunteer." Although it was specialized, moreover – "a dynamic conflict within a highly specialised field" – this professional narrowing down was not a treasonous withdrawal from broader loyalties but, on the contrary, an extension of loyalty outwards: one's first loyalty, the fellow spy declares, had to go to the "human species" (316).

In the later confrontation scene, *Loyalties* reverses the earlier alignment; here it is an intransigent son who accuses his intellectual father. But the accusation is in the name of the same values: Wales

138

and the working class, "shared existence and shared knowledge." "No authentic act for socialism can distance itself, let alone hide, from these ties of its own people" (358). The son's words echo the socialist humanism of E.P. Thompson, or of Williams himself, while the father's answer, in the mode of professional expertise, accepts an Althusserian "distance" from "experience" that is seen as largely error: "That I should be loyal to ignorance, to shortsightedness, to prejudice, because these exist in my fellow countrymen?" (360). Judging from the keywords, one would have to place Williams on the side of the son and closely shared ties as against distance and what he calls, in *Border Country*, "longsightedness" (244). But here Williams introduces a symbol that mediates between the two positions. The novel's major metaphor is a pair of binoculars, emblematic of the tactical power of longsightedness (itself Williams's continual metaphor for academic work). The binoculars first belong, appropriately enough, to a Cambridge student. But distance also means, here, the internationalist commitment that sends this student off to Spain to fight for the Loyalists. When he is killed, this double emblem of intelligence at a distance is carried home by the hero's adoptive working-class father. Thus it is passed on, or back, to the Cambridge-educated son. It is Williams's one *acceptable* symbol of Cambridge, which is to say of action involving (like the father's railway) distance as well as closeness.

Here, as so often, the issues of professionalism and internationalism overlap. Like Steiner, Williams locates the far-seeing spy as a figure of and after the Second World War. Norman becomes a spy in the course of the anti-fascist struggle in Spain. But unlike Steiner, Williams takes Spain and its anti-fascist alliance as the war's central meaning: a moment of "temporary fusion" drawing together otherwise irreconcilable social classes and groups in a common struggle, sending Welsh miners and Cambridge undergraduates off together to fight a distant enemy who would ordinarily be invisible. This is something like what David Hare (who was tutored by Williams at Cambridge) was suggesting in the play and film *Plenty*, the war (and, coincidentally, undercover resistance work) recalled as a sort of Golden Age of significant collective action, from the standpoint of which the routine and compromises of post-war work seem mean and meaninglessness. And it is something like Le Carré's reading of espionage in the post-war context, which presents spies like Philby as just what "the Establishment deserved. Philby is a creature of the postwar depression, of the swift snuffing out of the Socialist flame, of the thousand year sleep of Eden and Macmillan."[33] At the end of the World War, the world falls back into its usual national rivalry, and according to the logic of Williams's narrative (though not according to his explicit commentaries), the opprobrium that is then heaped on spies would result from the sudden and arbitrary criminalizing of what had been the war's international solidarity. In this sense, the spy is keeping the "fusion" of the war alive into the fallen post-war period.[34] Put in terms of the problematic of work sketched out above, the spy (or professional) would be the figure who, continuing to respond to solidarities that have grown distant or invisible, continues to invest work with public, political meaning, to hold public and private together. Or, more exactly, whose problematic loyalty and moral status register the strain of holding them together.

Williams's own military service during the war is perhaps another clue to this opening up to professionalism via internationalism. In *Loyalties* he gives that experience to the working-class Welshman (the adoptive father of Norman's son) who, having barely survived Spain, is horribly wounded in a skirmish between tanks in Normandy. Armor, artillery, mechanized mobility: the constellation of terms characteristic of tank warfare leads away from the language of rootedness, openness, and proximity we have been led to associate with Williams. And the experience does seem to have marked Williams in an unfamiliar direction. In *Politics and Letters*, his brief discussion of his military experience includes uncharacteristic praise of specialization. As an officer commanding a crew of five in his tank as well as three other tanks, he found that because each had "technical jobs to do," relations were "not so hierarchical." Specialization creates social cohesion without hierarchy; within its limits, it is egalitarian. Moreover, its efficiency contrasts with Williams's rage at the "incompetence" of his leaders (55).

In the thriller genre, as in the Westerns discussed by Will Wright, the birth of a new local solidarity that is separable from larger national loyalties, and conceivably larger, more internationalist than they are, is also a recognized phenomenon of the post-war period. Before the war, according to Myron J. Smith, in its "Innocent Age," the spy thriller pitted upper-class amateurs against clearly defined national enemies.[35] After the war, in the "James Bond" era, professionals of dubious morality or problematic loyalty, like Le Carré's heroes, tend to be set against other professionals, elite against elite, with no clear national enemy. Jerry Palmer's *Thrillers: Genesis and Structure of a Popular*

Genre (1978) presents a similar argument: "professionalism is a feature of all thriller heroes" (211). In Forsyth's *The Day of the Jackal*, for example: "The world in which the Jackal himself moves is entirely dominated by professionalism. Amateurs who impinge on it are victims" (207). More to the point, Palmer sketches out a dialectic of isolation (individual freedom) and participation or allegiance which casts the professional, who is "capable of membership in a group" (14), in the role of synthesis. Michael Denning's *Cover Stories: Narrative and Ideology in the British Spy Thriller* (1987) insists in the same vein that there is more to all this professionalism than loss of purpose, both personal and national. In his reading of the thriller as "a tale of the political contradictions of white-collar, professional work" (151), Denning points out the utopian appeal of this synthesis, which promises an intertwining of "public and private" (131) that seems elsewhere inaccessible.

The political thriller thus offers something beyond the range of the Welsh trilogy. There, community meant closeness, and action was enclosed by the community. Here, imagining that the stuff or substance of community can be spread more widely, can be distributed differently, Williams seizes the possibility of action at a distance, and solidarity at a distance. He tries to grasp a solidarity that would not only be to him (and others) what Wales is, but would help him and them to act upon the forces working against Wales, as working *within* Wales might not allow them to do. I hope it is clear that I am not speaking, as I think Williams is not speaking, of the peculiarities of espionage, but rather of professional work in general. Like professionalism, espionage involves professional secrets, a monopoly of information and control over its flow, a narrowing down of community that paradoxically also claims to expand or universalize loyalties. It also represents a professional ideal: political activity in the midst of what appears to be political quiescence, or acquiescence.

3. "From a high place"

"You speak for yourself, but I speak for Britain." "Where is that?", you may think to ask, looking wonderingly around. On a good day from a high place you can see about fifty miles.

Raymond Williams[36]

Like espionage, professionalism more frequently appears to Williams as a variant of rootless cosmopolitanism. In the capsule history of

"Cambridge English" in *Writing in Society*, which was cited in Chapter Two, he refers to literary study as it has emerged from its origins in modernist "estrangement" as "the profession of a stranger."[37] It is statements like these that permit Terry Eagleton, in a moving obituary, to affirm that Williams "had little or no sense of himself as part of a 'profession.'"[38] And again: "what some left academics sometimes like to feign – that they are merely passing through the system, dipping in and out, fundamentally detached – was in his case oddly true" (7). What is oddest here, however, is not Williams's very real loyalties outside his profession, which are shared in kind if not in the same degree by many of his professional colleagues, but rather the profession's general eagerness both to "feign" such detachment from itself and to praise, as Eagleton does, those who seem genuinely to achieve it. To see detachment from the profession as a persistent convention of professional eulogy is to see Williams's ambivalence, which he himself saw in class and national terms, as an ambivalence that is also intrinsic to the profession itself, at least in its recent historical form. Eagleton more or less admits as much when he describes Williams as "always haunted by the border he had crossed from the 'knowable community' to the life of educated intelligence" (6). Put in these terms, the haunting (which is what Williams's fiction is all about) seems not a quirk of Williams's autobiography but a general phenomenon of professionalism. And perhaps what is most frightening in it, both for Williams and for Eagleton, is the implication that the "life" of "educated intelligence" is not after all a privilege of the newly isolated individual but a "community" in its own right – that one may have joined a new, less "knowable" community in the act of (or without) leaving another behind, and that the two communities may share common loyalties. If for Williams the lives of intelligence agents, like those of other professionals, seem to hover near tragedy, in that they transgress or threaten to trangress a very powerful loyalty, at least *Loyalties* comes closer to a successful reconciliation of loyalties than any of Williams's previous writings (except perhaps *The Country and the City*, which works hard to relativize the story of the lonely urban intellectual's departure from a rural home). At any rate, it is certainly a large step away from the inchoate self-hatred of the autobiographical novels, a step toward consciously inhabiting one's professional life rather than pretending it is someone else's, and toward seeing even the academy as not, like Steiner's extra-territoriality, an excuse for non-affiliation, but as a place where new affiliations can (and must) come into being.

In his inaugural lecture as Professor of Drama at Cambridge, from which the lines above are taken, Williams addressed himself to another sort of drama, the "theatrical ruling show." "On what is called the public stage, or in the public eye," he said, "improbable but plausible figures continually appear to represent us. Specific men are magnified to temporary universality."[39] What the political leader acts out, Williams noted, is the false universality of the nation. "'I speak for Britain' runs the written line of that miming public figure, though since we were let in on the auditions, and saw other actors trying for the part, we may have our reservations; we may even say, 'Well I'm here and you don't speak for me.'"

Coming to Cambridge from Wales and from the working class, Williams had some reason to be suspicious of "English" universality, whether in politics or in literature, and much of his writing was an effort to break it apart, to expose the exclusions that it disguises, to speak up against the powerful voices that claim it. Perhaps it is this effort which generates a sort of uneasy echo in the words of the inaugural lecture. When Williams says that "specific men are magnified to temporary universality," he could be speaking of the very occasion in which he is participating. When he speaks of how much you can see "from a high place," he could be discussing the institutional place to which he has at that moment ascended.

In speaking against the pretense of universality, Williams is speaking at cross purposes to himself. The inaugural lecture cannot entirely disavow universality. As a paradigmatically professional genre, it is committed to laying out a program of work, and the meaning of any program of work can only be defined by locating it on a broad map of neighboring fields, knowledge already acquired, research already in progress. When Adorno explains "The Actuality of Philosophy" in his inaugural lecture at the University of Frankfurt in 1931, he feels obliged to situate it in relation to competition from the rising science of sociology.[40] He was not so crude as to say that "everything" was philosophy, but he had to see almost "everything" spread before him in order to say what philosophy could and should claim to be, where it could and should fit in. Foucault begins his inaugural lecture at the Collège de France by expressing extreme discomfort at the intense personal surveillance which the ritual of elevation makes him undergo, but the program of work he lays out in his lecture is among the most comprehensive, almost omniscient displays of cross-disciplinary erudition ever staged. Looking far out across the specialties, it demands a perspective like the watcher in the tower of Bentham's Panopticon. And what is true for these ideal instances is true in principle for the genre as such. An inaugural lecture must look "from a high place."

Williams's discomfort with the high professional place in which he found himself is not only a discomfort with "longsightedness," with the presumption of privileged perspective; it is also a refusal of the idea of "speaking for others," of being representative. This refusal aims at the very heart of literary criticism. In his two retirement lectures of 1983, Williams reminds his hearers that "English" as a course of study has substituted for a problematic whole (English as nationality and language) a still more problematic part (English literature). What is now meant by "literature," he says, is in fact the thin, specialized margin that has slowly been torn away from the full working culture of English people. In the definition of the word there has been, "first, a restriction to printed texts, then a narrowing to what are called 'imaginative' works, and then finally a circumscription to a critically established minority of 'canonical' texts."[41] What's wrong with this is more than the suppression of ordinary culture and the propagating of minority culture. If the nineteenth-century move from literature as both fact and fiction to literature as merely fiction meant a weakening of its ties to social actuality, hence also of its public authority, the further specialization to a highly selective canon meant, paradoxically, a new claim to social authority and representativeness for those who taught it. For a selective canon requires and empowers an elite of interpreters, that "virtuous minority, against commercialism" (188) who thus become guardians of the distilled essence of the national heritage that is called "English literature." English teachers, like political leaders, implicitly draw power from the claim to represent the entire nation, to be "the minority carriers of a common tradition, an 'Englishness' of the literature which was made to stand for the 'Englishness' of a people" (221).

No one has been as eloquent a critic of criticism's pretense to national representativeness as Williams.[42] But the real force of the critique does not target representativeness as such. According to Terry Eagleton in *Criticism and Ideology* (1976), the difficulty of Williams's style can only be explained by its own peculiar aspiration to universality. It is "an elaborately formal, resoundingly public discourse in which an abstractive habit has become an instinctual reflex," a "magisterial" style that seeks to assume "an unruffled, almost Olympian impersonality."[43] The personal trajectory is there, but it is assimilated or projected into a larger whole. In short,

"Williams is resolutely offering his own experience as historically representative. Such a discourse rests on a rare, courageously simple belief . . . that the deepest personal experience can be offered, without arrogance or appropriation, as socially 'typical' " (23).

This is precisely the move that, as Williams demonstrates, the teacher of English shares with the political leaders of Britain, those "specific men" who are "magnified to temporary universality." It is also the animating principle behind Williams's extraordinary chef d'oeuvre, *The Country and the City* (1973).[44] *The Country and the City* is a history of decolonization – the decolonization of literature. Literature begins as a colony of the ruling class, a place where they do what they want. As in *Heart of Darkness*, the colonists need not worry about how it all looks from the natives' point of view. The extermination of brutal reality is, for the moment, total; no sign remains to reveal, for example, that Sidney's *Arcadia* was written in a park formed when a village was enclosed and all its inhabitants expelled. But gradually the reality of the inhabitants forces its way into the picture, and as literature comes to listen to people who live on the land that it converts into pastoral, comes to include reality it had ignored, the narrative turns into a progress. The paradigmatic progressive moment is, as one might expect, in the nineteenth century. The chapter entitled "Knowable Communities," for example, progresses from Jane Austen's restricted circle of visitable neighbors to George Eliot, who shows us real country people at work. Dickens takes the reader to London and begins to reveal, behind the shock and abstraction of city stereotype, webs of connection and community linking together the working lives of ordinary people. This literary history follows a trajectory of displacement much like Williams's own. More important, it makes that trajectory representative. For this narrative of progressive democratization is both a personal myth and a generalizable narrative of vocation. Paralleling the rise of realism with the extension of political representation in an ever-expanding democratic inclusiveness, it includes any would-be critic who comes from the provinces to the metropolis. Realism tells us, in effect, that the critic's upward mobility is acceptable and even commendable. Although the profession does constitute an elite, it is also socially responsive, socially representative. For if literature in the past has gradually come to represent the public, as realism guarantees it did, then we who represent that literature are also representive. In vulgar sociological terms, professionalism's necessary claim to public service can thus be satisfied.

I have no quarrel with either the narrative of democratization or with its professional usefulness. My own argument will fit pretty comfortably within it. The difficulty lies in the paternal point where the process of democratization is arrested.

Like Lukács, Jameson, and Moretti, Williams offers a paradigmatic moment of *retreat* from the project of democratization, beginning as early as George Eliot's withdrawal into private subjectivity in *Daniel Deronda*. Thinking back to the scene on the railway platform in *Border Country*, we can describe this moment of arrest as an interpellation in the name of the Father-as-Culture. Richard Johnson once summed up a question that many British socialists had expressed, he said, about Williams and E.P. Thompson: "Why did they choose to write about their deepest political convictions through the presentation of significant persons, mostly long dead?" His explanation of this detour was, in effect, that they placed excessive importance on "culture," and that they did so because "culture" corresponds well to what is required by "English intellectuals," who are "removed from" the "morality and purposes" of "industrial capital", in order to fit themselves into the intellectual division of labor – in other words, to define for themselves a specialized vocation.[45] It is this sense of vocation, constituted out of political blockage, whose genesis can be observed on the railway platform. Not "long dead," but soon to be dead, the father of Williams's hero represents to him the culture of the Welsh working class. He illustrates the redefinition by which Williams, as critic, was to take "culture" away from Matthew Arnold – patriarch among the line of fathers that Raymond Williams himself was assembling in *Culture and Society*, with love and hate, while writing *Border Country* – and bring it into the present: culture as a "whole way of life." But culture as "whole way of life" is curiously indistinguishable in its effects from culture as detour through dead men. By the logic of the narrative (if not the logic of Williams's conscious critical beliefs), there can be no movement beginning in either culture that is not a movement away from culture, which is to say a betrayal of and a fall from it.

The consequences of this arrest are not too much representativeness, but too little. For the blockage of the vocational narrative of democratization in *The Country and the City* coincides with a new problem, simultaneously global and professional. At the end of the book, Williams extends the titular terms to the imperialist world-system: city becomes metropolis, and country becomes periphery. To extend the terms, however, is immediately to face a difficulty in the narrative that came before. For the British Empire was of course in the process of construction *throughout* the period that narrative covered, not just at the end; and the economic interests, racial beliefs, and so on that went into constructing it came both from the city and from the country. This is to say that, from quite early on, all of Britain, including what Williams calls "the country," was already playing the role of "city" to the Third World's "country" within the international division of labor. The colonized at home were also, simultaneously, colonizers abroad. The narrative of progress, obscuring not just those as yet unrepresented, but those being newly conquered in those same years, was itself a narrative of domination.

This is invisible in the book, perhaps even more so than, say, the similar split in Williams's historical subjects introduced by the *sexual* division of labor; Joan Scott's analysis of E.P. Thompson's *Making of the English Working Class* is a suggestive parallel.[46] It is invisible not just because it is simultaneous and Williams is working with a linear narrative, but because he is limited by the representativeness of "experience," "culture," and "knowable communities." Country people in the nineteenth century had little or no first-hand experience of Empire; hence, by Williams's definition, it was not part of their culture. Yet this did not stop them from being part of it, nor stop it from being part of them – through a network of distant, mediated connections that are not available to "experience."

My point is not that Williams should have carried further an unease with the professional work of representation that was correct in principle. As I've suggested, loyalty to "experience" carries its own tale of upward mobility, its own allegory of vocation; but that allegory is also a grounding of the critic: it means no "high places." And in the era of the integrated world economy, "high places" and longsightedness cannot be foregone.

4. "Half my right of speech": James Agee

In May 1939 *Partisan Review* sent a number of American writers and intellectuals, including James Agee, a questionnaire about their social role.[47] Agee shared *Partisan Review*'s conception of the intellectual as an amateur rather than a professional, but he was infuriated by the questionnaire's implicit vanguardism, its assumption of social leadership, and he sent in answers that *Partisan Review* judged unprintable. Agee printed them himself, not long after, in *Let*

Us Now Praise Famous Men (1940), his documentary book about southern tenant farmers in the Depression.[48] Reviewing that book, Lionel Trilling objected – in an otherwise positive assessment – that there had been "a failure of moral realism." The problem was "Agee's inability to see these people as anything but good."[49]

How do we break out of this impasse? Trilling gives his assumption of superiority away when he defends, in contrast, "the relatively fortunate middle class that reads books and [sic] experiences emotions" (99). On the other hand, he is clearly right about Agee's helpless, self-effacing emotions of reverence. And to his critique could be added the same factors of self-interest and self-aggrandizement that Trilling himself betrays. The excess of democratic respect that Trilling complains of in Agee was also Agee's way of grounding or legitimating his role as an intellectual. There is vocational self-interest hidden in his reverence.

When Agee went exploring among the poor tenant farmers of Alabama, it is clear that one thing he was looking for was his father. As we learn in Agee's autobiographical novel *A Death in the Family* (1957), which makes an enlightening counterpart to the family descriptions of *Let Us Now...*, he felt that his father's death in an automobile accident had estranged him forever from the simple mountain folk of that side of the family.[50] He was looking, that is, for a return to that folk, to "the people," a literal embodiment of a sacred memory and source of infinite moral obligations which he idealized much as he idealized his father. The passage from which his title is taken goes on: "Let us now praise famous men, *and our fathers that begat us.*"

Agee is willing to distort the lives of the tenant farmers in order to make them the supporting antithesis of himself. Work is "the very essence of their lives" (31), Agee writes, "the heart and center of living" (34). Agee recognizes elsewhere that a main problem of tenant farmers was in fact *not* having *enough* work, but still he describes their lives, over and over, as stretched to the very limit of Necessity, with absolutely no time for leisure, as lives of *pure* work. It becomes clear that (like "the people") work is a constructed necessity, a hypothetical stable ground invented in order to serve, by contrast, as the foundation of Agee's very different sense of his own work.

He experiences the relation between their work and his work in two modes. On the one hand, as shame and guilt; before the "necessity" of their work, he feels that his own work is arbitrary, contingent, meaningless. Talking for a living, he is to his silent father as his loquacious mother was to her husband. And he despises himself for it. But on the other hand, what is Agee's proud amateurism but a claim of *not* being tied down by the usual bonds to society, of being independent of Necessity? The creation of their necessity is simultaneously the creation of his own freedom, which he of course jealously and zealously defends. And vice versa: his freedom produces and maintains their necessity, or the exaggeration of it – forces them to abide within the borders he has drawn for them.

Within the terms of this opposition, Agee was necessarily blind to the common ground between himself and the people he writes about, especially the common ground of action. On the *Partisan Review* survey, he was furious at question #2, about audience, because the editors dared to assume that writing can somehow *make a difference* in the world. If "the people" is necessity, then he himself must be the opposite, an amateur both undetermined and undetermining, incapable of determining any outcome, producing any results. The "people," written about, cannot ever be the "public," written to or for. Thus he declares that he doesn't want his book to be "popular" while at the same time asking his publishers to print it not on glossy *Fortune*-like paper but on cheap newsprint. His book should appear to come from the people, but not go to the people. Always delayed, deferred, absent from any action or interaction, the people for Agee is obliged to serve as the noble stasis defining his own ignoble mobility.

Having written himself into this bind – the bind of the "free-floating" intellectual – Agee proceeds to *drive* himself into it. In the middle of *Let Us Now Praise Famous Men*, he describes himself, driving his car through the southern landscape, as if he were floating freely above it. He slows down "into this nearly noiseless floating at five miles per hour" (344); on the next page he drives in "the slow flotation of silence." Suddenly he has to fight an urge to crash the car. This impulse to merge with his father, and with what his father represents, suggests the high cost, for the free-floating intellectual, of mooring himself to those who are trapped in necessity. And what actually happens is only slightly less drastic. Searching to ground himself in the *terra firma* of the people, the free-floating intellectual runs aground. As Agee is driving away from the Gudgers' house, the car "seemed," he says, "more to float and sail than to go on the ground" (370) – until, that is, he "half-contrives" to get it stuck in the southern mud. "Stationary in the middle of a world of which all the members were stationary," he abandons the car and is taken into the Gudgers' house, where he decides that he is "at rest in my own home." In the Gudgers, he decides, he has found his "own parents" (376). Or, more precisely, he has found his father and his father's side of the family. "For half my blood is just this," he writes, "and half my right of speech . . ."

This narrativizing of the quest for vocation provides an extraordinary moment, but it is fortunately not the end or summation of what Agee offers. This return to the land restores, as he notes, only *half* his right of speech. The word "half" invokes something missing from the whole, and one thinks immediately of his *mother's* half. In Agee's familial inscription of the intellectual and the people, loyalty to the father means disloyalty to the mother, who is excluded from the people's silent essence and forced to stand for a talkative fallen nature, for the impure language that her son must work in once he has been severed from the purity of his father's silence. She stands for his "professional" self as opposed to the higher yet unrealizable self of "vocation." The harsh treatment of Agee's mother in *A Death in the Family* is evidence enough that he was not the only victim of his professional self-hatred. Hating the self for not being the Father means hating the Mother – and at the same time hating the wordy, sordidly material self of professionalism. Misogyny and anti-professionalism go hand in hand.

There is no image quite as striking as the car-in-the-mud to convey the less realized idea that Agee might yet ground himself in a whole or rather doubled right of speech, the bequest of both his parents – that he might give up his anchor in the necessarily unchanging because necessarily ideal figure of the father and make the "people" include the educated, educating, self-expressive mother.[51] (That is, that he might see himself as both intellectual and professional.) But there is at least one of Agee's most persistent metaphors: the felicitously mixed metaphor of the Gudger *house* as a *boat* and of the (masculinized) *land* – the same southern earth he's just gotten stuck in – as a (feminized) *sea*. I quote one of many instances. Describing the Gudger house, Agee writes: "beautiful it seemed in a particular time, as if it were a little boat in the darkness, floated upon the night, far out on the steadiness of a vacant sea, whose crew slept while I held needless watch" (382). Agee continues to insist that his watch, his consciousness, is unnecessary. But the metaphor of the ship on the sea says he *is* necessary – though no more so than anyone else. Or rather – in a Gramscian formulation – what is necessary is watchful-ness, the *function* of the intellectual, now detached from any specific category of people. Watchfulness reminds us that there is no pure freedom in this floating: at sea as on land there are constraints, determinations to make and to accept. Absolute stasis is written out of the metaphor; movement and change are shared. Agee remains a "free-floating" intellectual only to the extent that *everyone* is afloat, at sea, without the security of anchorage. Instead of "the people" as ground (earth, Father) and the intellectual as free-floating, we have flotation as a general condition, a shared, fluid sort of grounding.

This is something less than a clear new position on what Jim Merod calls "the responsibility of the critic," the intellectual's relations with those they teach and to whom they are accountable. There is not even a clear enough opposition to the mandarin vanguardism of *Partisan Review*, which denied all accountability as such. What there is, following out Agee's hints, is the beginning of a revision of accountability. Democracy is not served, we can suggest, when the intellectual grounds himself in "the people" as undiffer-entiated whole. Exposing how the foundational metaphor of ground-ing leads to gender injustice, to class immobility, to professional self-hatred, we need not therefore give up on the metaphor, however. Rather, we can point toward a decentered or polyphonic account-ability. Like Weber in Jameson's reading, we can consider vocation not as an anachronistic attempt to restore the moment when the calling was transmitted from Father to son, but as a complex gift from fathers and mothers to daughters and sons – as a modern, secular, democratic response to a multiplicity of callers. We cannot escape the universe of authorities, but we can try to divide, distribute, and discriminate those authorities.

5

The East is a Career:
Edward Said

"The East is a career." The quotation, from Disraeli's 1847 novel *Tancred*, is briefly and brilliantly offensive. Activating the convention by which an empty, immobile point on the compass is held capable of condensing millions of undescribed personal destinies, the sentence equates these missing millions with a single individual's rising curve of professional accomplishment. The individual who is to enjoy the career is elided, as if in pretense of equal exchange for the elision of the colossal human diversity that is to be its raw material, and in the space of symmetrical impersonality thus cleared the static East can be spurred into movement, metamorphosed into the kinesis of a (Western) "pursuit." In this outrageous incongruity of scale, the quotation mimics the almost unimaginable overriding of the reality of "the East" by the self-interested systems of Western "experts" that Edward Said exposes in *Orientalism* (1978), to which it serves as acutely ironic epigraph.[1]

But today we must add to this sentence another, further irony, newly and eccentrically literal. Thanks largely to the path-breaking work of Edward Said, it is now possible for intellectuals from what used to be called "the East," as well as from the metropolis, to make a metropolitan academic career out of transmitting, interpreting, and debating representations of what is now called (with no more precision) the "Third World." Giving due weight to the fact that such careers are often visibly contestatory – though rarely as much so as Said's own – it is now almost possible to say, in the flip shorthand of academic fields, that "the Third World is a career."

There are good reasons why this sentence remains not quite sayable. But there is also at least one bad reason – a reason of some significance for the politics of intellectual work. This is the assumption that success in professional career-making is at best an embarrassment to any scholar who, like Said, makes a career while and by maintaining a commitment to radical social change. Careers, that is, are suitable for more or less irreverent *ad hominem* or *feminam* gossip; they may be stripmined for easy ethical inconsistency or psychological insight, but their dynamics are not subject to properly social or political analysis. Few thinkers – Said himself and Perry Anderson are among the exceptions – have sought to generalize with political seriousness from the individual trajectories of scholarship. But now, when so much of the left's intellectual work is carried out in universities and within an ideological context of professionalism, there is intense need to revitalize the genre of scholarly biography (which accounts for much of Said's own most animated prose) and to examine our highest examples of politicized scholarship on the principled level they deserve. To bring the perspective of professionalism to bear on this exemplary leftist career is not to diminish in any way Said's achievement. Rather, following his own Foucauldian insistence on the social structuring that constrains but also enables individual achievement, it is to show how his success reflects meaningfully both on him and on the profession which he has helped to change.

1. Representation and Theory

Orientalism's other, equally ironic epigraph comes from Marx's description of petty landowners in *The Eighteenth Brumaire of Louis Bonaparte*: "They cannot represent themselves; they must be represented." This sentence has become a touchstone of the new anti-representational common sense that – until quite recently at least – has helped bind together the poststructuralist left's otherwise divergent moral and epistemological impulses. Between theory, asserting that there is no escape from representations which can never coincide faithfully with their objects, and the new social movements, which have shaken the claims to representativeness of those false universalities that had silenced and excluded them, but have done so in the name of their own capacity to represent themselves, the common ground has been an almost uncontested ethico-epistemological denial of anyone's right or ability to represent *others*. As a result, it is widely believed (in Derrida's pithy phrase) that "representation is bad," and that the disciplines most directly based on it, like anthropology, have consequently lost their rationale or vital principle.[2] There has been little desire to face the contradictions of this position for those most likely to hold it, oppositional scholars whose *raison d'être* and daily business inescapably involve (however mediated through texts and concepts) the representation of others.[3]

As one outstanding representative of the poststructuralist left in the US today, Edward Said is often identified as a source or center both of this modified anti-representational common sense and, more specifically, of the position on professionalism that seems to result from it. *Orientalism*'s two epigraphs help explain why. Taken together, they seem to form a parable of professionalism-as-domination. The West projects onto those it has subjugated degrading stereotypes that naturalize the West's rule as well as its monopoly on representing them, and – once the field is cleared of their protest or self-expression – representing and ruling them can become a career for enterprising Westerners. This logic, like *Orientalism* itself, has had an enormous effect – perhaps its greatest effect – outside the field of Middle Eastern area specialists and policy intellectuals, on those for whom it is only a "case" of a larger principle to be applied to very different topics, especially the arguably different issues of representation for women, people of color, gays and lesbians, and so on.[4] What is perhaps the most absolute case of non-representation, that of the Arabs of the Middle East, is taken as definitive and generalized accordingly. In its broadest extension, the logic of Orientalism is thus often held to illustrate the view that *all* professional scholarship, inherently elite and undemocratic, is similarly based on a denial of self-representation to oppressed groups, making possible a monopoly of uncontested and degrading representations of them by authoritative, self-accredited professionals, which in turn allows those groups to be more conveniently ruled. Professional careers are made, the logic goes, by representing those whom the career-maker keeps from representing themselves.

Once this version of common sense is in place, however, the way is open for the same accusation to be leveled even at those professionals, like Said, whose professional success has depended on drawing legitimacy and authority from previously unrepresented others, and who are thus charged with disciplinary self-promotion (for example, by Paul Bové). Or else, on the same basis, Said and others like him can be charged, symmetrically, with *keeping* the unrepresented from representing themselves, substituting their own elite intellectual work for the voices of the oppressed even as they claim to represent those voices (for example, by Benita Parry).[5] A still more reductive version of the same argument animates Aijaz Ahmad's charge that *Orientalism* served the "professional assertion of the middle-class immigrant and the 'ethnic' intellectual" in the metropolis, thereby displacing the non-metropolitan working class (or, one supposes, its legitimate representatives).

> What the upwardly mobile professionals in this new immigration needed were narratives of oppression that would get them preferential treatment, reserved jobs, higher salaries in the social position they already occupied: namely, *as* middle-class professionals, mainly male.[6]

The energy behind these accusations could be put to better use, however, if the accusers would acknowledge that they share the same professional base of operations with the accused, along with the same work of representing at an inescapable if not identical remove from those represented. As Jim Merod comments, "Lamentably, everything Bové says about Said's self-promotion can be turned against Bové also."[7] This professional base draws on the same resources of authority and legitimacy. The critic who accuses another of speaking for the subaltern by denying that the subaltern can speak for themselves, for example, is of course also claiming to speak for them. In the professional context, the belief that the subaltern can speak becomes a belief that they can speak *through us*, through our mediatory interpretations of their texts. However pure, self-effacing, and anti-representational we may try (mistakenly) to appear, we are thereby assigning ourselves a job of work – work that is justified by public interests but is also something added onto the mere existence of any constituency, and that must be accepted in its specific weight, concreteness, supplementarity. We can neither deny representation nor self-effacingly make ourselves transparent so that others can fully and immediately represent themselves. While working toward greater democracy of representation – an effort that should not of course be taken for granted – we can only affirm the value of one own mode of representation over another; we cannot stop representing. As Jonathan Arac concludes, "People do it all the time, and the crucial issue is by what means, to what purpose, with what effect."[8] The one satisfactory answer, in other words, is to strike down the assumption that a representational logic linking "the East" to a "career" is inherently and absolutely unacceptable.

Before pressing this argument further, it is important to say that the identification of professionalism with domination by means of representation is not in fact Said's own position on the matter. To begin with, it is not his position on representation. This makes sense for various reasons. In the struggle over the aspirations of the Palestinians to self-determination, the position that treats the link between the Palestinians and their representatives as illegitimate has been one major means of denying them representation, thus prolonging "the fate of every Palestinian, which is both to be *there*, and yet not to be accounted for politically."[9] Said describes the strategy of being "for Palestinian rights in general but against Palestinians and their representatives in particular." So Walzer and Howe, for instance, "speak openly against Begin – excellent – but simultaneously speak cold-bloodedly ... of *destroying* the only authentic representatives of Palestinian nationalism."[10] In questioning the political motives of a critique whose sole determination is to pry open some gap, *any* gap, between representer and represented, making no distinctions in the doubt it casts on the legitimacy of all representation, Said insists that representation *can* be "authentic" and legitimate. Thus he stands apart from certain trends in poststructuralist theory.

But this position is by no means a matter of practical political expediency alone. It is also entirely consistent with his theoretical stance toward professional work. In this respect he rejoins the Marxist tradition, which assumes neither that the only acceptable representation is self-representation nor that the ability to represent oneself can be taken for granted. (In the epigraph from *The Eighteenth Brumaire*, for example, Marx's irony is clearly complex; it includes some scorn at the *incapacity* of the petty landowners to represent themselves.) Said writes, for example:

> if you believe with Gramsci that an intellectual vocation is socially possible as well as desirable, it is an inadmissible contradiction at the same time to build analyses of historical experience around exclusions, exclusions that stipulate, for instance, only women can understand feminine experience, only Jews can understand Jewish suffering, only formerly colonial subjects can understand colonial experience.[11]

Any sense of "intellectual vocation," then, will *require* accepting the task of analyzing, understanding, representing the experience of others.

There is only one problem with this statement. By not specifying who if anyone might historically exemplify such a vocation, it permits itself to be taken exclusively as exhortation, as an ideal of how things *should* be rather than a fact about how things already are. Thus it is possible to neglect the senses in which representation of others is not merely potentially and desirably but *necessarily* part of the job of professional scholarship, and therefore already part – if not a sufficiently large part – of its present. A useful example of this neglect is Said's well-known account of literary theory. That literary theory "has turned its back" on "the social world," Said writes in *The World, the Text, and the Critic* (1983), "can be considered, I think, the triumph of the ethic of professionalism" (4). Along with "guild consciousness, consensus, collegiality, professional respect" (20), he targets "a cult of professional expertise whose effect in general is pernicious" because it accepts "the principle of noninterference" (2–3), an ignoring of "connections between texts and the existential actualities of human life, politics, societies, and events" (5).[12] One can agree that much of this is true about the profession we know and still want to insist that literary theory would not have enjoyed the professional success it has, indeed would not exist at all, if it were as cut off from "the social world" as Said suggests – if it did not somehow help accomplish, however unsatisfactorily, a necessary task of representing others in a defensible way.

If this point has yet to become common sense, the cause is perhaps, ironically, theory itself and its effect on the conceptualizing of professionalism. Said's description of literary theory is remarkably and unexpectedly similar to his description of Orientalism, a discipline one would have thought more closely connected – in the service of the wrong interests, of course – to the actualities of "politics, societies, and events." It is almost as if the image of theory had both controlled the definition of professionalism (as isolated and self-enclosed "system," like representation itself) and had been projected onto Orientalism, so that the actual existence of "the East" makes no difference to the professional authority, legitimacy, or procedures either of the literary theorist or of the Orientalist scholar – and need not therefore become part of even the *critique* of Orientalist scholarship. But where, then, does the critic of Orientalism stand? Trying to work his way around this problem of self-placement – appropriately enough, in the passage where he explains the "East is a career" epigraph – Said allows the (negative) notion of the profession as totally hermetic, self-contained, protected from any accountability, to reproduce itself in or on the critic's own (affirmative) premises:

> it would be wrong to conclude that the Orient was *essentially* an idea, or a creation with no corresponding reality. When Disraeli said in his novel *Tancred* that the East was a career, he meant that to be interested in the East was something bright young Westerners would find to be an all-consuming passion; he should not be interpreted as saying that the

East was *only* a career for Westerners. There were – and are – cultures and nations whose location is in the East, and their lives, histories, and customs have a brute reality obviously greater than anything that could be said about them in the West. About that fact this study of Orientalism has very little to contribute, except to acknowledge it tacitly. But the phenomenon of Orientalism as I study it here deals principally, not with the correspondence between Orientalism and Orient, but with the internal consistency of Orientalism and its ideas about the Orient (the East as a career) despite or beyond any correspondence, or lack thereof, with a "real" Orient. My point is that Disraeli's statement about the East refers mainly to that created consistency, that regular constellation of ideas as the preeminent thing about the Orient, and not to its mere being, as Wallace Stevens puts it. (5)

Both at the beginning and at the end of this passage, there is a surprising eagerness to discuss what *Disraeli* meant by his statement – as if Disraeli's opinions about the Orient, rather than the premises and procedures of his own book, were what Said had been explaining or what the reader wanted to know. The momentary uncertainty as to who is speaking here, Disraeli or Said, or Disraeli for Said, will be familiar to literary critics, who are used to playing with the possibilities for indeterminacy and polyphony created by the convention of commentary on an author. But here the convention covers an unlikely complicity: the duplication by the critic of an object strenuously criticized. If Disraeli and Oriental scholarship treat the East as a "career," that is, so does Said's *Orientalism*, which analyzes (and refuses to go beyond) "internal" and "created consistency," "regular constellation," in short, formal coherence in isolation from the reality of the Orient.

Said knows very well, of course – and it is thanks to him that many of us know it – that Orientalist scholarship most often in fact "represented" extra-professional interests and constituencies, most notably those of the colonial powers, and took authority and legitimacy in part from its usefulness to colonial and neo-colonial projects. Why, then, should he seem to present the discipline as if – like literary theory in his view – its authority and legitimacy were based on nothing more than guild loyalty and formal coherence? Why make it seem totally arbitrary that the Orientalists said what they said and not some other thing, that in misrepresenting the East, the West was constrained by nothing but the formal or aesthetic coherence of its own created system?

The most obvious answer is that it is only in this way that *literary critics*, who specialize in formal or aesthetic coherence, can claim the subject-matter of Orientalism as an appropriate object of study and commentary. Against the claims of other, more obviously pertinent disciplines like political economy or history to isolate, explain, and criticize the abuses of Orientalism, and *mutatis mutandis* of other fields, an imperiously expansive literary criticism has marshalled poststructuralist theory's assertion that "everything is" (the terms are not interchangeable, but close enough) language, textuality, discourse, narrative, rhetoric, or representation. Thus it could expose the cultural (linguistic, textual, discursive, etc.) constructedness of apparently "natural," "empirical" knowledges. In this (surely unconscious) tactic of disciplinary aggrandizement, there was a substantial political gain, and not just for the members of one discipline. Still, if we do not adopt that one discipline's perspective, the political value of asserting that knowledge is *only* representation is no longer self-evident. For if *everything* is representation, then the ubiquity of representation is not a scandal. Or if *all* representation is a scandal, then no particular representation is especially scandalous – and in protesting Orientalism's "coherence," we are not protesting in the most useful direction.

This would explain why Said's two epigraphs might conceivably be read, removed from his own unmistakably indignant voice, as strangely, structurally *lacking* in indignation – as an uninflected account of how things are rather than a protest. No, they *cannot* represent themselves. Yes, the East *is* a career. So? Sadik Jalal al-Azm, who is not a good judge of Said's politics, is nevertheless acute on this point in his essay "Orientalism and Orientalism in Reverse":

> Said himself admits readily that it is impossible for a culture, be it Eastern or Western or South American, to grasp much about the reality of another, alien culture without resort to categorisation, classification, schematisation and reduction – with the necessarily accompanying distortions and misrepresentations. If, as Said insists, the unfamiliar, exotic and alien is always apprehended, domesticated, assimilated and represented in terms of the already familiar, then such distortions and misrepresentations become unavoidable.... He even finds "nothing especially controversial or reprehensible" about the domestication of an exotic and alien culture.... If, as the author keeps repeating (by way of censure and castigation), the Orient studied by Orientalism is no more than an image and a representation in the mind and culture of the Occident (the representer in this case) then it is also true that the Occident in so doing is behaving perfectly naturally and in accordance

with the general rule – as stated by Said himself – governing the dynamics of the reception of one culture by another.[13]

One can conclude, therefore, that literary critics confuse colonial and neo-colonial injustice with epistemology or "internal coherence" in order to give criticism – with its predisposition to believe, as al-Azm puts it, "in the magical efficacy of words" (14) – a particular or privileged grasp over its diagnosis and exposure. This is how the subject-matter of (post)colonialism is assimilated into a new sub-discipline, very much under the sway of criticism and poststructural-ist theory, called "colonial discourse" – that is, grasped specifically *as* discourse.

My point here is not to argue that Said's own critique corresponds to a particular professional logic and is shaped by (even as it reshapes) the professional exigencies of a particular discipline. This can be taken for granted about anyone, however innovative and transgressive, working within a scholarly discipline or disciplines. Since it can be taken for granted, it is not in itself a critique. Critique might begin, for example, by pointing out how a "colonial dis-course" sub-field with so much of the aesthetic in its constitution might tend, at worst, to repeat a Romantic respect for particulars for their own sake, perversely recoding a discredited Arnoldian "cul-ture" as Third World "difference," and thus renewing it while neglecting, say, capitalism as a world system and the common elements of struggle against it around the world, whether First, Third, or (already upon us) Second. But any such criticism would also have to weigh the political *benefits* of this particular professional logic. It could not walk away, its task accomplished, once the contaminating presence of the professional had been identified; it could not assume that professionalism by definition precludes public or political benefits and encourages only private gains at the public's expense.

2. On the Career of Claude Lévi-Strauss

Formal coherence is, it seems, one foundation for professional authority. Indeed, it can even support such authority in a negative and backhanded way. To the extent that any critic draws authority in proportion to the magnitude and significance of the object treated, whether that treatment involves praise or blame, even oppositional critics may well be tempted to exaggerate, for professional reasons, the systematic, totalizing coherence of what they oppose, tempted to exclude from it any untidy discrepancies or counter-hegemonic utterances that, in mitigating its gravity or systematicity, also compromise the critic's authority. But careers do not rest on "internal consistency" alone. Here I open up a sizable digression from Said's career in order to make this case with regard to Claude Lévi-Strauss. Famous for his extreme formalization of the study of myth, from which the formalist current in theory and the interdisciplinary imperialism I have been discussing in large part descend, Lévi-Strauss is a far less political figure than Said, both in his writing and outside it. To suggest the limits of "internal consistency" in explaining *his* career, therefore, is to suggest something quite general about the politics of career-making.

In *Reinventing Anthropology*, edited by Dell Hymes in 1972, a collection that served as the major expression of 1960s protest on the part of radical anthropologists against their field, there is a passage from Lévi-Strauss that is quoted twice. The first time is in the Introduction:

> Anthropology . . . is the outcome of a historical process which has made the larger part of mankind subservient to the other, and during which millions of innocent human beings have had their resources plundered and their institutions and beliefs destroyed, while they themselves were ruthlessly killed, thrown into bondage, and contaminated by diseases they were unable to resist. Anthropology is the daughter to this era of violence.[14]

A powerful indictment of an entire discipline, the passage is an important precedent for Said's *Orientalism*. However, in the penultimate chapter, written by Stanley Diamond, the same quotation prefaces an attack on Lévi-Strauss as the quintessential "professional" – an "alien" whose ultimate values are "academic and ethnocentric" (403–5). This is the charge – with some geographical allowance – that Lévi-Strauss has made the East a career. This point has been made too often not to contain an important truth. Any reader of Lévi-Strauss will be aware that the level of intelligibility of myth, in his view, has little to do with the conscious "experience" or opinions of the native informant. On the contrary, Lévi-Strauss defined myth in such a way that it could be comprehended only by the expertise of a European professional like himself, far removed from face-to-face contact with the "primitive." Indeed, he makes no secret of the self-serving vocational motives behind his research. As

Clifford Geertz writes in "The Cerebral Savage," "no anthropologist has been more insistent on the fact that the practice of his profession has consisted of a personal quest, driven by a personal vision, and directed toward a personal salvation."[15] In *Tristes Tropiques* (1955), Lévi-Strauss himself is unusually frank about his own desire, in setting sail for Brazil, not to intervene against colonial injustice but to resolve a vocational crisis, a crisis of a sort that was to become familiar to the students of the 1960s.[16] He has never studied anthropology, but other subjects (including philosophy, which he is supposed to be teaching) leave him cold, and he doesn't quite know what to do with himself. The Indians of Brazil solve his problem.

For Geertz, as for other commentators, Lévi-Strauss's anthropology seems first and foremost, or perhaps exclusively, a professional solution to this personal search for satisfying work. The characteristic imagery of this low-key satire of hyper-professionalism is that of enclosure. It is only the assumption that the "primitive" universe is closed, Geertz says, which permits the closure of myth. From the closure of myth follows the definition of (enclosed) "system" or "structure" that is the true object of narrative analysis. From the boundedness of "system" and "structure" follows the satisfying sovereign enclosure of professional territoriality. What makes anthropology, in Lévi-Strauss's words, "one of the few true vocations" (354) is that, like music and mathematics, it detaches itself from the messiness of history in order to reach a high degree of order, which it identifies with reality itself. "'To reach reality we must first repudiate experience'" (356) – in particular the experience of contact with the Other. The retreat from contact with the outside is not so much the price Lévi-Strauss pays in order to achieve professionalism's internal coherence as the formulation of the professional project itself.

In 1981, after the death of Sartre, Lévi-Strauss was voted the most influential French intellectual alive. According to David Pace, this pre-eminence should be interpreted as the replacement of the "philosophe" by the "academic" and by "the ideology of the university."[17] Perhaps. But if this story, like Geertz's narrative of professionalization and like the sad, familiar tale of the academicization of the 1960s that we have seen numerous versions of in this book, presumes that a new tendency in the academy can make its way, or an older one can sustain itself, by means of a politically self-indulgent withdrawal into self-enclosure, then it mistakes professionalism in general, as we have seen. And it also mistakes Lévi-Strauss

162

in particular. It is true, as Geertz says, that objectivity and "coherence" are major vocational desiderata for Lévi-Strauss. He dislikes law, another vocational option, because "it seems unable to find any basis for itself that is at once solid and objective" (45). On the other hand, Lévi-Strauss tells us that he rejects philosophy, for which he didn't have a "genuine vocation" (42), because its results were judged in terms of "technical perfection or internal coherence" (43) – that is, because "Expertise replaced the truth" (44). His life's work, then, must be able to claim a professional authority *higher* than mere "coherence."

What authority? This question can be rephrased as the question of why structuralism struck when and as it did. The ideas of Saussure and Russian formalism came considerably earlier. Why the lag? Why the explosion of the 1960s? A literal-minded explanation – by chance Lévi-Strauss meets Jakobson in New York City during the war, thus acquiring the linguistic paradigm for his redefinition of myth – still leaves us with another more than fifteen-year lag before the phenomenon picks up any real interdisciplinary momentum. What is roughly specific to the 1960s, on the other hand, is the context of global decolonization. While Lévi-Strauss was writing, France was losing wars of national liberation in Indochina and Algeria, wars which clearly belonged to the global pattern, since the Second World War, of self-assertion and independence by former colonies. In the intellectual domain, all of this is accompanied by a critique of Eurocentrism and a growing openness in the First World to Third World voices. Lévi-Strauss's effort to break down the loaded opposition between history, which belongs to Europe, and myth, which characterizes the so-called "savage mind," is an obvious and significant example, if also a troublesome one. The concept of "structure," which is the common denominator between history and myth and the immediate predecessor of "narrative" as a new conceptual common language, gives to "peoples without history" a possibility of self-representation, holds and preserves the experience of those who hadn't had access to the "higher" genres. Yet unlike myth, which already did some of this work, it cannot be opposed and subordinated to the self-consciousness of "history" or "fiction." While the criterion of self-consciousness was hierarchical, the abstractness of narrative structure (which of course downplays questions of consciousness) makes it democratically inclusive, equally appropriate when applied to Third World myth, First World discourse about that myth, or anything else. When Lévi-Strauss and his followers asserted something like the proposition that "everything is narrative," they were leveling the playing field of scholarly discourse. At least within the confines of this field, they proposed in effect a two-step redistribution of authority: the self-representations of the newly independent peoples could be afforded greater respect, while the positivist truth claims of European inter-preters of those representations must be relativized. It seems likely, if hard to verify, that the political pressure which made such a redistribution of authority possible then and there, which authorized and sustained this formalist effort to define and extend a common ground between Europe and its "others," came from the struggles of national liberation that were so dramatically remaking the political map of the world in those years, and the climate of opinion they fostered even in the former colonial powers.

I have ignored the manifest political difficulties posed by Lévi-Strauss in order to bring out the less visible work of cultural relativizing that he accomplishes, with its oblique but real claim to improve the political conditions of representation for colonialism's victims. In so doing, I am less interested in measuring the scope or endurance of his achievement than in illuminating its principle: his discovery of a professional authority higher than mere coherence. I want to suggest, in other words, that his appeal to an abruptly expanded post-colonial public sphere, his implicit claim to provide theoretical concepts that were more adequate to this new public sphere (as distinguished from any more direct claim to represent its new constituencies), is inseparable from his revitalizing of the anthropological profession – just as appeals like it, as we have seen, are part of professionalism in general. What permitted him to speak for and help produce an anthropological renaissance – the epigraph to *Reinventing Anthropology* cites his proposition that "Anthro-pology will survive in a changing world by allowing itself to perish in order to be born again under a new guise" – was reaching outside the discipline to the wider post-colonial public in whose eyes anthropology had to win its new social legitimacy. In this sense *Tristes Tropiques* itself is a quintessentially professional book: a book written in order to legitimate the profession to non-professionals.

This tactic of furthering his discipline's interests by demonstrating that it is neither self-enclosed nor self-sustaining is not confined to the rhetoric of Lévi-Strauss's best-seller. In the classic exposé of structuralism, "The Structural Study of Myth," we find the same provocative indeterminacy about the line separating the profession's inside and outside.[18] In the essay's first paragraph it is clear Lévi-Strauss is defending its interests against "amateurs," whether from other disciplines or not: "because the interest of professional anthropologists has withdrawn from primitive religion, all kinds of amateurs who claim to belong to other disciplines have seized this opportunity to move in, thereby turning into their private playground what we had left as a wasteland" (206). Later in the essay, however, his own central exhibit, a reading of the Oedipus myth, makes no claim to be "an explanation acceptable to the specialist" (213). Does myth belong within disciplinary boundaries or not? Do disciplines *have* boundaries? "French sociology," he declares elsewhere, "does not consider itself as an isolated discipline, working in its own specific field, but rather as a method, or as a specific attitude toward human phenomena. Therefore, one does not need to be a sociologist in order to do sociology."[19] In explaining the attack on Sartre in *La Pensée Sauvage*, however, he writes, "I was simply obliged to clarify certain things, when Sartre, leaving his own domain, proposed to reveal to ethnologists the deep nature of their profession."[20] Is thought tamed by its "domain" or "profession," or is it a wild thing that roams freely? To judge from Lévi-Strauss, one would have to conclude that the opposition is a false one; the profession and its outside have no firm boundary but are mutually interdependent.

Again, the example can be generalized. Explaining the circuitous careers of four scholars of myth (Lévi-Strauss, Cassirer, Eliade, and Malinowski), Ivan Strenski declares that history in the first half of the twentieth century

> made normal professional life impossible. Professionals engaged in the study of myth might want to ponder the historical fact that perhaps the most creative thinkers in the field were nurtured intellectually – at least, for significant parts of their lives – *outside* their professions.

This leads him to note

> a great irony. As soon as they succeeded in re-establishing themselves professionally, they did so with a certain "vengeance"; all, except Cassirer, founded the major "schools" in their respective fields; as a result, they became responsible for entirely new enterprises of professionalization in those fields.... In each case the result was the production of "professionals" who developed and disseminated the concepts of myth associated with their great mentors. Small wonder that the discourse in this field is as imperialistic as it is.[21]

This is well observed, but Strenski's interpretation is debatable. Yes, these scholars made their breakthroughs by bringing into their professions something of what they had learned from twentieth-century history. But there is no "irony" in the fact that the result was "new enterprises of professionalization" so forceful in their impact as to be described as "imperialistic." For better or worse, this is how "normal" professions work. Those who have the vision to retool professional procedures and protocols in response to or anticipation of great historical shifts and newly emergent versions of the public interest – by no means a mechanical feat, of course – are vastly more likely to set the professional agendas of the future, force professional paradigm shifts, realign the competing disciplines among themselves and (in so doing) in new relation to worldly power. For professions – even the notoriously unworldly literary theory – are not self-enclosed and self-sustaining, however much they would sometimes like to believe it. The outside constitutes the inside, and vice versa.

3. Michel Foucault: "the professionalism of intellectuals . . . can be envisaged in a new way"

Presiding over the resuscitation of an endangered discipline by speaking, with exceptional force, both inside and outside it, Lévi-Strauss set an influential example. Foucault, Didier Eribon tells us, often stated his admiration for the way in which Lévi-Strauss "was able to explode the boundary separating academic work's specialized public and the broad educated public."[22] Foucault's own example is of course significant both for Said's thinking about careers and the institutions in which they take place and for his own career. His effort to articulate a left-wing critique of Foucault that would not reject all Foucault's premises in favor of Marxist doxa, a sort of critique of poststructuralism from within, is another of his essential contributions to the formation of a poststructuralist left that would obviously include but not be restricted to the academy. The public question of common ground and common sense is therefore crucial.

Unlike Foucault and poststructuralist orthodoxy, Said has dissented from any over-totalizing system that threatens to leave insufficient room for the assertion of human will. Unlike most Marxists, he has never found much use for "capitalism" as an explanatory term (except indirectly, through "reification," about which more below). The term he shares with both, however – and through which, perhaps, he has managed so well to draw both groups together – is "work." From *Beginnings* (1975) onward, it is "work" that offers a version of "will" that need not deny "system."[23] Even Orientalism must be seen, he says, "as a kind of *willed human work* – not of mere unconditioned ratiocination" (15). But if the workplace is where will can uniquely be exercised, then the implicit social model would seem to be the relative autonomy of a *professional* workplace, and professional autonomy would seem to be the socially specific target of appeals for change.

In this respect Said and Foucault are perhaps closer together than they otherwise seem. The readers addressed by Foucault, Jim Merod writes in *The Political Responsibility of the Critic* (1989), are "the professionals who own the disruptive potential on which his strategy depends" (158). "In effect the centerless power [Foucault] opposes resides precisely here, among those he calls on to disrupt a system they hold by expertise that circulates outside political inspection and political accountability" (159). For Merod, who takes Said's side in the debate between them over will and "autonomy," this strategy is a mistake: "by restricting political struggle to professional combats, Foucault enhances divisions between experts and nonexperts" (189). But he points us toward a Foucault with whom Said has less reason to disagree. The aim of Foucault's concept of the "specific intellectual" is to invigorate local and professional action that was disabled and downgraded by the burden of universality. For Foucault, in *Power/Knowledge* (1980), the fact that such action may be restricted to the university, that it may deal with "a specialist matter which doesn't concern the masses," or (even) that it "serves the interests of State or Capital" is no longer decisive in itself. Thus "the question of the professionalism of intellectuals ... can be envisaged in a new way."[24] Each point holds for Said as well.

As Colin Gordon comments in the same volume, a crucial step in Foucault's analysis is his provisional but powerful amoralism:

> His object is not to arrive at a priori moral or intellectual judgments on the features of our society produced by ... forms of power, but to render possible an analysis of production itself. It turns out that in fact this scrutiny of power in terms of knowledge and of knowledge in terms of power becomes all the more radical ... through its rigorous insistence on this particular brand of neutrality. (237)

The shock of reading Foucault is partly the shock of this neutrality in unexpected places, a neutrality which distinguishes him at once from the garden-variety breeds of anti-bureaucratic thought in current circulation. And if it makes sense to consider Edward Said – in spite of their disagreements – as a Foucauldian critic, it is because he produces a similar shock and sustains a similar discrepancy: the shock of positing institutional modernity as the non-negotiable terms in which modern action must be carried out, and the discrepancy of this position for someone who cannot forget the absolute urgency of intervention.

The jolt of unexpected neutrality makes itself felt from time to time in a slight lexical estrangement. Certain key words, such as "affiliation," "worldly," and "career," seem peculiarly and inexplicably *inoffensive* as weapons with which to attack the ethic of professionalism. For example, in *The World, the Text, and the Critic*, the term "affiliation" defines the endpoint of a narrative in which modernist exile is institutionalized in the academy. In the careers of modernist writers like Joyce, Eliot, Freud, and Lukács, Said plots a three-step pattern: (1) an initial break with natural filiation – the unchosen, almost biological relationships enmeshing the individual in a given culture – leads to (2) a "pressure to produce new and different ways of conceiving human relationships," artificial and compensatory social bonds – for example, Eliot's turn from *The Waste Land* to the community of the Anglican church, or Lukács's championing of class consciousness and vanguard party as answers to alienation – which now, however, assume (3) all the authority of the old filiative order, becoming "no less orthodox and dominant than culture itself" (16–20). But does "affiliation" become oppressive with a tragically rapid and universal inevitability? In places it is a synonym for "system," a word that is never used with approval. Yet the coinage itself is a move in the direction of neutrality, and in other places "affiliation" seems entirely neutral – for example, as the realm of "social and political conviction, economic and historical circumstances, voluntary effort and willed deliberation" (25). Or it is presented in such a way that it *need not* end in dominating system: "The second alternative for the critic is ... to show how affiliation sometimes reproduces filiation, sometimes makes its own forms" (24). Are all "new forms" as oppressive as filiation, or only some? Since modernism's new affiliation is with the university, the main force of this equivocation falls on the profession of literary criticism.

In *Beginnings*, the term "career" sets the writing life apart from ordinary life as a form of modernist expatriation. Yet it weights this neo-romantic exile down with heavy semantic baggage: the homeliness of the beaten track (the grooves of the carriage road, the circled limits of the race-course) where achievement is circumscribed by a pre-established framework, a path traced in advance. It is very much a professional term, and it grants the modern writer exactly the measured "dehumanization" and the consequent freedom of action that professionalism grants. In "The Limits of Professionalism," Samuel Weber argues that the career replaces "the lateral ties of earlier local communities" with its "progressive initiation, mastery, and exercise of a profession," thus both permitting and producing "individual performance within an institutionally defined framework."[25] Defending members cut off from "earlier local communities" against the cold winds of the market, the profession offers them (in limited supply) use values instead of exchange values. Thus, on a minor scale, it could be said to overcome reification. Like modernism, in other words, the professional career substitutes for a lost or broken filiative order a new set of affiliative bonds that are both constraining and enabling. This is to say that in refusing the immediacy of inspiration and restoring the multiple mediations, the trans-personal determinants that make any literary achievement possible, Said is not setting modern writing against the bureaucratic modern world but, on the contrary, defining it as an instance of post-entrepreneurial modern labor.

Like "affiliation" and "career," "worldliness" seems slightly and provocatively out of control. In introducing the term, Said's intention is clearly to break open the hermetic, inward self-enclosure of the profession. His vocabulary for the profession, as for modernism, suggests an activity that is incestuous or sterile. He wants to send criticism forth into "circumstantial reality." But it is equally clear that the force of "worldliness," and its hint of Foucauldian amorality, come from closing off, not opening up. In the context of a polemic against critical otherworldliness, one can still hear in it the sense of "devotion to worldly affairs to the neglect of religious duties or spiritual needs" (OED). To recast this in the affirmative is to approve a tabling of spiritual or existential questions in the interest of getting on with mortal business, a suspension of paralyzing ultimates in favor of less dramatic daily activity. In effect, it is to call for a version of professionalism. On the secular plane, the same stress on what is taken for granted within a closed system, on the enabling exclusion of outside concerns, is conveyed by Peter Brooks in *The Novel of Worldliness* (1969): "By 'worldliness' I mean an ethos and personal manner which indicate that one attaches primary or even exclusive importance to ordered social existence, to life within a public system of values and gestures, to the social techniques that further this life and one's position in it." The emphasis falls on exclusiveness, on "the one world that counts" and on "man's way of being within its limits and in its terms: what we may call man's worldliness, or *mondanité*."[27] Parsimonious, local solidarity and strategically localized action bring worldliness back together with the professionalism against which it was marshalled.

Despite its apparent expansiveness, then, which permits Said to identify the worldly with the homeless, worldliness leads to a new investment in the local, a word Said uses frequently and approvingly. For example, in *The World, the Text, and the Critic*, Swift's "fairly strict, not to say uninteresting conservative philosophy" (74) is declared immaterial and replaced by an exhibition of "Swift the activist": "too many claims are made for Swift as a moralist and a thinker who peddled one or another final view of human nature, whereas not enough claims are made for Swift as a kind of local activist, a columnist, a pamphleteer, a caricaturist" (77). Considered as a "kind of marginal, sporty political fighter" whose writing is almost entirely "occasional" and "parasitic on what it responds to" (77–8), Swift is liberated from retrospective judgment in terms of ideological universality. In the same way, the concept of the professional career, whose institutional framework limits but also shapes possible actions, saves the individual's accomplishments from being immobilized by the crushing standards of universal justice or truth.

The homology with professionalism is clear, but incomplete. In using the local to free an activist Swift from the Tory Swift (though one might have thought Swift was an activist *because* he was a Tory), Said does what professions do: by a willed, selective blindness to socio-moral universals, to the aims and consequences of action as they would appear to a hypothetically global perspective, he makes a place where action can be accomplished. In this sense the professional, like the local, can be described as a position that, falling short of the ideological purity of homelessness, receives in exchange a purchase on the world. The barter of a rationed amoralism for rational agency is certainly part of Said's own professional worldliness. Yet this localism is also an *affront* to professionalism. Said disengages Swift from the trans-historical content of his ideas by re-engaging him in the "particular struggles of a very limited sort" (83) in his own time that have now disappeared or lost their significance. He thus associates Swift with "the scandal . . . that what is being said is being said at that moment, for that moment, by a creature of that moment" (87). As an exemplar of pure localism, Swift becomes "perhaps the most worldly" of writers (88), abandoned to secular interventions that will not survive their occasions, from which we can wring no transcendence. The scandal of worldly-ascetic writing that in submitting itself entirely to action would be entirely subsumed by the past, leaving no residue for the reader of the present, is also the scandal of writing on which the profession of literary criticism could no longer be based. For criticism's persistent professional rationale has stressed the import of transcendent or trans-historically valued writing from an over-supplied past into a needy present.

Thus the local both underwrites and undermines professional logic. Or rather, it is inscribed in contradictory professional logics. For writing that dissolves ascetically into its local occasion without residue becomes, by Said's mediation, itself the residue, supplement, or transcendence of its occasion, an instance of trans-historical transmission, an allegory of vocation. Swift the local activist emerges from the past to function as a model for the intellectuals of the present. Swift is what the emergent professional critic of today might look like, according to Said's allegory, if the profession could stop imagining its vocation as the guardianship of the cultural archives. But it is only thanks to his own residual guardianship of the archives that we can benefit from Swift's example.

4. Communities of Method

If only because it circumvents the issue of representation, it is clear that "the local" cannot simply or exhaustively stand for the professional. As Said presents it, professionalism's local logic calls out for a complement – if not necessarily for universality, then for some "express" logic that valorizes discontinuity and distance. But in thinking through the disparity or apparent inconsistency of these logics, we must bear in mind the value of the initial leap. "Thinking local" helps account for Said's ability to curb his otherwise powerful impatience with professionalism and to generate terms and concepts that are uniquely serviceable under modern, professionalized conditions of intellectual work. Whether these conditions are ineluctable or open to contestation and change remains a politically significant question. But the provocative notion of an oppositional thought that in being local would be in *harmony* with its conditions of production deserves separate and serious reflection. For such a notion exposes something about our professional logics that has not been much noticed: how often oppositional thought has in fact been defined specifically by opposition to its conditions of production *rather than to anything else*. What would a criticism look like that did *not* take its opposition to its own social circumstances as the central, definitive, and exhaustive fact of its oppositionality? In telling professional critics to be paradoxically both "local," on the one hand, and "worldly" or "universal" or "humanistic," on the other, this is perhaps the question Said is posing.

It is the holding together of contradictory professional logics under the heading "Traveling Theory" that has made that essay and title so widely influential.[28] The central voyage in question is a fall: the fall of theory from direct, authentic politics – exemplified by Lukács's theory of reification in *History and Class Consciousness* (1923) – into academic routine, illustrated in the reworking of Lukács's ideas by academics Lucien Goldmann and Raymond Williams. The difference between Lukács's theory of reification (produced as a weapon in the heat of battle) and Goldmann's application of it (in homologies between seventeenth-century literature and theology) is academicization: "Lukács writes as a participant in a struggle (the Hungarian Soviet Republic of 1919), Goldmann as an expatriate historian at the Sorbonne." Theory has been domesticated "to the exigencies of a doctoral dissertation in Paris" (235–7). After a relatively rapid passage from the ideal immediacy of revolutionary action to the predictable over-mediations of habitual scholarly practice, it works only "to shake up a few professors of literature" (238).[29]

Yet for all its political bravado, this anti-academic narrative also duplicates an enabling academic myth – the myth, precisely, of the trans-local guardianship of the archives. Though he begins with the *theory* of reification rather than with the thing itself (so to speak), Said's second-degree version follows the same structure as Lukács's original. Like Weber's "rationalization" (which was a major influence on it), Lukács's reification depicts the transition to modernity as institutional mechanism, instrumental rationality, and cultural sterility, a horror unrelieved except by the highly theoretical prospect of the proletariat's eventual arrival at universal consciousness. In so doing, it sets off from, and sets off, a past comparatively rich in genuine relationships, organic community, cultural vitality. That is, it offers a more politicized version of what is still the strongest

172

professional logic that the humanities possess: the narrative of "culture" dying in a modern wasteland where only a few select misfits still recall and preserve its fast-fading glories. However oppositional, this narrative obviously lends itself to a self-serving rationale for professional humanists.[30] As I have argued earlier, a narrative of decline that indicts the status quo for multifariously neglecting the cultural truths, beauties, and values of the past, now best known to the guardians of the archives, is a rather well-chosen means of shaming society into paying for the maintenance of those archives. If to be oppositional is to propagate such a narrative, then to be oppositional is not only not opposed to being professional; professional activity nearly requires it.

This is one logic, in fact, that makes "careers" out of "the East." When Lévi-Strauss laments the disappearance of native cultures, in part because of the activities of anthropologists themselves, he is both accusing his discipline and providing it with a version of legitimizing vocation. As James Clifford writes, "Traditions are constantly being lost. But the persistent and repetitious 'disappearance' of social forms at the moment of their ethnographic representation demands analysis as a narrative structure. . . . Ethnography's disappearing object is . . . in significant degree, a rhetorical construct."[31] The profession is sustained by protest against this repetitious disappearance, which it thus has an interest in sustaining or constructing. The continuity with the humanist decline narratives of Arnold and Eliot is clear. The logic that links professionals to the disappearance of their objects is even manifest in the poststructuralist premise that, in Said's innocuous words, "the written statement is a presence to the reader by virtue of its having excluded, displaced, made superogatory any such *real thing* as 'the Orient.'"[32] Here, in a rarefied, textualized form of Lévi-Strauss's position, "representation" as such replaces the primal act of violence that makes the cultural object disappear, thus calling for the politically ambiguous but nonetheless necessary services of those who interpret representations, and ensuring the value of those services. One reason for the relative success of the sub-field of "colonial discourse" is the ease with which geographical displacement ("the East") can substitute for temporal displacement (the past) in the professionally foundational narrative of disappearing culture(s).

At the same time, of course, Said is well and justly known for his uncompromising refusal of "culture" as an enclosed, exclusionary concept and his courageous, controversial embrace of "the great modern or, if you like, post-modern fact, the standing outside of cultures."[33] If the titular argument of "Traveling Theory" is that travel – here, the wrenching of theory out of its European context and its recontextualization in the US academy – is dangerous, travel also belongs to Said's continuing polemic against cultural rootedness. It defines the uprooted critic as an oppositional figure. Nothing could be less characteristic of Said than a secure, comfortable, stick-in-the-mud localism that would restrict interpretation to its context of origin. He is manifestly uninterested, for example, in reporting at any length on the original French context of Foucault. One has the sense that he would be more engaged by the eccentric, defamiliarizing fact that in Tunis, where Foucault taught from 1966 to 1968 while working on *The Archaeology of Knowledge*, Foucault seemed a pure "représentant du technocratisme gaulliste."[34] Such facts, unavailable to the scholarly stay-at-home, nourish the roving appetite for risk and disorientation that Said celebrates as "criticism."

What follows for the imagining of academic work? It hardly needs to be said that the ideal homelessness of "criticism" does not exclude, and indeed encourages, that the critic be "placed" in the university. In the name of "travel," the academy can either be condemned as a place of drowsy rootedness and inactive belatedness, or, on the contrary, it can be defended as the one place – really a non-place – where criticism can be truly itself: non-totalizing, perpetually alert and self-critical, pure. This is the twist that Said gives to the academicizing narrative of "Traveling Theory" when, after seeming to idealize the revolutionary intensity of Lukács's reification at the expense of later scholarly apathy, he ends by censuring the over-totalized oppressiveness of the concept of reification and by crediting the critique to Raymond Williams – in particular to the "virtue" of Williams's academic "distance."[35] As a place of "critical distance," the academy illustrates the merits of "travel" rather than either its perils or the perils of situatedness.

This revisionary move is neither complacent nor uncomplicated. Though Said criticizes the theory of reification for its inability to account for its own (oppositional) existence, he is committed to applying that same theory of reification to describe the institution in which his critique of it comes into existence. In the conclusion of "Orientalism Reconsidered," for example, academic reification seems the inescapable diagnosis, as much for well-established fields like criticism as for emergent sub-fields like colonial discourse:

But there remains the one problem haunting all intense, self-convicted, and local intellectual work, the problem of the division of labor, which is a necessary consequence of that reification and commodification first and most powerfully analyzed in this century by Georg Lukács. . . . This is where we are now, at the threshold of fragmentation and specialization, which impose their own parochial dominations and defensiveness.[36]

On the other hand, in the course of complaining about the current fragmentation of the disciplines – our "professionalized particularism" (103) – he also complains that "world history as a discipline" is "essentialist universalism" (102), and he praises the work of "fragmenting, dissociating, dislocating, and decentering the experiential terrain covered at present by universalizing historicism" (102). Here the desideratum is "plurality of terrains, multiple experiences, and different constituencies" (105). The apparent inconsistency (is totality what we have to get rid of or what we are lacking? is fragmentation a problem or the solution to a problem?) makes an invaluable point. Reification, it appears, is not something universally to be opposed. For it can open up the academy as well as enclose it. From the point of view of a Third World constituency, what might otherwise look like the reification of the humanities – their further specialization or fragmentation – is more correctly seen as *representation*. One might expect Said to challenge reification's Eurocentric assumptions, thereby reserving the non-European world as that "world of human agency outside the reach of reification" which Lukács overlooks.[37] Instead, his local, exclusive concentration on the academy exposes the hidden representational links between academic careers and "the East." If "fragmentation" can be desirable when it liberates a Third World constituency, say, from the false universality that had represented it, it can be desirable *in much the same way* when it permits a given discipline or sub-discipline to break free from given scholarly assumptions and realign itself in regard both to other disciplines and – most pertinently – to a previously underrepresented constituency. "Feminism," "Afro-American studies," and "colonial discourse" might all be taken as cases in point.

To set limits to opposing reification is in effect to overthrow the entire fall-narrative of literary professionalization. For as I noted above, reification is one version of the profession's enabling myth; it defines "culture" as a perfect professional object, both missing and indispensable. In so doing, it has been a good provider of professional legitimacy to intellectuals. Reification is capitalism for those who do not suffer economically from capitalism; it makes their non-economic suffering – the fragmentation of life without the wholeness of "culture" – the representative and determining instance. As Richard Johnson put it (in a remark already quoted), "The problematic of culture expressed the dilemmas of some English intellectuals sufficiently removed from industrial capital, in situation or sympathies, to distance themselves from its morality and purposes." In other words, it was itself a product of "the increasingly differentiated functions of intellectual labor" to which it seemed the antithesis. "Culture" was the claim, on the part of a social group that was already and increasingly marginal, that the privileged knowledge that group possessed was what all of society needed. The very indistinctness of culture – like "language" and "discourse," it could not easily be *opposed* to anything – made it more easily universalizable.[38]

But the profession's basis in "culture" also restricts its oppositionality to whatever political value the resupplying of this object might have. If the past proximities of "culture" are the foundation of the humanities in a time of inhuman distances, then criticism remains a stay-at-home, grounded in but also by its single founding gesture, unable to make the distant connections that Said prescribes for worldliness. It is also set in contradiction with its conditions of production, that is, the intellectual division of labor that defines it as a discipline. To the extent that it *is* a discipline – divided from other disciplines, and dividing territory with them – in calling out for the wholeness of "culture" it is calling for its self-destruction. Few of our professional narratives are as successful as the narrative of "Traveling Theory" in fighting off their impulses to do precisely that.

One might conclude that because professionals *must* present themselves as representative, there is no alternative to the sort of inconsistencies and self-hatred that surround the professional imagery of culture and reification. One of the many interests of Said's writing, in the moment-by-moment richness of its undaunted textual energies, is the assurance that alternatives exist, even when they manifest themselves only as a mode of inhabiting contradictions that for the moment remain unsolvable. For further and final contrast with the narrative of professionalization-as-decline, consider the narrative of "Third World Intellectuals and Metropolitan Culture" (1990).[39] In this essay, the map of ironies is filled in: "the East" is again a career, but this time for its own intellectuals.

Said's subject is "the work of intellectuals from the colonial or peripheral regions of the world, intellectuals who wrote not in a native language but in an "imperial" language, who felt themselves to be organically tied to a mass effort at resisting imperial rule.... These figures address the metropolis using the techniques, the discourses, the very weapons of scholarship and criticism once reserved exclusively for the European. (29)

Taken together, such figures form a "culture of resistance" (27). Beneath this relatively straightforward exposition, the deeper problematic would seem to be how to define the originality, resistance, and independence of intellectuals who are "apparently dependent (some would say parasitic) on a mainstream discourse like history, political science, economics, or cultural criticism" (29), that is, on European scholarly disciplines. But a still deeper structure appears when we break up the last phrase. Insisting on the need for ex-colonials to counter *Europe* is one thing; it is less evident that "resistance" should or even can happen *within scholarly disciplines*.

The allegory of vocation emerges from the essay's narrative structure. In an ambitious periodization of Third World intellectuals from the 1930s to the 1960s and 1970s, Said passes from C.L.R. James and George Antonius, writing "works of scholarship and advocacy" in the 1930s "from within a national movement for independence" (32), to Ranajit Guha and S.H. Alatas, writing in the 1960s and 1970s "postcolonial and specialist works ... that address a smaller audience" (32). Again, as in "Traveling Theory," we move away from direct (anti-colonial) politics and toward greater submission to the specialization of the academy. Through Guha, this endpoint is even associated with poststructuralist theory. But this is not a narrative of decline.

> The contrast between James and Antonius on the one hand, and Guha and Alatas on the other, is not that the earlier writers were more immediately involved in contemporary politics whereas the later two are involved mainly in scholarly disputation in newly independent states, but that history itself has changed the terms and, indeed, the very nature of the argument. (33)

What is this change? It is not a new separatism, though James and Antonius claim "Western" culture as their own, while Alatas and Guha see colonized and metropolitan cultures as "radically antithetical." What defines the new stage, rather, is the recognition that the intellectual's own class has been formed by and within metropolitan culture, and that it is this very class which must be opposed – from within, so to speak, and with its own tools. The project of rescuing "the suppressed native voice" is now aimed specifically at the "nationalist elite," at the intellectual's own class. To be both of this class and critically detached from it is, it seems, what it means to be "academic specialists" like Guha and Alatas (39).

According to Johannes Fabian, Lévi-Strauss's anti-experiential structuralism corresponds historically to "the demise of direct colonization demanding personal and direct involvement in the *oeuvre civilisatrice*" and to the rise of neo-colonialism's more indirect hegemony.[40] Neo-colonialism, which is to say capitalism as a world system, also seems to underlie Said's revalorization of the academy, which takes its cue from the confusion in which natives can be enemies and foreigners allies. It is this interiority of the struggle, within the class of the Third World intellectual, as opposed to the dramatic exteriority of earlier nationalist struggles, that produces the intermediate position, the embattled margin of detachment, that Said defines and defends for "academic specialists." If ex-colonial scholarship seems secondary and belated in relation to European scholarship, it seems still more secondary when narrativized against the predecessors' immediate solidarity with anti-colonial struggle. In confronting the first figure of originary authority, Said is also confronting the second. Aligning the academic and the colonized, he defends both forms of secondariness together. The hero of his narrative is the anti-colonial intellectual as academic, the academic as anti-colonial intellectual.

The space thus cleared for the dignity of scholarship is open to all. The avant-garde metropolitan formations of twentieth-century modernism, Said suggests, have to be considered "an extension into the metropolis of large-scale mass movements.... The contest over decolonization has moved from the peripheries to the center" (30). His example is the Algerian war of independence – an example that suits admirably the argument above about Lévi-Strauss's highly mediated (indeed, high modernist) career-making intervention in global and disciplinary representation.[41] Like the metropolis which gives them a local habitation, the scholarly disciplines are a place of "overlap and interdependence" rather than "the reactive assertion of a separate colonial or native identity" (30–1). In a striking phrase, Said describes the process that produces this new kind of place as "adversarial internationalization" (31). The phrase describes what might otherwise be called "professionalization" – the substitution of dispersed professional community, joined only by "method," for the tight, mobilized unity of given "culture" or nationalist conflict: "if the grand and nourishingly optimistic narratives of emancipatory nationalism no longer serve in the 1960s and 1970s to confirm a community of culture as they did for James and Antonius in the 1930s, a new community of method – more difficult and exigent in its demands – arises instead"(43).[42] Whether or not such a "community of method" has already come to pass, it is arguably one of the most useful of images for students and scholars currently seeking a sense of their own vocation.[43]

The last words of "Third World Intellectuals and Metropolitan Culture" are "toward community." In his debate with Michael Walzer as in his critiques of professional enclosure, Said has always publicly insisted on the terrible injustices that are ratified daily in the name of even the most modest or progressive local solidarity. It has been harder to see that in so doing, he has also been helping to define new "affiliations," new means and modes of community that can live and work with this knowledge. Yet his unflagging commitment to a scholarly and critical vocation – to "the belief that the study of literature has a crucial but insufficiently defined intellectual and critical role to play in the contemporary world" – and the superb power of both his commitment and his achievement to inspire so many fellow professionals must remain entirely mysterious unless we understand how the big world of East and West, North and South, is always already inscribed in, and is sometimes contested by, the making of academic careers.[44]

6

Comparative Cosmopolitanisms

In the much-publicized backlash against the left's influence in the academy, there has been a strange coincidence.[1] On the one hand, literature departments are accused by the right of abandoning "Culture" capital C in favor of *multiculturalism*, defined by the *New York Times Magazine* as "the drive to include non-Western materials in every possible course."[2] On the other hand, in variants of the sad, familiar story of academicization-as-decline, literature departments are also accused of falling from the commonness of culture into the privacy of *professionalism* – self-enclosed, jargon-ridden, hyper-theoretical, ignoring the common reader and lacking any general human concern. Academics as a professional "conspiracy against the laity," minority constituencies who blindly insist on seeing their numbers and cultural differences recognized in the curriculum, without concern for the value of their cultural exhibits as judged by any more general standard – in each case the target is the same: the particular as opposed to the universal, the "special interest" pressing for its own advantage at the expense of the common good.

There is some reason to be skeptical about any version of the common good that can ally against it two such unlike terms as "non-Western cultures" and "American professionals." But this is just the alliance that I want to examine. My premise will be that the right is right. Not in its opposition of the universal and the particular, about which more below, nor in its tendentious versions of professionalism or multiculturalism. It is right in the (perhaps unconscious) implica-tion that the new worldliness of the Anglo-American humanities, our[3] recent reaching out to world literature and to colonial, post-colonial, and minority discourse, is somehow related to the local self-interest, the social or institutional being of critics as a group. To this premise must be added, however, the question of whether to relate them is, as both right and left often assume, necessarily to make an accusation. I will answer that it is not. Cultural criticism in the United States has often claimed to be oppositional by virtue of its *un*worldliness – its joint appeal to a restricted, elevated canon and to

Arnoldian or Weberian disinterestedness. Both appeals have been largely discredited in recent years. (Perhaps because it became increasingly difficult to believe, with the increasing academicization of intellectual life, that institutions servicing so many thousands of people a year could be entirely staffed by, and engaged in producing, mavericks and outsiders.) But the brouhaha in the press over multiculturalism and the continuing vulnerability of tenured and untenured radicals to attack, not least from themselves, suggest that no alternative description of where intellectuals think they stand (especially when they are not being Eurocentrists) or what intellectual activities they engage in (especially when they are speaking about other cultures) has successfully taken the place of the former ideal. This chapter is an attempt to explore an alternative description. Now, perhaps, it is time to consider the new brand of intellectual oppositionality that might be emerging from what I call our new worldliness – worldliness in the two senses of (1) planetary expansiveness of subject-matter, on the one hand, and (2) unembarrassed acceptance of professional self-interest, on the other.

1. Belonging, Being Situated, Being Specific

The right is clearly wrong – indeed, it is contradicting itself – when it suggests that multiculturalism and professionalism are related as parallel versions of particularism. Applied to these two objects, the charge of particularism indicates not a parallel but an intersection. For if professional critics *were* hermetically sealed in an ivory tower, then why *would* they respond to "pressure" from "minorities"? If academics were as self-enclosed as we are told (and as some of us appear on occasion to believe), then why would they *support* multiculturalism? Between these two cases of supposed particularism, there would in fact seem to be some sort of communication, some common language, common interest, common ground. But what ground could that be?

When we speak today of world literature or global culture, we are not naming an optional extension of the canon. We are speaking of a new framing of the whole which revalues both unfamiliar and long-accepted genres, which produces new concepts and criteria of judgment, and which affects even those critics who never "do" world literature or colonial discourse at all – which affects all critics, that is, by shifting criticism's whole sense of intellectual enterprise. In an unprecedented and somewhat mysterious way, what it means to be an intellectual or a critic seems to have become worldly or trans-national or – to use a wilfully provocative word – cosmopolitan. But this cosmopolitanism does not yet seem to have moved forward to the stage of conscious self-definition, nor has it been seized upon, therefore, as a possible means of self-legitimation or self-defense. If the neo-conservatives have been quick to attack the emergent or perhaps already dominant sensibility which supports multicultural inclusiveness, they have been allowed to keep the term cosmopolitan-ism for themselves. Contrasting it to particularism or "cultural egocentricity," Dinesh D'Souza's "Illiberal Education," for example, cites it with full approval.[4] But the left meanwhile, groping for a line of defense stronger than "diversity for diversity's sake," has almost completely shunned the term.[5] And this is in large part, I think, *because* it connects international or global subject-matter with the embarrassingly local placement of intellectuals in relatively privileged institutions.

Beyond the adjectival sense of "belonging to all parts of the world; not restricted to any one country or its inhabitants," the word "cosmopolitan" immediately evokes the image of a privileged person: someone who can claim to be a "citizen of the world" by virtue of independent means, expensive tastes, and a globe-trotting life-style. The association of cosmopolitan globality with privilege – classy consumption, glossy cleavage, CNN, modems, faxes, Club Med, and the Trilateral Commission – is so deeply unattractive to us, I think, because deep down we tend to agree with the right that, especially when employed as academics, intellectuals *are* a "special interest" group representing nothing but themselves.

This is not to say that the privileges associated with cosmopolitan-ism can be, as the saying goes, "left unexamined." The first entry under "cosmopolitan" in the *Oxford English Dictionary,* from John Stuart Mill's *Political Economy,* suggests why left-wing critics have recoiled from it: "Capital," Mill writes in 1848, "is becoming more and more cosmopolitan." Cosmopolitanism would seem to mimic capital in seizing for itself the privilege (to paraphrase Wall Street) of "knowing no boundaries." Which is also the gendered privilege of knowing no bodies: of being, in Donna Haraway's words, "a conquering gaze from nowhere," a gaze that claims "the power to see and not be seen, to represent while escaping representation."[6] We may also remember that the gendered and classed privilege of mobile observation in a world of tight borders and limited visibility corresponds to a traditional self-image of criticism itself – criticism as disinterestedness, neutrality, objectivity – that the left rightfully shies away from. The very act of comparison, as in comparative literature, can seem to signal a liberation from insularity and national prejudice into the one true judgment. And when the international range of comparison suddenly and dramatically expands to include the world outside Europe, there is the danger that, under cover of the most democratic intentions, what will be re-invented is the old "free-floating intellectual" and/or an even older version of privileged impartiality. The most visibly ineligible example is perhaps V.S. Naipaul, who has recently been singing the praises of what he calls "our universal civilization."[7] Naipaul presents himself (in Rob Nixon's words in "London Calling") as "the ultimate literary *apatride*, the most comprehensively uprooted of twentieth-century writers and most bereft of national traditions."[8] And he does so in order to lay claim to Arnoldian objectivity, to a "secure, reputable tradition of extratraditionalism" (11) – that is, to "detachment" in the geographical, empirical, and political senses of the word (3).

As an image of criticism, detachment is deservedly obsolete. It is an article of our contemporary faith that, like Naipaul, intellectuals and academics are not detached but *situated* – for many of us, say, situated as metropolitans, or situated as professionals. To say this, however, is already to feel some impious stirrings of doubt. What precisely do we mean by the situatedness we devoutly claim to believe in? What excess baggage does it carry? How tightly does it restrict access to the other places we may come from, the other places we communicate with? How far can this metaphor of locality be reconciled with the expansive awareness or worldliness that we also aspire to?

In an effort to begin thinking through this piece of piety, let us consider, for example, Tim Brennan's application of the term "cosmopolitan" to Salman Rushdie. Brennan speaks of the "almost boastful cosmopolitanism" of "third world metropolitan celebrities," including Rushdie, who are celebrated at the expense of "the domestic or indigenous artist in the process of an actual anticolonial struggle."[9] In "The National Longing for Form," he places Rushdie in a group of "cosmopolitan commentators on the Third World, who offer an *inside view* of formerly submerged peoples for target reading publics in Europe and North America in novels that comply with metropolitan tastes."[10] The message of such cosmopolitans – a critique of Third World nationalism and Third World elites – "is very familiar to us," Brennan concludes, "because it has been easier to embrace in our metropolitan circles than the explicit challenges of, say, the Salvadoran protest-author Manlio Argueta." Thus the metropolis understands the Third World in terms of a "disengagement" and a "rootlessness" that are "not at all characteristic of the 'counter-hegemonic aesthetics' of much Third World writing" (64).

This argument might be classified as strongly reader- or reception-determined. According to Brennan, the decisive reality of the text, a social reality pinpointed with the authority of a lexicon borrowed from market research, is the "target reading publics" of Europe and North America: the "tastes" of the metropolitan consumer. In much the same way, Rob Nixon argues that Naipaul is not an exile but *really* a metropolitan. "The introduction of the category 'metropolitan' helps dispel the myth of Naipaul's homelessness" (27).

To catch an author in the act of belonging to the metropolis, even one who claims to belong nowhere, is a two-finger exercise, given that we believe in advance that everyone belongs somewhere, that there is no alternative to belonging. But the exercise becomes more complicated as soon as we ask what it *means* to belong, or how many different ways of belonging there may be. Absolute homelessness is indeed a myth, and so is cosmopolitanism in its strictly negative sense of "free[dom] from national limitations or attachments" – as the doctrine, in George Boas's words, "that nationality is insignificant from every point of view."[11] But this negative sense of "cosmopolitan" coexists from the outset in tension with more positive ones: with the scientific sense of "world-wide distribution," and with the more general sense of "belonging" to parts of the world other than one's nation. In any given case, it seems reasonable to try to sustain this tension, valuing the negative relation to nationality without giving up an insistence on belonging – an insistence that includes the possibility of presence in other places, dispersed but real forms of membership, a density of overlapping allegiances rather than the abstract emptiness of non-allegiance.

After all, we know in other contexts that "grounding," "placement," and "location" are tricky metaphors. Whether mediated by the Marxist global division of labor or the psychoanalytic model of selfhood, the notion that we are where we are not is an equal and opposite constituent of the new common sense. If our supposed distances are really localities, as we piously repeat, it is also true that there are distances *within* what we thought were *merely* localities. No localization can be assumed to determine absolutely. If it could, then the charge of "metropolitanism" that falls on "celebrities" like

Naipaul and Rushdie would also have to fall on the metropolitan critic who *makes* that charge, whatever his or her own political intentions and degree of celebrity.[12] Situatedness would indeed be our faith, in the most dogmatic sense, if we allowed it to suggest the surrogate divinity of a single, absolutely determining cause, and if we did so, moreover, largely as a masochistic means of punishing and paralyzing ourselves.

Not enough imagination has gone into the different modalities of situatedness-in-displacement. And one of the places where we must learn to see a more complex function or "office" of placement is the university. It says something about the humanities as institutionalized in the university, for example, that they can both over-appreciate the rootlessness of the world's Naipauls and, *for reasons that are no less institutional*, feed off what Brennan calls "protest-authors" as well. It says – and this is the beginning of an answer to the right's charge that professional scholars esoterically ignore the general welfare – that critics have to legitimate themselves to the public, that they do so as transmitters of cultural artifacts whose value to the public is a site of interpretive contest, and that those who criticize Naipaul as a metropolitan are simply engaging in that contest, which is to say behaving in no less "professional" a manner, obeying no less "professional" a logic, than those who delight to see their prejudices confirmed by Naipaul's trashing of the post-colonial nations. The political differences that count are not differences about professionalism as such.[13]

Professional self-legitimation can of course proceed by universalizing those values ("Western culture") of which the critic is custodian and transmitter. But professional self-legitimation can also base itself on the premise that all universals are merely particulars in disguise. The anti-cosmopolitan jargon of the authentically particular and the authentically local provides no escape from or political alternative to the realm of the professional. It simply conceals the exemplification, representation, and generalization in which any intellectual work, professional or not, is inescapably involved, its own included.

Consider, to take another example, how the piety of the particular functions within the most basic and apparently neutral of scholarly concepts: the concept of specificity. In her seminal essay "Under Western Eyes: Feminist Scholarship and Colonial Discourses" (1984), now reprinted in *Third World Women and the Politics of Feminism* (1991), Chandra Mohanty objects that first-world feminist scholarship has often used the category "woman" in a universalizing way "with little regard for historical specificities."[14] Her objection to "ethnocentric universalism" (336) in the name of specific situations was extremely useful then, and it remains indispensable now.[15] Nevertheless, it entitles one to inquire into the specific situation in which it itself is formulated and received. What about the (presumably "Western") logic which values and rewards this insistence on ("Eastern"?) specificity? Why should the professional discourse of metropolitan critics greet the call for specificity with such suspiciously unanimous enthusiasm?

One answer to these questions appears in Mohanty's counterexample of scholarship that is *not* "ethnocentric universalism," the example of a "careful, politically focussed local analysis" of lacemakers in Narsapur, India. This analysis leads to the conclusion, Mohanty says, that

> There is no easy generalization in the direction of "women" in India, or "women in the third world"; nor is there a reduction of ... the exploitation of the lacemakers to cultural explanations about the passivity or obedience that might characterize these women and their situation.... These Narsapur women are not mere victims of the production process. (345)

I am in full sympathy with what I take to be Mohanty's intent here, but the possible consequences of her phrasing go far beyond that intent. If we agree that there is "no easy generalization," don't we want to retain the right to *difficult* generalization? Critics other than Mohanty might easily conclude, otherwise, that generalization *as such* was politically undesirable, whereas generalizing is precisely what Mohanty is doing. What she uncovers among the Narsapur women is not so much a set of particulars as an instance of a rather general rule: the rule that exploitation will always be met with resistance. As Mohanty herself notes, the finding of active agency among the Narsapur women registers nothing but that specific generalization which symmetrically opposes Orientalist generalizations about women's "passivity" and "obedience." "Specificity," in other words, functions here as an innocuous mask which hides not only a claim to epistemological authority, but also, more significantly, the unnecessarily camouflaged transmission of *counter*-universals, *alternative* generalizations.[15]

I am trying to suggest three things. First, that the act of finding "agency" in text after text corresponds to a logic which is as much a part of our "professional" or "metropolitan" situatedness as the act of neglecting or denying it would be. Second, that a critic's transmission of this (or any other) cultural value should not disguise itself as a defense of the particular, the local, and the specific, since it involves generalizations that are no less dramatically synthetic – the people united will never be defeated, the unconquerable human spirit, or whatever – than the Orientalist stereotypes they are marshalled against. And third, that if we do not need "easy generalizations," we do need difficult ones – for example, the more difficult though less pious procedure of *not* assuming agency to be everywhere present, but trying to explain why it is where it is and why it isn't where it isn't.

It is arguable that, as a critical procedure or paradigm, the formulaic recovery of inspirational agency may foster political quiescence, while a more politicized criticism might in fact result from a focus on vaster, less anthropomorphic, less hortatory structures. After all, why *do* we all value agency so highly? As an abstraction that lends itself equally well to the Marxism of Lukács and the humanism of Matthew Arnold, agency legitimates the specific politics of neither one. What it does legitimate is the public representativeness of criticism as such, its responsiveness to the active voice or will of the people. When the academic humanist pulls this particular rabbit from his or her text, the point is both that the people make their own history and also, however implicitly, that the academic who is representing them as so doing, by transmitting this tidbit of the cultural heritage, is himself or herself acting in the interests of the people thereby, including the people who make much of that academic's own immediate history – the public legislators and private funders who pass judgment on academic legitimacy.

However desirable agency may be, there is at any rate no inherent connection between it and the particular, the specific, the local.[17] Here an edifyingly unliterary parallel presents itself: the so-called "localities" debate which has raged over the past few years among radical geographers. The move in geography to study the smaller, sub-regional units known as localities came at a time when the worldwide restructuring of the capitalist economy seemed at once to be increasing the scale of global interconnectedness and, in direct proportion, to be decreasing the power of the human agents concerned to grasp or resist its operations. In scaling down the size of the units studied, geographers were hoping to draw on the empirical authority of the particular, or rather were hoping *through* that authority to sustain a waning illusion of agency. Hidden away in the miniaturizing precision of "locality," with its associations of presence and uniqueness, empirical concreteness, complete experience, accessible subjectivity, has been the nostalgia for a collective subject-in-action that is no longer so easy to localize. As one essay in the debate concluded, "*We do not have some privileged access to understanding patterns of human agency simply by studying localities*" (original emphasis).[18] Thinking small is not enough; agency is not to be had so predictably. The unit of coherence where transformative energies have the best chance of seizing hold is not predictable in advance; it might well be larger, not smaller. As Neil Smith writes: "it is not clear in the current restructuring that, in economic terms at least, coherent regions continue to exist as subdivisions of the national rather than international economy."[19]

This suggests the case for a certain cosmopolitanism – not one obsessed with embodying a preconceived totality, but one which does not judge in advance the macro-political scale of its units, which sees "worlding" as a process, to quote Gayatri Spivak, and a process in which more than one "world" may be realized, where "worlds" may be contested.[20] "Cosmos" (world) in "cosmopolitan" originally meant simply "order" or "adornment" – as in cosmetics – and was only later extended metaphorically to refer to "the world." Cosmetics preceded totality. Worlding, then, might be seen as "making up" the face of the planet – something that can be done in diverse ways. At the same time, the case for this more modest cosmopolitanism is also a case for a certain professionalism – a professionalism which, without presumption of ultimate totalizing certainty, believes in its own intellectual powers of generalization, abstraction, synthesis, and representation at a distance, and in the process of putting them to use. Which believes, one might say, in its own *work*.

2. Discrepant Cosmopolitanisms: James Clifford

Here, then, is a task: to drop the conversation-stopping, always reversible charge of "privilege" and instead to discriminate degrees of complacency, degrees of service to the general welfare, within an overarching acknowledgement that the professional producers and transmitters of knowledge are *of course* not motivated solely (if at all) by pure disinterested altruism. This effort can begin where the cosmopolitan's privileges are most grossly accepted. In the recent volume *Global Culture*, there is an essay called "Cosmopolitans and Locals in World Culture," written by Ulf Hannerz, which defines the figure of the cosmopolitan by a series of exclusions.[21] "Anybody who moves about in the world" (238), the author writes, is not a cosmopolitan. Nor is it sufficient to have "a willingness to engage with the Other" (239). Cosmopolitans are not tourists, for whom they are likely to be mistaken, since "tourists are not participants" (242). They are not exiles, since the exile's involvement with another culture has been "*forced*" (242). "Most ordinary labour migrants are not cosmopolitans either. For them going away may be, ideally, home plus higher income; often the involvement with another culture is not a fringe benefit but a necessary cost, to be kept as low as possible" (243). "The perspective of the cosmopolitan must entail relationships to a plurality of cultures understood as distinct entities" (239).

At this point, if not before, one becomes aware of how self-serving this process of definition is. Imagining cultures as "distinct entities" makes them into objects of artistic appreciation for the passing connoisseur; it is a way of imagining that all privileges of mobility and comparison inhere in the cosmopolitan observer. As the definition narrows further, it accumulates still more privileges. Cosmopolitans, like expatriates and ex-expatriates, "are people who have *chosen* to live abroad" (my italics). They know "that they can go home when it suits them." Today, this knowledge is less often guaranteed by independent means than by their occupations. "Transnational cultures today tend to be more or less clearcut occupational cultures" (243). What occupations? The climactic example of transnational occupational culture is – to no one's surprise – the intellectuals.

This more or less shameless use of the new "global culture" to re-invent or re-legitimate Mannheim's "free-floating" intellectuals seems to corroborate, once again, the fear that cosmopolitanism is only a screen for privilege and self-aggrandizement. But this is not the precise moral I draw from it. The essay's criteria for true cosmopolitanism share a good deal with traditional aesthetics. In its view, cosmopolitanism becomes an autonomous, unforced appreciation of coherence and novelty among distinct cultural entities. The editor of the volume in which this essay appears, Mike Featherstone, stresses the same point when he describes "transnational intellectuals" as those who "seek out and adopt a reflexive, metacultural or *aesthetic* stance to divergent cultural experiences" (9 – my italics). In my own view, it is this aestheticism, with its presumption of inequality and its spectatorial absence of commitment to change that inequality, which disqualifies the essay from representing the new transnationality of intellectual work. What we have to object to, in other words, is the particular position that the essay tries to legitimate, and not the effort of self-legitimation itself.

By producing a new, international pedigree for the old idea of the intellectual as autonomous critic, this essay joins the genre of the allegory of vocation. What I have been calling allegories of vocation are critical works which, while doing whatever other interpretive tasks they set themselves, also perform a second, most often implicit function: they invent and arrange their concepts and characters so as to narrativize and argue for the general value and significance of the intellectual vocation they exemplify. Examples include Raymond Williams's *Culture and Society*, which tells the story of how leftist critics like Williams himself arose from Romanticism to write works like *Culture and Society*, or Gilbert and Gubar's *The Madwoman in the Attic*, which turns *Jane Eyre* into a paradigm for the rise of the twentieth-century feminist critic. But I have not *criticized* any of these works by identifying the genre they belong to. If we accept the premise that we *want* to do significant work – that we want the privilege, if you like, of doing work that is more significant than earning a living – then we must desire and value texts which help explain, to ourselves and to others, why a particular sort of work is meaningful and valuable. We can criticize the aestheticism of this cosmopolitan, in other words, but not the fact that the essay makes a case for intellectuals. What should be set against it is another case for intellectuals that mobilizes cosmopolitanism differently.

As a more desirable alternative within the same genre, then, I will take up the rich and influential work of historian of anthropology James Clifford, which has been inspiring to students seeking a sense of intellectual vocation in the confusingly transnational space of contemporary knowledge. It has been as inspiring as it has, I think, in part because it has struggled in an exemplary way not only with our ambivalence about cosmopolitanism, but also, less visibly, with our ambivalence about professionalism.

Clifford's position on cosmopolitanism seems to be expressed unequivocally in his influential review of Edward Said's *Orientalism*.[22] There the term "cosmopolitan" is unmistakably derogatory. "Said's basic values," Clifford says, "are cosmopolitan." This statement concludes Clifford's case that "humanist common denominators ... are meaningless, since they bypass the local cultural codes that make personal experience articulate." "The privilege of standing above cultural particularism, of aspiring to the universalist power

190

that speaks for humanity ... is a privilege invented by a totalizing Western liberalism" (263). What must always be avoided, Clifford declares, even if the concept of culture itself is eventually abandoned, is "the positing of cosmopolitan essences" (274–5).

In this context, "totalizing Western liberalism" seems to name what is wrong both with cosmopolitanism and with professionalism. Clifford's essay "On Ethnographic Self-Fashioning: Conrad and Malinowski," first published in 1985, has thus been taken as an undermining of the scientific model of ethnographic authority that Malinowski did so much to make the professional standard, an undermining carried out in large part by invidious juxtaposition with the messily literary, unsystematic, unprofessional figure of Conrad.[23] "By professionalizing fieldwork," Clifford writes, "anthropology transformed a widespread predicament into a scientific method" (95). Conrad, who acknowledges the same (cosmopolitan) predicament without escaping into scientific method, thus seems to embody the literary as an alternative to the professional.

If this were all, it would be manifestly insufficient. For, as Paul Rabinow pointed out in his contribution to *Writing Culture*, it would leave Clifford no way of acknowledging the fact that, however "literary" his style, in relation to the anthropologists who are his subjects, he too is playing a professional role.[24] "There is only one 'professional,' so to speak, in the crowd," Rabinow comments. "For, whereas all the others mentioned are practicing anthropologists, James Clifford has created and occupied the role of ex officio scribe to our scribblings ... Clifford takes us as his natives" (242). A "new specialty is currently in the process of self-definition," Rabinow says (242). But Clifford's "own writing and situation," which define this specialty, "are left unexamined" (244).

This sort of tit-for-tat, in which injurious epithets like "specialist," "professional," and "metropolitan" are asked to stand in for substantive political judgment, must always be the result as long as it is assumed that to go ahead and *examine* one's professional "writing and situation," to open one's eyes finally and painfully to the "situatedness" of a metropolitan or a cosmopolitan, is ipso facto to judge oneself intolerably contaminated and self-contradictory. One of the extraordinary strengths of Clifford's work is that this is an assumption he has come increasingly to question. If one looks more closely at the Conrad/Malinowski essay, one sees that in fact neither "professional" nor "cosmopolitan" functions there as a term of opprobrium. A struggle with "cosmopolitanism" (95), we are told, is something Conrad and Malinowski have in common. And the essay is about a "difficult accession to innovative *professional* expression" (96 – my italics) that they also have in common.

And Clifford himself has this in common with them as well. The last line of this extremely moving essay is an ambiguous quotation from Conrad's Marlow: "You see me, whom you know." The point of the ambiguity seems clear: the essay is itself an allegory of vocation describing a "difficult accession to innovative professional expression" shared not only by Conrad and Malinowski, but by Clifford too, along with many of his readers. One might think of the essay, then, as just that act of professional self-examination that Rabinow found lacking in *Writing Culture*. Much of its power comes from the extra work it does to redescribe and legitimate the work of the *historian* of anthropology along with that of the anthropologist, the professional, second-order work of criticism as well as the "primary," "unprofessional" work of the novelist.

In Clifford's allegorical reading of Conrad, *Heart of Darkness* becomes an alternative model of writing that is no less professional than Malinowski's professional ethnography. The decisive difference between them is that Conrad includes the experience of fashioning and self-fashioning, the activity of selecting and discarding, that is usually suppressed from ethnographic writing. His fiction includes the exclusions – the Lie to the Intended, the tearing off of Kurtz's "Exterminate the brutes!" from the official report – that are inevitable in all professional discourse. Professional discourse, the moral would seem to go, cannot be purified; it can only be saved by its ironic self-consciousness of its impurity.

We may or may not feel that this solution "works" – that it rises above, say, irony as a mode or style of living with exclusion too comfortably. But in fact this is only one of two resolutions to the dilemma of professional exclusiveness that the essay explores. Why *is* exclusion inevitable? On the one hand, Clifford suggests that, like fiction, even the most scientific discourse selects and fashions and invents. Here only self-consciousness will help. On the other hand, however, he also suggests that the Lie to the Intended and the tearing off of "Exterminate the brutes!" are exclusions produced not by representation in general, but more precisely by the writer's or professional's deliberate act of loyalty to the arbitrary limits of his or her chosen culture. Marlow, Clifford says, "learns to lie – that is, to communicate within the collective partial fictions of cultural life" (99). Clifford tries to restrict the damage this will do as a paradigm of professional ethnography. The "ethnographic standpoint" is better represented, he adds, not by Marlow but by the second narrator, silently listening to him, who "salvages, compares, and (ironically) believes these staged truths." But this distinguishing of narrators does not seriously affect the result: professional writing seen as "local, partial knowledge," or more strongly (but relegated to a footnote), as "a positive choice for the 'lie of culture'" (99). "[L]ike Marlow's account aboard the *Nellie*, the truths of cultural descriptions are meaningful to specific interpretive communities in limiting historical circumstances" (112). The arbitrary, exclusive cultural wholeness that Malinowski imposes upon the Trobriands results from an arbitrary, even absurd act of self-defining allegiance to the professional community of English anthropologists. The ethnographer lies about his cultural objects, presenting them as more "local" than they are, in order to make himself a member of the "local" culture of his fellow professionals.

This is a dead end of professional self-definition from which ironic self-consciousness offers no hope of rescue. But Clifford does trace a way out of it. The logic of self-rescue goes from "culture" to the "post-cultural" and finally back to the "cosmopolitan." If it is no longer feasible to think of the cultures studied by ethnography as distinct entities, as Clifford repeatedly suggests, then why assume that the professional culture *of ethnographers* is a distinct entity? If we must learn to see other cultures not as distinct, different wholes, but as mobile, fluid, hybrid, and inclusive, then why insist on a necessary and absolute exclusiveness in studying the culture that studies those cultures? In writing himself out of "culture" as an absurd but necessary (and necessarily exclusive) order, Clifford also writes himself out of "the profession" as a similarly necessary (and exclusive) absurdity. Instead of a dichotomy of professional describers of culture, on the one hand, and their non-professional objects of description, on the other, Clifford now assumes a "post-cultural" space where the subjects and objects of description are at least potentially reversible, where the mobility required for observation and comparison is not monopolized by one side, where the word "local" has lost much of its contrastive force. His name for this space – a space that is not exclusively professional – is "cosmopolitanism."

In the work that has followed *The Predicament of Culture*, Clifford has radically revised his opinion of cosmopolitanism.[25] Rather than speaking in the name of the local, as in the review of *Orientalism*, he has been pointing out the manifold abuses of "thinking local," the distortions involved in taking "the field" and "the village" as localizations of culture. He has been calling on anthropologists to bring back into their ethnographies the "cosmopolitan intermediaries" who intervene in and help constitute them, and "to focus on hybrid, cosmopolitan experiences as much as on rooted, native ones." Clifford can approve of cosmopolitanism because he has been seeing it, and teaching others to see it, as neither the consequence nor the prerogative of "totalizing Western liberalism." He has been seeing it as something he himself shares with his subjects. It is not only gentlemen travellers, but the people of color who were the servants of those travellers, who have "specific cosmopolitan viewpoints." Even the organized coercion of migrant labor produces "cosmopolitan workers." "The notion that certain classes of people are cosmopolitan (travellers) while the rest are local (natives)" is only "the ideology of one (very powerful) travelling culture." Questions of power aside, "they" and "we" can no longer be divided as "local" and "cosmopolitan."

Thus the latter term becomes available again for general use. Instead of renouncing cosmopolitanism as a false universal, one can embrace it as an impulse to knowledge that is shared with others, a striving to transcend partiality that is itself partial, but no more so than the similar cognitive strivings of many diverse peoples. The world's particulars can now be recoded, in part at least, as the world's *discrepant cosmopolitanisms.*

How can comparative attention to "discrepant cosmopolitanisms" help us to respond to the current backlash? In the *New Yorker* article mentioned in the Introduction, an article which does its bit for this backlash, Cynthia Ozick comes to the following conclusion on multiculturalism: "I would not wish to drop Homer or Jane Austen or Kafka to make room for an Aleutian Islander of lesser gifts, unrepresented though her group may be on the college reading list."[26] I take Clifford's reversal on cosmopolitanism as a hint that one of the various moves we might make against this use of the Aleutian Islander as an empty figure for pure particularity, and against the label of cultural particularism in general, is to fill the figure in, not just *as* a particular (worthy of the same respect as every other particular), but also, perhaps, as the carrier and embodiment of a certain cosmopolitanism. One might, for example, bring forward an essay by Claude Lévi-Strauss called "Cosmopolitanism and Schizophrenia" which discusses the syncretic mythology of Native Americans along the Pacific Northwest coast. Or, apropos of the putative Westernness of the Great Ideas, one might emphasize the word "Egypt" on the first page – unfortunately, *only* on the first page – of an article called "The Greek Origins of the Idea of Cosmopolitanism," which reads as follows: "The earliest recorded formulation of this idea is supplied by modern archaeological discovery at Tell el-Amarna, in Egypt. Inscriptions have been found there, written by Akhnaton (pharoah of Egypt from 1375 to 1358 BC). . . ."[27] Or one might counter ethnocentrisms both right and left with cosmopolitanism like that of the last page of *I, Rigoberta Menchú*: "[M]y commitment to our struggle knows no boundaries nor limits. That's why I've travelled to many places. . . ."[28]

The scholarly project of accumulating instances of cosmopolitanism from around the globe – in Arjun Appadurai's words, "to fish for cosmopolitanism in the raw" – would help clinch the point that the concept is neither a Western invention nor a Western privilege.[29] When the right suggests that, after all, there is ethnocentrism everywhere, that is, in the Third World too – the inevitable prelude to the suggestion that, after all, only in the West has there been any move away from it – we can then say not just that unequal power has made Eurocentrism qualitatively different in its effects from other ethnocentrisms, but also that we *value* the move away from ethnocentrism – in all the many places, Western and non-Western, where it has occurred. To take an empirical route out of the oversimple binary of universal and particular, rather than performing a merely logical or deconstructive exercise on it, would put the matter across to a broader audience, and it would also have the advantage of distinguishing cosmopolitanism from an abstract, ahistorical universalism.[30] For it would bring out many diverse and overlapping syncretisms and secularisms[31] for which the term is an umbrella. (The opposition between religion and secularism itself might be one casualty of such a project.)

The limits of the term are among its conjunctural virtues. No one actually is or ever can be a cosmopolitan in the sense of belonging nowhere. Who can say, in Jonathan Arac's helpful twisting of a familar phrase, "I am an alien; everything human is alien to me"? Nor can anyone be a cosmopolitan in the sense of belonging everywhere. If such a thing were conceivable, it would not be desirable, for as Donna Haraway has pointed out, it could only exist in the form of complete cultural relativism.[32] The interest of the term cosmopolitanism is located, then, not in its full theoretical extension, where it becomes a paranoid fantasy of ubiquity and omniscience, but rather (paradoxically) in its local applications, where the unrealizable ideal produces normative pressure against such alternatives as, say, the fashionable "hybridization." Its provocative association with privilege is perhaps better understood, in this context, as the normative edge that cosmopolitanism tries to add to the inclusiveness and diversity of multiculturalism – as an attempt to name a necessary but difficult normativeness.

The term is not as philosophically ambitious as the word "universalism," though it does some of the same work. (It makes room for moments of generalizing, one might say, without offering license for uninhibited universalizing.) Nor is it as politically ambitious as the word "internationalism." But it does start us asking what form such an internationalism might best take. The academy-bashing journalists have been suggesting that multiculturalism is nothing but an attempt to revive the naive Third Worldism of the 1960s, with its automatic division between Imperialist Bad Guys and Newly Independent Good Guys. It seems to me that the term cosmopolitanism better describes the sensibility of our moment. Now, as opposed perhaps to two or three decades ago, anti-imperialism has been and must be newly careful, skeptical, measured in its support of any nation. Recently and paradigmatically, it has had to learn to oppose Bush's war in the Persian Gulf without defending Saddam Hussein. More generally, it has been to school with movements in the name of gender, class, and sexual orientation which, in Jean Franco's words, "have sprung up on the margins of the nation state" and "no longer couch cultural or political projects in national terms."[33] Our moment, one might say, is that of the globalizing of such movements – a moment to which there would correspond, ideally, some new, de-nationalized internationalism.

If cosmopolitanism cannot deliver an explicitly and directly political program, it is at least a step toward this sort of internationalist political education. By suggesting that there is no right place to stand, it can take some of the moralism out of our politics. Better still, by doing so it can liberate us to pursue a long-term process of trans-local connecting that is both political and educational at once. And in the midst of the short-term politico-educational crisis where we now find ourselves, it can designate a teaching of culture capable of mobilizing the energy and enthusiasm of a broad front of people who are not all or even predominantly leftists, whatever the right may think. As a practice of comparison, a range of tolerances and secularisms, an international competence

196

or mode of citizenship that is the monopoly of no one class or civilization, it answers the charges of "particularism" and "loss of standards." As a positive ideal of interconnected knowledge and pedagogy, it elevates rather than lowers existing educational standards. It presents multiculturalism as both a common program and a critical program.[34]

3. The Composition of Cultural Capital: Gayatri Spivak and Pierre Bourdieu

Clifford's critique of the notion of culture as a rooted, distinct entity, his refusal to allow this anthropological concept of culture to do the same professional service as the Arnoldian concept that it resembles and miniaturizes, and his urging that we replace both with a "post-cultural" or cosmopolitan model of mobile, reciprocal interconnectedness – these propositions emerge from one writer's extraordinary individual effort, but they also belong increasingly to the common sense of cultural workers both inside and outside the academy. And the fact that Clifford's voice is not sole and solitary poses an interpretive problem. For the "salvage paradigm" cannot explain how it is that, with the rise of cultural studies, the *critique* of the salvage paradigm should also arise. If culture has been the capital of the intellectuals, according to Pierre Bourdieu's well-known metaphor, if they have made use of culture in order to define themselves, legitimate themselves, reproduce themselves, if culture has been a base or foundation for them, then what happens from the moment – it seems to be our moment – when intellectuals accept the validity of critical analyses like Bourdieu's and Clifford's? How can we explain the *success* of these analyses among those very intellectuals whose base or foundation the analyses seem to remove? Have the intellectuals been voluntarily renouncing their capital? Or are they sustained by some economy of legitimation that has yet to be recognized as such, a new form of post-cultural capital that supports them by some as yet undetermined means?[35]

It is too soon to expect satisfying answers to these questions. But there are nevertheless reasons to test them out, if only in a tentative fashion. And one obvious object of such inquiry is the work of Gayatri Chakravorty Spivak. Spivak is perhaps the most brilliant exponent in her generation of what Edward Said calls "adversarial internationalization"; no one else except Said has done as much to mobilize the energies of young cultural critics for the study of colonialism and post-colonialism or to offer them working tools and paradigms. But while Spivak is clearly a source of immense vocational inspiration, she pushes away questions of vocation and legitimation decisively, as if to challenge their continued pertinence. Her writing often seems to imply that it *ought not* to be as inspiring as it is – that proper criticism should do everything possible to throw itself into question, to fight a legitimacy that is always already too-well-established, to accept its own groundlessness. Ideally, she suggests, criticism should remain illegitimate.

This position is implicit in one of Spivak's most influential critical performances, a reading of *Jane Eyre* as a double narrative of legitimation. In this characteristically dazzling essay, "Three Women's Texts and a Critique of Imperialism," first published in 1985, Spivak reads Brontë's novel as a double allegory: an allegory of Empire and an allegory of professionalism. Jane Eyre rises out of domestic servitude to become her master's wife and equal, Spivak argues, not just by her virtues or by means of an inheritance extracted from the colonies; she rises by her "virtuous" involvement in the same imperial logic that helped seize and rule the colonies. Jane discovers meaningful work in training and disciplining peasant girls, then in preparing herself for the "missionary" role of converting and civilizing the Hindu heathen. And it is this work, according to Spivak, which is realized in the destruction of the first Mrs Rochester, the violent, brutish, uncivilized creature from the colonies who must be removed so that Jane can occupy her place. The alternative ending, in which Jane would go to India to join St John Rivers' "civilizing mission," is in fact the key to the actual ending. The novel makes Jane into "Mrs Rochester" only by doing to one colonial subject what Jane had been training herself to do to other colonial subjects: eradicating their unchristian animality and replacing it with civilization. Only so high a mission, Spivak suggests, could offset the social transgression that would otherwise be entailed by the plot's raising up of the "other woman" at the expense of the legitimate wife.[36]

Alongside this argument about the constitutive role of imperialism in *Jane Eyre*, and more generally about its role in the literature of the nineteenth century, Spivak also makes an argument about the criticism of the twentieth century. As read by a certain tendency within feminist criticism, she suggests, the story of Jane's rise has become an allegory of feminist criticism's own rise. It has been mobilized in order to secure and legitimate the similarly transgressive emergence of feminist criticism as an institutional power, a rise which Spivak, extending her argument, accuses of the same complicity with imperialism, the same degradation of (post-)colonial subjects, that she found in the original. *Jane Eyre* has become "a cult text of feminism," she suggests, because it can be used to make "feminist individualism" seem to stand for "feminism as such" (244), an "emerging norm" in which "the 'native female' . . . is excluded from any share" (245).

There is tremendous power in this stereoscopic mode of reading. After Spivak's essay, it is difficult not to see Gilbert and Gubar's immensely successful *The Madwoman in the Attic* (1979), which subtitles its *Jane Eyre* chapter "Plain Jane's Progress," as an allegory of the bourgeois or mainstream feminist critic's passage from rage and rebellion to academic or institutional acculturation.[37] This "pilgrim's progress toward maturity" (339) passes through encounter with that rage and rebellion, in the figure of Bertha, but leaves Bertha and anger behind. It ends in the achievement of contented equality with the master, equality which is also self-conscious superiority to the other servants. "[I]solated from society but flourishing in a natural order of their own making": Gilbert and Gubar's description of the marriage suggests a withdrawal into professional community as a compensation for the lack of renewed community in the world – a professional community which leaves out Bertha Mason as figure both for feminist anger and for the Third World subject.[38]

At the same time, of course, we have no reason to believe – and Spivak herself does not suggest – that her own argument is exempt from some such logic. The fact that feminists have received Spivak's own work with so much admiration and have increasingly sought to follow her example, relating issues of gender to issues of Empire and thereby producing criticism which has everything to do with feminist anger and Third World subjects, is evidence enough that compensatory isolationism is hardly the whole story of feminism's professionalization. So one asks oneself: what is the next episode? How can this story be stretched to include Spivak herself, along with her many admirers? If some vocational logic informs *her* narrative of nineteenth-century literature, connecting it with *her* version of twentieth-century professional criticism, what logic might this be? From what base or foundation does the cosmopolitan post-colonial critic speak?

As I said, Spivak does not invite such questions. She implies, on the contrary, that one must *not* offer young feminist internationalists a Jane-Eyre-like sense of legitimate vocation. And at the root of this modest disavowal, I think, lies a parallel between professionalism and imperialism – a parallel which is misleading about both topics.

It is strange, after all, that the two halves of Spivak's argument are linked by so parallel a logic. The brutality of the Empire, which is decorously screened from view by the marriage plots of domestic fiction, returns like the repressed and is revealed as constitutive – constitutive, first, of the domestic plot and, second, of scholarly, professional interest in that plot. The self-constitution of imperialism, like the self-constitution of professionalism, occurs by means of exclusion. The West has become what it is by othering the non-West. The profession is what it is because it excludes and denigrates the layman, the non-expert, the ordinary citizen.[39]

As far as professionalism is concerned, Spivak's reading of *Jane Eyre* as a zero-sum allegory, an ascent of the social ladder achieved only by pushing someone else down or off the ladder, corresponds well enough to the received wisdom. In her highly respected book *The Rise of Professionalism* (1977), Magali Sarfatti Larson describes professionalization as "a collective process of upward social mobility" – in a sense, as *Jane Eyre* on a larger scale (xvi). More recently, the authors of *Power in the Highest Degree* (1990) have declared:

> Professionals argue that power based on knowledge is natural and justifiable, unlike power based on wealth or coming from the barrel of a gun. Through professionalism, the argument goes, the "best and the brightest" are justly rewarded; hence everyone is encouraged to develop his or her human potential. But professionalism . . . also erodes the rights of those not certified as experts, bringing its own threats to democracy and equality. The shadow side of professionalism is the creation of a new dispossessed majority: the uncredentialled. (4)[40]

As I have tried to suggest throughout this book, however, this logic of self-constitution by means of exclusion cannot be taken for granted. It is true, of course, that credentials are only meaningful if someone else does not possess them. Yet there is a very long step from this truth to the more questionable notion that the unequal possession of credentials is necessarily unjust. There is another long step to the more dubious assumption that unequal credentialing is the central principle of injustice in our unjust society.[41] And when we turn from professionalism to imperialism, or rather to the discourse produced by or about imperialism, the pertinence of this zero-sum logic is more questionable still.

200

In the realm of international political economy, zero-sum logic is exemplified by so-called dependency theory. "Dependency theory," in Jean Franco's summary, "is based on the assumption that underdevelopment is structurally linked to development in the dominant nation. . . . It is no longer possible to treat the two terms as if they were separable." This line of thinking helped expose the deep and complex entanglement of colonialism in the making of the developed countries. At least in its strong form, however, it also went further, proposing "that the very same mechanisms which set off underdevelopment in the 'periphery' are prerequisite to capital accumulation in the 'core.' Capitalist development cannot take place in the core unless underdevelopment is developed in the periphery."[42] This version adds to economic analysis a certain moral satisfaction, for its direct and continuous causal link between First World riches and Third World poverty suggests that there is no credit on one side of the ledger that is not precisely matched by a debit on the other. Politics, arranging itself around the primal opposition of Third World to First World, thus takes on the enviable transparency of an ethical balance sheet. Unfortunately, as Robert Brenner has pointed out, the actual development of world capitalism has been a much messier and less systematic process. Economic innovation and social conflict in the European core, for example, determined the course of capitalist development there in ways that did not always involve the extraction of surplus value from the periphery. And underdevelopment at the periphery similarly depends on the state of class relations *at* the periphery as well as on the global relations between periphery and core. In short, it cannot be assumed that development and underdevelopment have always been two sides of a single, unified historical process, even if the assumption of unity helps moralize and simplify political choices. Capitalism is not a single, unitary whole.[43]

What any zero-sum logic takes for granted is of course just this: that whatever happens, happens within a single, unitary whole. A larger slice for you necessarily means a smaller slice for me only if we are dividing one whole pie into two slices. It would be politically dangerous to assume in any given instance that the pie is *not* whole; that is why the left so often counters the right's assumption of abundance with an instinctive, contrary assumption of scarcity.[44] But there exists no rule that covers all instances. Sometimes there will be scarcity; sometimes there will be abundance; sometimes the issue is not quantifiable at all. So we have to ask: what is in fact the case for professionalism in general, and for professional discourse about colonialism in particular?

As I suggested earlier on, "discourse" is one candidate to fill the "everything is x" slot in post-Arnoldian moments of professional rationale. But when it stands for "everything," it becomes a version of dependency theory's capitalist world system: a single unified whole whose very existence marks the symmetrical absence of Third World self-representations. In choosing this carrier to transport the political urgencies of colonialism and neo-colonialism into the humanities, then, one runs the paradoxical risk of giving the West too great, if also too guilty, a role. In asserting the guilt, one also asserts the greatness. It is necessary to say, therefore, that the West never did fill all discursive space with its projections. Subaltern voices spoke, even if the West could not hear them. What was missing was not these other voices but rather a common space, a transnational public sphere, where all voices could come together, where competition could have taken place, where the West could have drowned them out. Nor could imperialist projections even occupy the West's own public sphere as entirely as is often assumed. For the imperial powers could not have successfully conquered and occupied so much of the world if the West had done nothing but project its suppressed contradictions and anxieties onto unresisting Eastern objects. Some degree of non-projective information about the East must be assumed to intervene, not thanks to the West's scientific objectivity but simply because it needed useful knowledge in order to rule with relatively efficient brutality.[45]

Freud's "return of the repressed" narrative, the Hegelian model of "self-constitution via degradation of the other," and for that matter the "world capitalist system" all share with "discourse" one founding premise. As models for culture's relation to imperialism, each assumes a single, comprehensive mind or *Geist* that is always already connected to each and every (psychic or cultural) event in its experience. In this center/periphery scenario, it would be impossible for culture *not* to register its connection with the empire, however deviously. The colonies cannot be absent. But without this possibility, any specific connections between metropolitan core and colonized periphery that a critic might want to demonstrate are presumed to exist in advance. Thus they lose not only their disconfirmability, but the usefulness that comes of being able to locate a vector of domination precisely in time and space, which is a precondition for developing the specific agency that can answer it.

To say, for example, that "in the nineteenth century, the Western Subject required colonized peoples for its consolidation," as a recent essay on Bharati Mukherjee proposes, is to forget any of imperialism's non-discursive or non-cultural dynamics. It is thus to misunderstand seriously the dividedness of the collective self or subject they emerge from.[46] Is it the case, as the verb "require" suggests here, that there could have been no consolidation of the "Western Subject" *without* deforming mastery over colonized peoples? Was it truly out of the question that domestic culture might have *ignored* the faraway sufferings that its imperialism caused? As Raymond Williams and his interviewers in *Politics and Letters* agreed some fourteen years ago, there is no way of deducing the Irish famine of the 1840s from the British novels of the 1840s, though the Irish who were starving and the novelists who were writing lived far closer together than the novelists lived to the rest of the Empire.[47] Who says the Empire is the "political unconscious" of the nineteenth century? On what grounds could we assume it is a repressed but definitive truth that could not help but return?[48]

The point here is not just that repression-and-return and other zero-sum models make for an oversimplified history of the imperialism/culture relation. It is also, to follow out Spivak's stereoscopic insight, that the supposed necessity for the empire to show up in domestic culture may be less an imperial imperative of the nineteenth century than a professional imperative of the twentieth century. For asserting Western culture's guilt, as I suggested, can also be a way of preserving Western culture's greatness.

When the universal, humanizing value of culture is challenged, as it notoriously has been challenged since the national liberation movements that followed the Second World War, since the women's and civil rights movements of the 1960s, and so on, what happens to the professional rationale of the humanities? Obviously enough, the definition of culture could expand, taking in forms of expression formerly seen as below or outside it and thus becoming more genuinely representative of the world's ways of feeling and thinking. This is of course what we have seen. For all the complexities and uncertainties that accompany it, this expansion of the culture concept nevertheless provides the democratic rationale, foundational and inescapable, underwriting the existence of all professional cultural workers today. (The present book is no exception.) But under these new conditions, the previous canon is suddenly at risk, not so much from its complicities with imperial hegemony as from its indifference.

Disciplinarily speaking, it is better to be complicitous with empire than indifferent to empire, for it is only if the traces of imperial exploitation can be shown to help constitute the homeland's canonical texts that those canonical texts can legitimately continue to serve as a discipline's object of study or knowledge base. To believe that the empire was constitutive of domestic existence is professionally enabling, for it authorizes us to go on studying the same texts without giving up the hope of propagating "the best that is known and thought" in a globally responsible way.[49] Asserting Western culture's guilt can also be a way of preserving Western culture's greatness, along with the legitimacy of the critics who preserve and transmit it. When imperialism, taking on the organic wholeness of culture, offers a theological guarantee that the repressed will always return, will always be accessible in the texts of the imperial culture, it provides a democratic legitimation for cosmopolitan critics.

This, then, is one possible answer, or part of an answer, to our original question of where Spivak stands, professionally speaking, and how she can inspire a sense of mission in critics who do not and perhaps cannot renounce their professional affiliations. By presenting imperialism as a densely packed, enclosed universe that abhors any vacuum, she presents already canonical texts as citizens of a larger world than they realized. And by demonstrating the unconscious cosmopolitanism of texts linked to distant peoples in a common but unrecognized citizenship of rights and obligations, she also validates her own conscious cosmopolitanism, along with that of other critics who do likewise.

Like the other instances of vocational allegory I have been accumulating, this point should be understood, as it is offered, not as critique but as a prior and lesser act, an effort to render explicit materials for which the eventual criteria of judgment are not yet in place. In such matters critique is almost sure to be premature. Consider, for example, the recent discussion of cosmopolitanism by Benita Parry in the journal *Transition*. Parry, one of Gayatri Spivak's least sympathetic critics, writes as follows: "there is a recognition that the 'global flows' of transnational cultural traffic have issued in 'public cultures' productive of an emergent *postcolonial* cosmopolitanism."[50] It is difficult to tell how Parry feels about this new non-Western cosmopolitanism. Her statement invites comparison, however, with her well-known attack on Spivak, cited in the last chapter. According to that argument, Spivak's deconstruction of the active, self-conscious Third World subject is nothing but a metropolitan intellectual's self-aggrandizement: "The disparaging of nationalist discourses of resistance is matched by the exorbitation of the role allotted to the post-colonial woman intellectual."[51] In Parry's version of the zero-sum logic of self-constitution, Spivak disparages the subaltern's speech in order to raise herself up. If intellectuals deny the agency and voice of the native, it's so that they themselves will be heard to speak better.

The answer to Parry's argument takes us one step closer to understanding the implicit alliance of "non-Western cultures" and "American professionals" with which this chapter began. It is true, I think, that to deny the voice and agency of the native can serve to affirm professional authority. But to *affirm* the voice and agency of the native can *also* serve to affirm professional authority. Spivak herself makes this point when she extends the *Jane Eyre* problematic to feminists, like herself, who highlight rather than neglect the "native female" subject. In terms of the position ascribed to the intellectual, to do the opposite of what *Jane Eyre* does, to preserve rather than destroy the Third World Other, is again a matter of imperialism, she argues – disciplinary imperialism. Considering "the Third World as distant cultures, exploited but with intact literary heritages waiting to be recovered, interpreted, and curricularized," she says, "expands the empire of the literary discipline."[52] Professional concern with Third World texts in the metropolis again means upward mobility, this time the upward mobility of a native elite – "the old scenario of empowering a privileged group or a group susceptible to upward mobility as the authentic inhabitants of the margin."[53] Intellectuals can hide their own self-interest behind a "positive" view of "the native," just as they can hide it behind neglect of "the native."

What then can or should intellectuals *do* with their self-interest, especially if they cannot ask anyone to believe they are not self-interested? Spivak is almost unique among contemporary critics in suggesting, however delicately, that they should *not* hide it. In "Can the Subaltern Speak?", she writes: "The banality of leftist intellectuals' lists of self-knowing, politically canny subalterns stands revealed; representing them, the intellectuals represent themselves as transparent."[54] They pretend, that is, that it is possible to *refuse* "the institutional privileges of power." And in so doing, they also refuse "the critic's institutional responsibility" (280). In this view, it is worse to pretend one can refuse the privileges of power than to acknowledge that those privileges exist and cannot be wished away.

Their materiality must be made visible, not left transparent, yet it must also be accepted. In the privileges of power begins responsibility.

Spivak expresses no absolute faith that consciousness of the privileges of power will indeed end in institutional responsibility. But she inspires a measured confidence that this is at least possible, for her work exposes the representativeness that, however deviously, reluctantly, and inadequately, goes into the making of our institutional materiality. One path leading back to representativeness is her modified version of the jeremiad. The refusal to ground the intellectual in the representation of others is an indictment of oneself, or of one's profession, for self-aggrandizement and abuse of professional privilege. But in a society based on the principle of self-interest, she who accuses herself of self-interest also removes herself from it, showing in the act of theoretical self-critique that she does not after all act in an exclusively self-interested way. In other words, theory does just what literature and culture were traditionally supposed to do, or at least it offers the same proofs of non-instrumental, not-for-profit virtue. At the same time, this theoretical reflexivity presses the rejection of market principles further. Assuming the inescapability of institutional placement, it offers less an unconditional refusal of representation than an indirect claim to represent better or more properly, a demand for conditions of representation that would be more stringent and responsible. In denying that I have any right to represent anyone, I demonstrate my qualifications as a representer, and will be so understood by all those who know that representation is the name of the game.

This logic, already touched on in Chapter Three, runs the risk of a representational regress whereby any interpretation which invokes the interests or, preferably, the oppression of a given social group in order to bring out a text's meaning and claim to our attention is immediately shown by someone else to have excluded or marginalized some other, preferably still more oppressed group. This critical response is then trumped in the same fashion. And so on. The professionally and politically debilitating prospect that such regress could become infinite has not escaped notice. What has not been much remarked, however, is how this professional deformation reflects on the normal functioning of the professional formation. If this deformed hyper-sensitivity *does* function, if the oppression and suffering of some collectivity can indeed become an intensely, almost embarrassingly desirable constituent of professional interpretation, it is because the work of interpretation is inevitably a work of representation in the political sense of the word – a sense that of course requires strenuous explication. One might even describe such representation, choosing one's metaphor carefully, as a quantity of cultural capital without which a critic cannot embark on his or her critical enterprise.

The attractiveness of Spivak's approach to this issue appears more dramatic if we contrast it with Pierre Bourdieu's concept of cultural capital and his superficially similar critique of legitimation. According to Bourdieu, in "Les usages du 'peuple'," both Spivak's argument and Parry's argument would correspond to options which are exercised all the time.[55] As a term, Bourdieu writes, "the people" can always be understood as "stakes in a fight between intellectuals" (178). The "negative" version (here, Spivak's, though Spivak does not actually make use of so crude a phrase) tends to appear in the discourse of relatively well-established professionals, who see "the people" largely as "obstacles" to their "monopoly of legitimate competence" (179). A more "positive" view (here, Parry's) tends to come from intellectuals who are "dominated in the field of specialists," and who therefore rehabilitate the people in order to gain leverage against other professionals and "to exalt themselves."

However reductive, this does not seem entirely off the mark. What Bourdieu does not say is where he himself stands when he rejects both of these self-authorizing views of the people. If invocation of the people can *work* as self-authorization, if it can actually help move someone up the ladder, then Bourdieu is clearly assuming a model of intellectual space in which there is more than one principle of upward mobility and social support – a space, to anticipate, where possession of cultural capital is not the only way of getting off the ground and staying there. And he is also assuming that ideas and intellectuals *require* support. If one occupies a position from which one's voice is heard in public, some force must have raised one up. To what force does he attribute his own elevation?

In a conversation with Terry Eagleton published in *New Left Review*, Bourdieu offers a revealing defense of the concept of cultural capital against the newly fashionable cultural studies and popular culture. He declares:

> It is a form of dominant chic among intellectuals to say "Look at these cartoons," or some other cultural item, "do they not display great cultural creativity?" Such a person is saying, "You don't see that, but I do, and I am the first to see it." The perception may be valid; but there

is an overestimation of the capacity of these new things to change the structure of the distribution of symbolic capital. To exaggerate the extent of change is, in a sense, a form of populism. You mystify the people when you say "Look, rap is great".... you forget what remains the dominant form, and that you still can't realize symbolic profits from rap, in the main social games.[56]

Bourdieu's curious will to reduce the motives of cultural studies to personal self-interest ("You don't see that, but I do, and I am the first to see it.") invites us to take a second look at self-interest, including his own. And what is thus revealed is paradigmatic. What is the source of Bourdieu's striking assumption that there indeed exists and has always existed a single "dominant form" of culture, a single source of "symbolic profits," a single set of "social games" that count? From New York, this assumption looks immediately counter-intuitive, and even in centralized Paris it can hardly be taken for granted. It is hard not to notice, therefore, that Bourdieu's interest in defending the notion of a single "dominant form" coincides with an interest in defending the "symbolic profits" that he himself has drawn from analyzing this dominant form, that is, from the discovery or the invention of "cultural capital." The threat to cultural capital posed by cultural studies is clear. For Bourdieu, culture is necessarily empty of any popular or democratic input. Its contents are arbitrary, fixed in advance by the state, and ruled only by the goal of allowing the dominant class to win at the "main social games" and thus maintain its privileges.[57] If culture's contents were *not* arbitrary (as indeed the metaphor of capital suggests), if "the people" had some special access, competence, or authority where culture is concerned, then the system could not work as he describes.[58] If the creators of rap could derive significant symbolic or social profits from their creation, for example, then it would be clear that the state is not the one dominant, all-determining factor, and the metaphor of cultural capital would collapse.

As far as the logic of legitimation is concerned, the crucial point here is Bourdieu's own relation to the state. How can he afford to be cynically amused by those who invoke "the people" or celebrate popular creativity? What resources give him the confidence to accuse these populists of self-interest without fearing that he will be tasked with self-interest in return? The answer is, of course, that he is backed by the limitless credit of the state. Or, to switch metaphors, that he has prostrated himself before a still higher authority than the people. The state, source of a lofty legitimacy which need not stoop to courting the populace, is the malevolent deity which pulls the strings of cultural capital. In discovering or inventing the notion of cultural capital, in other words, Bourdieu was not only professing faith in a superhuman power, but seizing the massive scale or scope of injustice it produces as the measure of his own legitimation. Its ability to persist in evil-doing becomes the guarantee that the arc of his own social ascent will not droop, that he will stay aloft. Monotheism guarantees his disinterestedness. If there is only one true god, then his heretic (or prophet – the two are almost inter-changeable) becomes a figure of altruistic universality, and the opponents of lesser or gentler gods, who are also one's own opponents, become mere self-interested imposters. Careerwise, malevolence works as well as benevolence, and denunciation of the deity works as well as the chanting of his praises. As a source of legitimation, the state, like the sublime, is beyond good and evil. Evil provides the same vocational results as good so long as Bourdieu can defend the state's sole, uncontested power.

I am not suggesting that Bourdieu, a professor at the state-supported Collège de France, is either wrong or right to rely on the state's implicit legitimation.[59] The state is not intrinsically more unworthy of such use than other authorities. Indeed, one possible explanation for the success of so-called French theory in the US, including Bourdieu's own success, is that it transported a highly statist mode of thinking – thinking that reacted against the state, of course, but for that very reason was saturated in the state's centralizing and totalizing powers – into a nation where the state apparatus is relatively weak or diffuse, where certain basic institu-tions of social democracy have never come into being, and where those centralizing and totalizing concepts could therefore serve a desirable purpose even while they were subjected to critique.[60] If, as one might argue, Foucault's narrative of an ever-expanding dis-ciplinary state has all but replaced Matthew Arnold as the major inspiration to cultural studies in America, one reason is that it too offers a negative or malevolent but parallel and proximate version of Arnold's beneficent cultural authority.[61]

For Bourdieu to allow the state to legitimate his refusal of legitimation is of course a form of bad faith. But its more serious fault is indolence. Bourdieu's deep, static pessimism, made possible by his forgetfulness of the organic composition of cultural capital, rests on the assumed constancy of the state.[62] He is so comfortable because he assumes the state will always be there to hate, and (either for that reason, or because it is such an evil power) that it cannot itself require legitimating, at least from left-wing intellectuals like himself. But these are lazy assumptions. The present crisis of the social-democratic state in Western Europe, along with the more dramatic collapse of the socialist states of Eastern Europe, has led to what Étienne Balibar calls "identity panic." These days we can take for granted neither the durable power of the state (vis-à-vis international capital, on one side, and the rise of the new racisms and nationalisms, on the other) nor its political malevolence, however comfortable for those who warm themselves in friction with it. The system by which biting the hand that feeds you is how you get fed therefore invites new scrutiny. Legitimation becomes a larger and more open question. In the US, twelve years of Reagan/Bush privatization, backed up by strong if hypocritical anti-statist rhetoric, have made legitimation that sets itself instinctively against the state look almost as politically misguided as the policy intellectuals' identification with the state.

This is not to say that, with the Clinton/Gore victory, intellectuals are now free to identify with the state. It is to say, however, that there is no simple opposition here between Bourdieu and Spivak. Spivak has elaborated a statist style of thought in a place – the US – where the state has been notoriously weak. The ambivalent secular vocations she has inspired are inseparable from this theoretical traveling. Unlike Bourdieu, however, she has made traveling a part of vocation. If Spivak's India-to-America *Bildungsroman* and her jet-setting cosmopolitanism, like Bourdieu's chair at the Collège de France, are always good for a cheap shot, they are also good for more than that. The world capitalist system may share some of the otherworldliness of Bourdieu's monotheist state, but it gets us beyond the nation's insularity, stretches the body of texts at hand so as to include new cultural constituencies. All the qualms about the right and the power to represent should not be allowed to camouflage the primordial, overwhelming drive toward representation that they escort and enable. Her project includes the democratic recomposition and redistribution of cultural capital.

If Spivak's accounts of international cultural interaction force us to rethink what we mean both by culture and by interaction, they simultaneously make both available, piercing the huge areas of motivated ignorance that surround and structure Western knowledge. If these results remain asymmetrical, as of course they do, and if they remain for the moment within the terms set by the profession, as they must, they are nevertheless a step toward an international public sphere, undreamed of by Habermas, where the phrase "citizen of the world" might be possible to pronounce without the usual pang. The cosmopolitanism of the contemporary American academy invites more cynical analyses: as the expression of an elite of apparently disinterested class aliens who refuse national limits, along with all other social membership, only to the extent that capital does, for example, or as the expression of an older class hierarchy that resists America's imperial nationalism in part because it sets its cultural standards above and against those of ordinary citizens. I prefer a third option: cosmopolitanism as the provocatively impure but irreducible combination of a certain privilege at home, as part of a real belonging in institutional places, with a no less real but much less common (and therefore highly desirable) extension of democratic, anti-imperial principles abroad. As Neil Smith has suggested, rethinking the imperfections of democracy requires rethinking space: the pertinent sub-national and supra-national units of agency and communication, differentials of scale that rule out many of our most frequent moralizing, universalizing gestures and demand a politics that is also differential. The most generous and useful way to begin rethinking cosmopolitanism, it seems to me, is neither as ideal unplaceableness nor as sordid elitism, but as a way of relativizing and problematizing the scale and the units of democracy.[63] As the invocation of citizenship in a unit that is phantasmatic or impossible, the term keeps us from forgetting that what is democratic progress at home is not necessarily democratic progress abroad. And that what may seem privileged on one scale may elsewhere be recognized as an extension of the constituency of knowledge, a genuine and even unprecedented pushing back of democracy's borders.

CONCLUSION

Aesthetics and Social Work

But the account, in the end, seems strangely undynamic, as if the
important conflicts have by now been resolved.
                                    Alan Brinkley

In *Literature, Politics, and Culture in Postwar Britain* (1989), Alan
Sinfield describes what he calls "left-culturism" in terms that should
recall a good deal of what has been said in these pages. Left-
culturism, for Sinfield, belonged to "middle-class dissidence." Like
other middle-class dissidence, it was animated by "hostility to the
hegemony of the principal part of the middle class – the businessmen,
industrialists and empire-builders."[1] The embodiment of this hostility was culture itself, which left-culturists understood as the antithesis of and the antidote to the self-interested world of the capitalist
market. This did not mean that they necessarily embraced culture to
the exclusion of other sorts of political activity. It did mean, on the
other hand, that out of the field of other political actors available,
they tended to ally or align culture with the one which best seemed
to represent a public or disinterested counterforce to the market:
namely, the state. "Most left culturists believed that commerce was
the problem and state funding the answer" (245).

According to Sinfield, the apogee of left-culturism came in the
1960s, a decade remarkable less for its "degree of disaffection than
for the persisting trust in the system.... In effect, there was a
persisting faith in social democracy, a belief that the state would
respond to just demands once they were sufficiently urgently
expressed" (248). But the 1960s also marked the "supersession"
(283) of left-culturism. With the advent of contestatory subcultures
(rock, gay, etc.) that defined themselves by means of, rather than
against, the market, the antithesis of culture and commerce began to
break down. "Left-culturists were disconcerted," Sinfield notes, "by
the combination of commerce and rebelliousness" in 1960s pop
culture. On the other hand, and partly as a result, faith in the state
as redemption from the market also began to disintegrate. During the

212

long, lean years of Thatcherism that followed, such faith could not have seemed more misplaced.

Across the Atlantic, as we have seen, much the same logic joins culture, commerce, and the left. The term that is missing from this list is the state, which doesn't seem to fit the American example. In Britain, on the other hand, Sinfield seems to have little need for the concept of professionalism that has seemed so indispensable here. The parallel breaks down. But perhaps its breakdown around these two terms can help specify some of the political assumptions and unresolved questions implicit in the foregoing discussion of American cultural politics.

In the 1960s, commercialized popular culture was in some respects more developed in America, or at least more organic to American oppositional feeling. Indeed, the perceived Americanness of already existing pop culture enabled British left-culturism to draw sustenance from a certain nationalist resentment. "The fact that 'mass' culture appeared to derive from the United States was convenient, for it meant that working-class culture had been interfered with and was not guilty of its own corruption" (241). At the same time, the immense value American intellectuals placed on the imported work of Hoggart, Williams, and Thompson suggests that left-culturism provided something that the American left was missing. The missing quantity was certainly not contempt for commerial pop culture. The Frankfurt School critique of the "culture industry" did not displease the American left; distrust of "mass" culture was at least as marked among the New York intellectuals, for example, as among Hoggart, Williams, and Thompson.[2] As always, the absence of a major American political party on the left must be factored into any contrast. But the clearest sign of difference is the lack of an American counterpart to that positive faith in the state for which Sinfield reprimands the British. American intellectuals cannot be so reprimanded, for no such faith is to be detected in them. (Its place was occupied, one might speculate, by faith in aesthetic modernism, a smaller-scale faith which could help organize a professional discipline but could not be expected to mobilize broader social and political influence.) If Sinfield's group portrait of left-culturism does not quite match the US, that is, one crucial factor is the underdevelopment of the American welfare state.

It is something of a cliché among sociologists that the late and/or weak development of the American state explains the relatively greater significance in the US of the phenomenon that Sinfield has

213

little cause to mention: professionalism. According to Dietrich Rueschemeyer, what distinguishes American from European professionalism is "the relative timing of the emergence of the modern state and the expansion of capitalist market exchange."

> Where a centralized bureaucratic state emerged in advance of full-blown capitalism, it set the cast for the expanding role of expert occupations; where the entrepreneurial transformation of exchange and production took place in the presence of a weaker administrative state apparatus, much more autonomous professional groups reorganized themselves so as to seize the new opportunities.

The latter description holds for the US, where professions are thus closer to the market and more independent of the state. The former description pertains on the whole in Europe, where professions

> kept a greater distance from the morality of the marketplace. Pre-capitalist and anticapitalist principles were generally strengthened by their orientation towards the state. Organizational loyalty played a central role in the state-centered professional ethos. This loyalty, more than the moral mission of an autonomous professional group, gave legitimation to the experts' claim to act in the public interest.[3]

Though the United Kingdom arguably has a weaker state apparatus than many other European nations, this contrast would still justify Jonathan Culler's observation: in Britain "teachers of literature are likely to think of themselves either as intellectuals or as university teachers" because "professionalization is considerably less advanced," while "in America the professor of English is perhaps above all a member of the profession."[4]

Roughly speaking, then, one might say that in Britain professionalism could less easily function, like the state, as a figure for the transcendence of private interest. Evelyn Waugh, ranting against "the new barbarism which lurks in academic byways," speaks of professionalism as the effort "to introduce rigid trades-unionism in the arts."[5] The same telling metaphor appears in the title of John Gross's diatribe against the "professional academic": "The Man of Letters in a Closed Shop."[6] From the heights of gentlemanly or state-sponsored culture, professionalism seems indistinguishable from trade unionism, itself looked down upon as the pursuit of crude private interest. Even the left-culturists of the 1960s, who did not share this view of trade unionism, had little more patience for professionalism than Waugh or Gross.

In the US there is of course a similar tradition of literary anti-professionalism. But those who identify with the high-minded, public-spirited amateurs of the past, whether left or right, lack comparable support from the lingering cultural influence of the aristocracy or from proximity to state power. And in part for that reason, a certain claim to public-spiritedness could devolve upon the distinctly decentered, non-governmental vocabulary of profession-alism. The movements of the 1960s are indicative. These movements are often violently anti-professional. But the very violence of the attacks testifies that, however negatively, the critics are honoring the profession's claims to public service. Their demand is for the profession to deliver on its promises. This is the precondition for the professions to retain their legitimacy – and it is clear that the critics usually wish them to retain it, if only so that they themselves can appropriate it and turn it to their own radical purposes. In *The Politics of Literature* (1970), a classic manifesto of 1960s sensibility, Louis Kampf and Paul Lauter take aim at "compulsive profession-alism" (15), "another professional doing his thing" (18), "the demands of professionalism" (20), "the growing disparity between the concerns of professionals and those of students" (29), and so on. Yet they also propose that teachers "should conceive as central to their *work* entering actively into political struggle" (44). Their *work* – the italics are in the original.[7] In this view, it is not necessary to get outside one's work in order to enter "actively into political struggle"; even or especially for white-collar professionals, the struggle is assumed to be always already at hand, right there at one's desk or lectern. "By the early sixties," Richard Flacks writes, "the search for an authentic career had become central for young intellectuals."[8] The word career speaks volumes about the trust that ideals of radical social change could reasonably be accommodated to the activity of earning a living, and even to upward mobility.

With the privilege of hindsight, it is tempting to chide the naïveté of this faith in professionalism, just as Sinfield chides the left-culturists for their faith in the welfare state. But this may not be the imperative that Sinfield's story supports most strongly. And there are other lessons to be drawn from its approximate parallels.

Sinfield's judgment of the moment of left-culturism is ambivalent. He appreciates the achievements that men like Hoggart and Williams left behind in influential institutions:

> left-culturism was far from ineffectual. It gained a powerful position in the academic and professional social sciences and humanities; all kinds

of contributions became best-sellers. Its attitudes filtered into the education system, and key texts went rapidly onto secondary-school syllabuses and stayed there. Left-culturism helped modernize and hence sustain the public service concept of broadcasting in Britain. (249)

On the other hand, Sinfield is critical of the structural blindness of the left-culturists to their own interest and location – a consequence of defining themselves on the basis of culture – that led them through a disingenuous affirmation of the working class. "For all their concern with working-class culture – indeed partly through that concern – left-liberal intellectuals were actually engaged in making their own culture" (260). Yet as the second thought ("*through* that concern") suggests, he does not profess to know whether they could have achieved as much *without* this affirmation, that is, without an implicit claim to represent others.

In conclusion, Sinfield enjoins the middle-class dissidents to follow the example of today's subcultures and "new social movements," often middle class as well. That is, they should be themselves:

> Middle-class dissidence has to recognize its own traditions, concerns and modes of operation, not to imagine itself as universal or as a misplaced version of someone else's politics and culture. It has to examine and build upon its characteristic resources; thus it may lose its apologetic tone and secure a basis for effective political analysis and action. (274)

But this imperative does not touch on the question of why being themselves should mean being on the left, why it should not mean being self-interested in the same sense as a corporate raider. Nor does it take up the question of whether being themselves might necessarily mean *continuing* to assert an ethic of public service, that is, representing more than merely themselves – as indeed Sinfield's broad survey might be felt to represent more than himself.

These ambivalences and hesitations can be summed up in Sinfield's attitude toward the state. He concludes: "Many people no longer believe in the capacity of government to deliver on the pact of welfare-capitalism" (282). Written under Thatcher, this conclusion carefully omits to judge whether these "many people" are correct, or more precisely whether or not the demand that the government deliver should be revived in today's politics. Sinfield's usefully corrective emphasis on local subcultures and on self-definition in rather than against the marketplace in no way excludes the possibility that, rather than abandoning the state which has already abandoned them, intellectuals should now answer Thatcherism by trying to take back the state, even in the compromised form of "welfare-capitalism."

This answer to the question of where to go from here undoubtedly offers the basis for an ample and progressive alliance. Harold Perkin, whose *The Rise of Professional Society* was also published in 1989, ended that book with a chapter about Thatcherism called "The Backlash Against Professional Society." Perkin's view of Thatcherism as "a reaction of one part of the professional class, the private sector managers of the great corporations and their allies, who had never felt the same degree of need for state support, against the other, public sector professions largely employed by the state," stretches the term professionalism too thin; expanding so as to contain all the decisive social phenomena, the concept of professionalism loses its tightness (ix). But Perkin helpfully suggests that the Thatcherite program of privatization and austerity has itself stretched the term, or the number of people who might be ready to identify with it. Those affected, or disaffected, by the withdrawal of the state make up a broad and impressive front, and their political potential seems worthy of attention. Reviewing A.H. Halsey's *Decline of Donnish Dominion: The British Academic Professions in the Twentieth Century* (1992), Perkin spoke more recently of a real "decline in wealth, status, and influence" due to budget cuts.[9] "The profession has been 'proletarianized', transformed from a community of scholars into the wage-labor force of a nationalized industry." And this has already had political consequences: "In politics academics have proletarianized themselves by voting increasingly like 'a fair sample of manual workers' rather than with the middle class to which they belong."

Thatcherism's winding down may do something to resuscitate a fading loyalty to the socialist project of reappropriating the state, while also spreading this project outward into the market and thus politicizing professionalism in a new way. And the end of the Reagan/Bush era may offer the symmetrical possibility of rechanneling American professional energies back toward the state – of stressing the politics in cultural politics. This speculation builds on the most unexpected outcome of the comparison with British left-culturism: the idea that the state may serve as the center of *both* national intelligentsias, though they have circled it at quite different distances. I am proposing, in other words, that perhaps American professionalism too must be measured and weighed in its relation to the welfare state, for each is entangled in the fate of the other. Remembering the weakness of social democracy in America, the comparison thus points toward the political project, which professionals would share with many other Americans, of reviving and enlarging those areas and purposes of state activity that are so strangely marginalized by the word "welfare."

This is to say, without entering into serious discussion of the extensive literature in the sociology of the professions, that debate over professionalism might profitably be extricated from the Weberian problematic in which it has been largely stuck. To ask how distinct professionalism is from state bureaucracies, how antagonistic it is to bureaucracies, or how successfully it resists the encroachment of bureaucracies is to ask the wrong question. For these questions make sense only if it is assumed, in the tradition of Weber, that the state is a principle of instrumental rationality coldly and relentlessly overrunning the warm, not-yet-disenchanted collegiality of professional community. In C. Wright Mills's words, "Bureaucratic institutions invade all professions."[10] Whether one argues for or against the proposition that professions can successfully stand up to bureaucracy, one accepts the doubly faulty premise that bureaucracies are necessarily the enemy and that professions are intrinsically a redeeming force. Thinking of professionalism and the state together again means recalling that both are the provisional results of struggles over representation. Look back to the anti-trust legislation of the Progressive era, for example, and to the popular struggles that went into placing the word "welfare" in the welfare state, and you are obliged to recognize some degree of popular will invested in the structures of the state, even if the compromised form they take is that of "corporate liberalism." As historian James Livingston writes, "it, too, was (and is) the effective creation of all parties to the bargain."[11] The welfare state has no eternal, essential identity as a tool of capital. Nor can professionalism be identified once and for all as a conspiracy against the laity, a meritocratic masking of social inequality, or, on the contrary, the revolutionary expression of some "New Class."[12] Both state and profession are sedimented composites of past social forces, democratic and anti-democratic, which the same forces continue to shape and reshape.

This alignment of professionalism and the state also runs athwart a common Marxist view. According to Magali Sarfatti Larson's *The Rise of Professionalism*, professionalization was "the process by which producers of special services sought to constitute *and control* a market for their expertise" (xvi). As Larson's market-oriented narrative approaches the present, however, control of the market becomes a much less significant factor, for professions increasingly find themselves attached to institutions which have already done their controlling of the market for them, at least provisionally. To take a pertinent example, this is the case for most academics. Unlike doctors or lawyers, academics don't have to address their market directly; except in moments of legitimation crisis or emergency, it is largely organized and controlled by the institution for which they work, the university. Partially protected from the open market by a host organization, whether public or private, they are professionals in much the same sense as social workers: dependent on the state, making their claims to the state and from within the state. Their true ancestors, that is, are not law and medicine but the clergy and the military. Yet Larson omits the clergy and the military from her discussion. As Terence Halliday comments, "one has the sense that the changes Larson finds in the character of professions as a whole, from early capitalism to its present form, are partially to be explained by taking into account a set of occupations in the latter half of the book whose structural forebears she refused to take into account in the first part."[13]

Where state institutions already control a market for expertise, professionalism must be interpreted differently. According to Larson, the new, second-order professionalization projects that arise in bureaucracies simply aim at winning the rewards of professional status, including prestige, income, and closure of access. But they are clearly more interesting than this – if not necessarily in their motives, then certainly in the social consequences of those motives. It is a remarkable fact about the "bureaucratic profession" of social work, for example, that its professional self-consciousness, like the recently publicized self-consciousness of teachers in the humanities and social sciences, tends to be intensely involved in some form of radical politics. Since the beginning, Richard Cloward writes in his foreword to Linda Reeser and Irwin Epstein's *Professionalization and Activism in Social Work* (1990), social work has been pulled apart by its dual identity "as a profession and as a social movement."[14] "To this day, the debate continues over whether social work is, or should be, a profession or whether it has abandoned its social action commitments to the poor and oppressed" (2). Though the question is posed as a choice, it is clear that neither option speaks as the true or single voice of the profession. The profession is best represented, rather, by the debate itself, which collectively clings to "social action commitments to the poor and oppressed" *and* to professional identity at the same time. And this double loyalty is precisely what the authors of this study discover when they inquire into the attitudes of social workers. Where one might expect professionalization to mean "political neutrality," the book reports that from the 1960s through the 1980s, only about 25 percent of social workers expressed the opinion that "social workers should avoid public expression of political values in professional roles" (88). Generally speaking, becoming "more professionalized" seems not to have meant, for social work, becoming "less activist" (xv).

There is no question that activism is also an assertion of professional identity and professional self-interest. Social work's perpetual posing of political questions about itself serves as a form of legitimation. It aims at keeping government bureaucracies from abusing social workers as they abuse other, non-professional wage laborers. It does so in part by reminding the government that it too draws its legitimacy from its supposed commitment to "the poor and oppressed," and could lose some of that legitimacy if it doesn't show more respect. This strategy need not be shown to have been extremely successful (it has had to overcome the lack of distinct expertise that is social work's major professional disadvantage), or even as successful as unionization, which it can also accompany, in order for its principle to be recognized.[15] Even inside the state, there are professional reasons to speak critically of the state and the status quo. And at the same time, there are professional reasons to defend and legitimize the state itself, for example against privatization and taxpayer revolt. To protect the state is to protect your job. In a routine sort of paradox, this is one thing social workers do, or fail to do, when they attempt to speak up for clients and *against* the state. All of this is compatible with self-interest – and all of it is arguably in the interests of the clients as well. It simply reaffirms the point with which the last chapter ended: that both state and profession exist in an organic and dynamic relation to a political constituency.

Examples outside social work might be multiplied. Myron and Penina Glazer have studied the "new tradition of dissent" which arose from "the struggle over the new regulations of the private sector in the 1960s and 1970s" and is embodied by the so-called "whistleblowers."[16] Largely professional, these were on the whole "conservative people devoted to their work and their organizations," men and women who had succeeded in building careers "by conforming to the requirements of bureaucratic life."

> Invariably, they believed that they were defending the true mission of their organization by resisting illicit practices and could not comprehend how their superiors could risk the good name of their company by producing defective products, the reputation of their hospital by abusing and neglecting patients, or the integrity of their agency by allowing their safety reports to be tampered with or distorted. . . . Also required was a belief that something could be done to rectify the illegal or unethical situation. (3–12)

This confidence or sense of legitimacy clearly extended beyond the bounds of the organization.

> They rejected a definition of professional ethics that required only a narrow range of responsibilities to colleagues and clients. Their brand of professionalism was enriched by a broad obligation to others deriving from humane, religious, and communal values. (70)

It would be a mistake, however, to see this "broad obligation to others" as "deriving from humane, religious, and communal values" alone. Professionalism is not simply "enriched" by obligations that come from elsewhere. One crucial fault of Larson's view of professionalism, and the many others like it, is this assumption that political opposition within the professions always has its source somewhere outside the professions, in some other loyalty, some other membership, some other set of values. It is true, of course, that loyalties and memberships overlap and that the friction between them can be a fruitful source of oppositional energy in one or the other. To belong to a particular church, class, race, gender, generation, and so on is to see one's other places of belonging with a different eye. And given the notion of professions as hermetically sealed against the outer world, there is some use in making this point. But the same regress that is applied to the professions can also operate on any of the above: as soon as you scrutinize it closely, as soon as this outside is explored as an inside, it too becomes a coherent, enclosed, balanced system that in turn demands some elsewhere so as to explain resistance, self-criticism, and movement inside it. The regress, which is undoubtedly a symptom of professional deformation, must be arrested somewhere, and the professions are as good as place as any to begin. Professional opposition in America is not a happy, untheorizable accident or the residue of a political moment like the 1960s whose energy came solely from outside. It is produced, along with much that is not oppositional at all, by what makes people professional in the first place.

And how much, finally, can be expected from professionalism? For every whistle-blower, how many other professionals remain silent and complicit despite professionalism, or even because of it? How far does professional responsibility ever extend beyond accountability to peers, and how effective is accountability to peers in protecting the public? According to Rueschemeyer in *Power and the Division of Labour* (1986), "professional privileges" are often not even "contingent on the delivery of competent service and the maintenance of a professional ethos. These privileges . . . are quite immune to a good deal of public suspicion and even plausible accusations of incompetence and unethical behavior" (120). If one looks at the Progressive Era's legacy of "bureaucratic organization" and "professionalization" in a Gramscian light, that is, as embodying in varying degrees the will, consent, and struggle of "intellectuals" and "politicians" as well as "the unionized sector of the working class," all of them "active participants" in the "convening" of "corporate liberalism," then what follows?[17] The immense influence of the result is clear, but what value are we supposed to place on it? Must we look upon the welfare state and find it good? How much power and motive for change do professionals actually display?[18]

These are questions to which I have no satisfactory answers. I have only a way of facing their openness. In another reading of the American heritage of Progressivism and pragmatism – a heritage that is deeply divided on the subject of professionalism, as my earlier remarks on Richard Rorty have suggested – Alan Dawley's *Struggles for Justice* (1992) asserts the existence of a split between progressive liberalism and managerial liberalism. The victory of the latter, by the end of the Progressive era, is for Dawley the regrettable victory of professionalism as we continue to know it. In his review of the book, Alan Brinkley remarks upon Dawley's inability to bring the ending alive: "the account, in the end, seems strangely undynamic, as if the important conflicts have by now been resolved."[19]

In making this sentence the epigraph to this conclusion, I have invited the reflection that the same may be true of my own argument. When I've tried to make arguments like this one in the past, I've come up against what I myself sometimes felt was a final insufficiency. Arguing that what professions are already doing is not objectionable in principle, even where I disagree with specifics, does not set up a strong tension or friction with the status quo. One feels the lack especially at that concluding point where by convention even the most routine or insipid arguments are expected to strike a hortatory note, to whip up a crusade or come down hard on the neglect of some virtue. We expect to be told in a conclusion why we should care, or at least what is urgent enough to need our immediate attention. One catches oneself wondering, therefore, if readers will find anything here but a strenuous complacency.

I would like to feel, on the contrary, that this book addresses itself precisely to the "undynamic" quality of professionalization stories of decline and fall, which have nowhere to go beyond that (early) endpoint and thus nothing to say about the near-universal paradox that they are themselves being written by professionals. The most dangerous complacencies are often those that accompany the harshest, most monotonously pessimistic readings of present history, thereby justifying in silence the space in the ivory tower that the writer does not otherwise acknowledge, and that the writer is therefore unmotivated to step outside of. There is no complacency, on the other hand, in admitting that the privileges of the university are real and sometimes useful, or that they depend on a relation to the outside that is both precarious and politically polyvalent.

One does not need to declare – there are good reasons for not doing so – that professionals constitute some new revolutionary class in order to restore the dynamism to a story that is very much a continuing one, morally and politically unresolved. It is hard to see, these days, what is and isn't the proper goal of a revolutionary politics. The division of labor, for example, which some take as synonymous with professionalism and specialization, no longer seems quite the appropriate target for revolutionary efforts. As Andrew Sayer and Richard Walker write in *The New Social Economy* (1992), it is a "differentiation ... which socialism must deal with (but cannot abolish)."[20] "Reformers and revolutionaries have too often relied on ideals of the new economic order that abolish the division of labor with a wave of the hand ... barring a general return to primitive economies, this is impossible" (9).

Is it enough, then, to claim that that middle-class radicals have interests in the state and in socialism and that these interests coincide in large part, here and now, with the interests of broad sections of the American people who have seen the state withdraw from them or who have never been extended its entitlements, protections, and rights?[21] In one sense, it is not enough. For the state isn't the single determining site or instance of political value. If the professions rose together with the welfare state, one might also say that they rose along with consumerism, the capitalism side of welfare capitalism, which generated needs professionals would fulfil just as the state generated standards they would enforce. As Sinfield and others have suggested, one can say, apropos of various subcultures, that the market expresses the public will, and one can say so with no more serious caveats than would be needed to say the same of the state. Perhaps the opposition between state and market matters less here than the claims that both market and state put forward on the public.[22] Taking the public as the definitive, more comprehensive category, one could relativize both state and market. Thus professionalism could perhaps be aligned with the new world of compromise formations that may come into view when future historians investigate the genealogy of market socialism.

Cultural politics today is not the sole or most important sort of politics around. But if it has less to do with the state than British left-culturism, like the subcultural successors of left-culturism it has helped the concept of culture acquire a lower-case, plural sense (if also a sense that remains a site of important controversy) that has no lack of political meaning. Opening aesthetics up so as to accommodate this sense of culture, or what George Yudice calls "practical aesthetics," it has also helped us think of the public in the same way: as multiple, concrete publics to which there correspond multiple responsibilities.[23] To do culture has thus meant to be in public, linked to real groups struggling in the real world, groups that make their demands not only in terms of culture, but to the state. The complexity of that link has yet to be explored, along with its actual and potential consequences on both sides. And the demands – for equality, recognition, expression, justice, material entitlements – have yet to be met. Both conditions offer significant work that has yet to be accomplished.

Notes

Preface

1. Antonio Gramsci, *Selections from the Prison Notebooks*, ed. and trans. Quintin Hoare and Geoffrey Novell Smith (New York: International Publishers, 1971), p. 324. Alan Wald, *The New York Intellectuals: The Rise and Decline of the Anti-Stalinist Left from the 1930s to the 1980s* (Chapel Hill: University of North Carolina Press, 1987), p. 4.
2. These quotations, representative of many others, are from Richard Hofstadter, Régis Debray, Jean Bethke Elshtain, and Russell Jacoby.

Introduction

1. Andrew Rosenthal, "Quayle Attacks a 'Cultural Elite' in Speech Invoking Moral Values," *New York Times*, June 10, 1992, pp. A1, A21. The speech was also perhaps a sincere expression of his feelings. After all, his early failure to achieve academic excellence has been widely reported, as have his more recent problems with spelling.
2. R.W. Apple Jr, "Dan Quayle Steps Front (and Right of) Center," *New York Times*, June 14, 1992, "The Week in Review," pp. 1, 3.
3. Dinesh D'Souza, *Illiberal Education: The Politics of Race and Sex on Campus* (New York: Free Press, 1991), p. 251.
4. Charles Derber, William A. Schwartz, and Yale Magrass, *Power in the Highest Degree: Professionals and the Rise of a New Mandarin Order* (New York: Oxford University Press, 1990), p. 4. In a sort of anarchist anticipation of Quayle, Donald Stabile warns that socialism itself has been a New Class project all along. Donald Stabile, *Prophets of Order: The Rise of the New Class, Technocracy and Socialism in America* (Boston: South End Press, 1984).
5. Shelby Steele, "The New Sovereignty," *Harper's*, 285:1706 (July 1992), p. 50 (pp. 47–54).
6. Russell Jacoby, *The Last Intellectuals: American Culture in the Age of Academe* (New York: Basic Books, 1987), p. 141.
7. Cornel West, *The American Evasion of Philosophy: A Genealogy of Pragmatism* (Madison: University of Wisconsin Press, 1989), p. 7.
8. Richard Rorty, "Habermas and Lyotard on Modernity," in Richard Bernstein, ed., *Habermas and Modernity* (Cambridge, MA: MIT, 1985), pp. 174–5.
9. Richard Rorty, "Reply to Andrew Ross," *Dissent* (Spring 1992), pp. 263–7.

10. See my "Tenured Radicals, the New McCarthyism, and 'PC,'" *New Left Review*, 188 (July/August 1991), pp. 151–7.

11. James Atlas, "The Changing World of New York Intellectuals," *New York Times Magazine*, August 25, 1985, p. 76.

12. In *The Joys of Yiddish* (New York: Pocket Books, 1968), Leo Rosten observes that the *Luftmensh* can have *too many* occupations (the "prototype" had twenty-six) as well as be "one without an occupation."

13. Paul Starr, "Pummelling the Professors," review of Martin Anderson, *Imposters in the Temple* (New York: Simon & Schuster, 1992) in *New York Times Book Review*, August 9, 1992, p. 10.

14. Richard Hofstadter, *Anti-Intellectualism in America* (New York: Knopf, 1963), p. 27.

15. Virginia Woolf, *Three Guineas* (London: Hogarth, 1986), p. 83.

16. Jane Gallop, *Around 1981: Academic Feminist Literary Theory* (New York and London: Routledge, 1992), pp. 4, 5.

17. In this sense, Roger Kimball's *Tenured Radicals*, which denounces from the right the fact that "yesterday's student radical is today's tenured professor or academic dean," comes closer to the truth than the many laments which see only the extinction of the intellectuals and the eclipse of the left: "the radical ethos of the sixties has been all too successful, achieving indirectly in the classroom, faculty meeting, and by administrative decree what it was unable to accomplish on the barricades." Roger Kimball, *Tenured Radicals: How Politics Has Corrupted Our Higher Education* (New York: Harper, 1990), pp. xiv–xv. For all the right's efforts to trivialize its enemies by presenting them as merely aesthetic (George Will speaks, for example, of "the striking of poses and the enjoyment of catharsis" in a "theater of victimization," and so on), it accuses them of successfully corrupting the country's youth and winning over administrators in the country's most prestigious universities. It treats the cultural left as a power in the world. The cultural left should learn from it.

18. The fact that the Fall is held to be from culture as well as from politics (just as it is largely a Fall into the universities in the US, but *from* the universities into the media in France) is certainly good cause for suspecting that we are dealing here with myth rather than historical actuality. This confusion also does an injustice to the brilliant historical achievement of the New York intellectuals, which in large part came from *sustaining the tension* between the disparate claims of art and politics. See, however, Andrew Ross, *No Respect: Intellectuals and Popular Culture* (New York: Routledge, 1989) for the high cost of defining intellectuals against popular culture.

19. Richard Johnson, "Culture and the Historians," in John Clarke, Chas Critcher, and Richard Johnson, eds, *Working-Class Culture: Studies in History and Theory* (London: Hutchinson, in association with the Centre for Contemporary Cultural Studies, University of Birmingham, 1979).

20. Cynthia Ozick, "A Critic at Large: T.S. Eliot at 101," *New Yorker*, November 20, 1989, pp. 119–54. The following paragraphs draw on

my "Othering the Academy: Professionalism and Multiculturalism," *Social Research*, 58:2 (Summer 1991), pp. 355–72.

21. Burton J. Bledstein, *The Culture of Professionalism: The Middle Class and the Development of Higher Education in America* (New York: Norton, 1976), p. 100.

22. The preceding paragraphs draw on my "Modernism and Professionalism: The Case of William Carlos Williams," in Richard Waswo, ed., *On Poetry and Poetics*, Swiss Papers in English Language and Literature, 2 (Tübingen: Günter Narr Verlag, 1985), pp. 191–205.

23. For further elaboration, see Gerald Graff and Bruce Robbins, "Cultural Criticism," in Stephen Greenblatt and Giles Gunn, eds, *Redrawing the Boundaries of Literary Study* (New York: Modern Language Association, 1993). On the contradiction between the aesthetic and intellectual disciplines concerned with the aesthetic, see Terry Eagleton, *The Ideology of the Aesthetic* (Oxford: Basil Blackwell, 1990), pp. 2–3.

24. David D. Cooper, "Beyond the Stockpiling of Criticism," *PMLA*, 106:5 (October 1991), p. 1183.

25. Brian McCrae, *Addison and Steele are Dead: The English Department, Its Canon, and the Professionalization of Literary Criticism* (Newark, DE: University of Delaware Press, 1990), pp. 12–14.

26. Sacvan Bercovitch, *The American Jeremiad* (Madison: University of Wisconsin Press, 1978). "The essence of the sermon form ... is its unshakable optimism. In explicit opposition to the traditional mode, it inverts the doctrine of vengeance into a promise of ultimate success, affirming the world, and despite the world, the inviolability of the colonial cause" (6–7). The jeremiad "joined lament and celebration in reaffirming America's mission" (11).

27. T.S. Klepp, "Every Man a Philosopher-King," *New York Times Magazine*, December 2, 1990, p. 57 (pp. 56 ff.).

28. West, p. 203.

29. Kenneth Burke, *Permanence and Change* (Berkeley: University of California Press, 1984), pp. 256–7, quoted in Paul Jay, "Kenneth Burke and the Motives of Rhetoric," *American Literary History*, 1:3 (Fall 1989), p. 543. The quotation continues: "and to have a vocation is to have an ethics or scheme of values, and to have a scheme of values is to have a point of view, and to have a point of view is to have a prejudice or bias which will motivate and color our choice of means."

30. Benjamin R. Barber, "The Civic Mission of the University," *Kettering Review* (Fall 1989), p. 72.

31. Henry Kissinger, *New York Times*, January 24, 1988 (verbatim).

32. Paul Johnson, *Intellectuals* (New York: Harper & Row, 1988), p. 1.

33. Richard Rorty, "Habermas and Lyotard on Modernity," pp. 84, 175.

34. Timothy Murray, *Theatrical Legitimation: Allegories of Genius in Seventeenth-Century England and France* (New York: Oxford University Press, 1987), p. 10.

35. Donald A. Davie, "Poet: Patriot: Interpreter," *Critical Inquiry*, 9 (September 1982), p. 42.

36. Wayne C. Booth, *The Vocation of a Teacher: Rhetorical Occasions,*

1967–1988 (Chicago: University of Chicago Press, 1988), p. 272.

37. This is close to Samuel Haber's argument: "What the professions do (and this helps account for much of their excitement and attainment) is to bring into the modern world ideals and standards that are premodern – both precapitalistic and predemocratic." This is the "special secret" of the professions, which are not "exemplary and up-to-date specimens of modernization," but "transmit, with some modifications, a distinctive sense of authority and honor that has its origins in the class position and occupational preoccupations of eighteenth-century English gentlemen." Samuel Haber, *The Quest for Authority and Honor in the American Professions, 1750–1900* (Chicago: University of Chicago Press, 1991), p. ix.

38. The same associations are celebrated by admirers of vocation, like political scientist Harvey Goldman: "The calling is, at bottom, a form of magic, elevating work into a totem of redemption when transformed into service and a higher ideal in the calling." Harvey Goldman, *Max Weber and Thomas Mann: Calling and the Shaping of the Self* (Berkeley: University of California Press, 1988), p. 205.

39. Bruce Wilshire, *The Moral Collapse of the University: Professionalism, Purity, and Alienation* (Albany: SUNY, 1990), p. xiii. "I am pure and wholly myself, and we are purely and wholly ourselves, because we are clearly other than those others – those uncertified by our professional tests" (xix).

40. Fredric Jameson, "The Vanishing Mediator; or, Max Weber as Storyteller," *The Ideologies of Theory: Essays, 1971–1986*, Vol. 2 (Minneapolis: University of Minnesota Press, 1988), p. 9.

41. Anthony Giddens, *Modernity and Self-Identity: Self and Society in the Late Modern Age* (Stanford: Stanford University Press, 1991), p. 195. Giddens is especially astute in his critique of Christopher Lasch, who holds that expertise and therapy are substitutes for religious authority. There are no substitutes, he argues, and that is why religion is very much still around. His critique of Braverman's version of deskilling is also pertinent to later stages of my argument.

42. Peter Novick, *That Noble Dream: The "Objectivity Question" and the American Historical Profession* (Cambridge: Cambridge University Press, 1988), p. 14.

43. Claude Lefort, *Democracy and Political Theory*, trans. David Macey (Minneapolis: University of Minnesota Press, 1988), p. 39.

44. James Atlas, "The Battle of the Books," *Sunday Times Magazine*, June 5, 1988, pp. 73, 75 (pp. 24 ff.). See also, on Fish, Adam Begley, "Souped-Up Scholar," *New York Times Magazine*, May 3, 1992, pp. 38 ff.

1. The Ambiguities of *The Professionals*

1. Louis Blumberg and Robert Gottlieb, "Garbage Wars: Citizens Take on 'The Experts,'" *The Nation*, May 28, 1990, p. 742.

2. An article whose argument and title are both pertinent is Robert Kanigel, "Angry At Our Gods," *Columbia* (October 1988), pp. 23–35.

"'Americans,' writes historian Nathan Hatch, 'have sustained a love–hate relationship with the role of the expert in democratic culture.' While they've aspired to professional status as a means of social mobility, they have also scorned professionalism because it carries a distinct elitist tinge, not an egalitarian one ... much clucking can be heard today about how professionals have become less gentlemanly – that the old sense of 'calling' is gone, replaced by a dollars-and-cents preoccupation little tolerant of the old-fashioned niceties" (28).

3. Max Weber, *The Protestant Ethic and the Spirit of Capitalism*, trans. Talcott Parsons (New York: Scribner's, 1958).

4. E.P. Thompson, *The Making of the English Working Class* (New York: Vintage, 1963). For the US, see Michael Denning, *Mechanic Accents: Dime Novels and Working-Class Culture in America* (London: Verso, 1987) and Fred Pfeil, *Another Tale to Tell* (London: Verso, 1990).

5. For Ruth Danon, "the myth of vocation" suggests "that work is the primary source of self-definition, psychic integration, and happy fulfilment available to a person." This has largely though not wholly been a gendered belief. Ruth Danon, *Work in the English Novel: The Myth of Vocation* (London: Croom Helm, 1985), p. 1.

6. Studs Terkel, *Working: People Talk About What They Do All Day and How They Feel About What They Do* (New York: Ballantine, 1972, 1974), p. 6.

7. P.D. Anthony, *The Ideology of Work* (London: Tavistock, 1977).

8. This section elaborates on my "Professionalism and Politics: Toward Productively Divided Loyalties," *Profession 85* (New York: Modern Language Association, 1985), pp. 1–9. There have been changes in this language since 1966. For the record, 1966 was also the year when Martin Luther King came out against the war in Vietnam and when the National Organization of Women and the Black Panther Party were founded.

9. Andrew Abbott, "Professional Ethics," *American Journal of Sociology*, 88 (1983), pp. 855–85.

10. One professional principle that is clearly overridden is the merely monetary relation tying them to their employer. Being paid, it would seem, is an insufficient principle of social cohesion. The surprise here is less that there are stronger principles of loyalty – like the loyalty to Maria Grant that leads both the goatkeeper and Señor Ortega, her husband's trusted emissary, to betray the plan of rescue to the guerrillas – than that professionalism itself contains a stronger principle.

11. Jean Baudrillard, *The Mirror of Production* (St Louis: Telos Press, 1975); Stanley Aronowitz, "Why Work?" in *Social Text*, 12 (Fall 1985); Jürgen Habermas, *Autonomy and Solidarity: Interviews*, ed. Peter Dews (London: Verso, 1986; rev. edn, 1992) ch. 5; André Gorz, *Farewell to the Working Class* (Boston: South End Press, 1982).

12. Note the similarity in the legalistic conclusion of *Robocop*.

13. On professionalism in the thriller, see, for example, Jerry Palmer, *Thrillers: Genesis and Structure of a Popular Genre* (London: Edward Arnold, 1978); Michael Denning, *Cover Stories: Narrative and Ideology in the British Spy Thriller* (London: Routledge & Kegan Paul,

1987); and the discussion of Raymond Williams's fiction in Chapter Four.

14. The existential account of revolutionary commitment that *The Professionals* puts in Raza's mouth suggests that, for better or worse, much of the politically radical or oppositional thought in contemporary Anglo-America has been invisibly reformulated under the influence of professional ideology. This is not the place to inquire whether and in what ways the reformulation is in fact for better or for worse – a task that would involve, inter alia, comparison with existing versions of politics and consideration of the constituencies appealed to, and that in any case will be pursued throughout the chapters to follow.

15. Will Wright, *Sixguns and Society: A Structural Study of the Western* (Berkeley: University of California Press, 1975).

16. Is Wright himself value-free in his own treatment? Or is he still a gunslinger on behalf of an old-fashioned society, as in the Western's classical plot?

17. *The* end, death, is a major presence in the film's argument about professionalism. For example, "the cemetery of nameless men" is a figure for the uselessness of all political commitment, and at the same time an argument for commitment, however arbitrary, as one way to earn and leave behind a name. The theme invites association with Weber's existential heroism and with the irreducibility of the individual life-span, the "career," as a unit of meaning.

18. Like the "professionals," the film's audience are also disengaged spectators of the execution, and it is tempting to push the parallel further. If our view through the camera is consistently identified with the privileged distance of their view through binoculars, if our pleasure in consuming their competence is no less motiveless than the competence itself, can we also identify spectatorial detachment as a version of professionalism? Here consumerism and professionalism would be opposed not to each other but rather to the simplicities of unmediated, pre-social production. The identification is also pertinent to a particularly American, particularly middle-class political situation: the imaginative challenge of Other People's Revolutions, or of revolution at a distance, revolution without personal motive. It is perhaps worth noting that when Dolworth appears on the horizon after the ambush, miraculously alive, Fardan tears off his binoculars – the end of spectatorship? – and pronounces him "the whirlingest dervish of them all" – an identification of the Western "professional" with the very type of "Oriental" irrationality.

19. Interview in Gerald Graff and Reginald Gibbons, eds, *Criticism in the University* (Evanston: Northwestern University Press, 1985), Tri-Quarterly Series No. 1, p. 113.

20. Barbara Ehrenreich and Deirdre English, *For Her Own Good: 150 Years of the Experts' Advice to Women*, (Garden City, Anchor/Doubleday, 1978).

21. Further evidence in the same direction comes from Regenia Gagnier's study of working-class women's autobiographies in mid nineteenth-century Britain: *Subjectivities: A History of Self-Representation in*

Britain, 1832–1920 (New York: Oxford University Press, 1991). Unlike many middle-class women, who felt abused by the power of the experts over them, working-class women were denied access to that expertise, and "demanded specialists" (62). In "demanding professional services," Gagnier writes, "they came close to rejecting the distinction between mental and manual labor."

22. Richard Wightman Fox and T.J. Jackson Lears, *The Culture of Consumption: Critical Essays in American History, 1880–1980* (New York: Pantheon, 1983), pp. xiv, 9.

23. For the zero-sum model of Taylorism as expropriation of knowledge in the interest of controlling the workers, see, for example, Benjamin Coriat, *Science, technique, et capital* (Paris: Seuil, 1976), pp. 110–32.

24. Barbara Ehrenreich, *Fear of Falling* (New York: Pantheon, 1989), p. 217.

25. Nancy Fraser, *Unruly Practices: Power, Discourse and Gender in Contemporary Social Theory* (Minneapolis: Minnesota University Press, 1989), p. 11.

26. Lisa Jardine, "'Girl Talk' (for Boys on the Left), or Marginalising Feminist Critical Praxis," *Oxford Literary Review*, 8 (1986), pp. 208–17. Jardine seems a bit unclear as to whether women *should* think of their work in professional terms, or whether those terms are inherently male: "there *is* no professional model for the woman who speaks with (her own) authority. Current male marxist teaching, on the other hand, tends to transmit an 'authoritative' counter-claim for readings silenced by the Establishment confraternity of teachers. In other words, the male Left appears still to be committed to Lit. Crit. as a *profession*" (214).

27. Jane Gallop, "Heroic Images: Feminist Criticism, 1972," *American Literary History* 1:3 (Fall 1989), p. 623 (pp. 612–36).

28. Barbara and John Ehrenreich, "The Professional-Managerial Class," in Pat Walker, ed., *Between Labor and Capital* (Boston: South End Press, 1979).

29. Thomas L. Haskell, *The Authority of Experts: Studies in History and Theory* (Bloomington: University of Indiana Press, 1984), pp. xv–xvi.

30. James Gorman, "The Doctor Won't See You Now," *New York Times*, January 12, 1992, Op-Ed section, p. 19.

31. John Hollander's diatribe is characteristic of a frequent, politically injurious, and entirely inaccurate conflation of the academic left, the free-market right, and the new market-oriented professionalism: "The *gauchisme* of many younger scholars reads like the deeply unpolitical cant of an exceedingly careerist generation. Many of the scholars wielding disproportionate power in the professionalized study and teaching of literature in universities today have the same character as CEOs who look only for the quarterly bottom line, as lawyers who have been contriving to give that profession an even – did it seem possible? – worse name." *ADE Bulletin* 98 (1991), p. 11 (pp. 7–13), quoted in Cooper, p. 1183.

2. Culture and Distance

1. Raymond Williams, "Distance," reprinted in *What I Came to Say* (London: Hutchinson, 1989), p. 40.
2. Walter Benjamin, *Reflections: Essays, Aphorisms, Autobiographical Writings*, ed. Peter Demetz (New York: Harcourt Brace Jovanovich, 1978), p. 85.
3. Edward W. Said, *The World, the Text, and the Critic* (Cambridge, MA: Harvard University Press, 1983), p. 15.
4. Raymond Williams, "Beyond Cambridge English," *Writing in Society* (London: Verso, 1983), p. 222.
5. There are notable examples of the battle as a paradigm of historical intelligibility in the French tradition: Chateaubriand, Stendhal, Hugo, and Sartre.
6. On experience, see Perry Anderson, *Arguments within English Marxism* (London: Verso, 1980), pp. 57–8.
7. Raymond Williams, *Culture and Society* (New York: Harper & Row, 1958), p. xiv.
8. Williams does not explicitly apply this logic to the issue of professionalization, and thus does not recognize any contradiction between seeing criticism as grounded on culture and seeing it as totally ungrounded. In "Beyond Cambridge English," he speaks as if "the profession of a stranger" needed no legitimation, as if it were natural and self-evident that capitalist society should finance a collection of free-floating extra-territorials.
9. Perry Anderson, "Components of the National Culture," *Student Power* (Harmondsworth: Penguin, 1968), reprinted in *English Questions* (London: Verso, 1992).
10. Richard Johnson, "Culture and the Historians" and "Three Problematics: Elements of a Theory of Working-Class Culture," in Clarke et al.
11. Ross, *No Respect*.
12. Edward Said, "Media, Margins, and Modernity," in Raymond Williams, *The Politics of Modernism: Against the New Conformists*, ed. Tony Pinkney (London: Verso, 1989), p. 196.
13. The canonical misunderstanding of Williams that plays down his own deep and early commitment to modernism (especially in drama and film) is explained by Tony Pinkney: "Make *Culture and Society* and *The Long Revolution* take a backward somersault over and behind *Drama from Ibsen to Eliot* and *Preface to Film*, implicitly reverse the order of their composition and publication in the very structure of one's discussion of Williams, and you magically produce a deeply-rooted native social theorist, as 'essentially English' (in that key Leavisite phrase) as the very intellectual lineage he discusses, but whose quaint, engaging, marginal hobby is collecting twentieth-century dramatists." "Raymond Williams and the Two Faces of Modernism," in Terry Eagleton, ed., *Raymond Williams: Critical Perspectives* (Oxford: Polity, 1989), p. 19.
14. Louis Menand, *Discovering Modernism: T.S. Eliot and His Context*

(New York: Oxford University Press, 1987), pp. 100–1. Another instance of the discourse of legitimation that recalls Bate's business-man-with-a-gun is Bertrand Russell's cable to Henry Eliot, again during the First World War, urging him not to insist that Eliot take his exams "UNLESS IMMEDIATE DEGREE IS WORTH RISKING LIFE" (quoted in Ozick, p. 130).

15. See, for example, James F. Knapp, *Literary Modernism and the Transformation of Work* (Evanston: Northwestern University Press, 1988). This paragraph also draws on my "Modernism in History, Modernism in Power," in Robert Kiely, ed., *Modernism Reconsidered*, Harvard English Studies No. 11, pp. 229–45 (Cambridge, MA: Harvard University Press, 1983), p. 237 and passim.

16. Andrew Abbott, *The System of Professions: An Essay on the Division of Expert Labor* (Chicago: University of Chicago Press, 1988), pp. 9–20.

17. The following pages draw on my "Modernism and Professionalism". They have been substantially revised.

18. Bledstein, pp. 90, 92; Malcolm Bradbury and James McFarlane, *Modernism* (Harmondsworth: Penguin, 1976), pp. 26–8.

19. Said, *The World, the Text, and the Critic*, p. 164.

20. Gerald Graff, *Professing Literature: An Institutional History* (Chicago: University of Chicago Press, 1987), chs 4–7.

21. John Crowe Ransom, "Criticism, Inc.," *The World's Body* (Port Washington, NY: Kennikat Press, 1938), p. 335. I'm grateful to Vincent Leitch for pointing this text out to me some years ago.

22. M.H. Abrams, *The Mirror and the Lamp: Romantic Theory and the Critical Tradition* (New York: Norton, 1953). William K. Wimsatt and Cleanth Brooks, *Literary Criticism: A Short History* (New York: Random House, 1957). Hazard Adams, ed., *Critical Theory Since Plato* (New York: Harcourt Brace Jovanovich, 1971).

23. Eric Havelock, *A Preface to Plato* (Cambridge, MA: Harvard University Press, 1963); D.A. Russell, *Criticism in Antiquity* (London: Duckworth, 1981); Harold Bloom, *The Art of the Critic: Literary Theory and Criticism from the Greeks to the Present*, vol. 1 (New York: Chelsea House, 1985). See also Chapter Three below.

24. This argument is developed at greater length in my "The History of Literary Theory: Starting Over," *Poetics Today*, 9:4 (1988), pp. 767–81. Abrams tries to take over New Critical objectivism on behalf of Romantic expressiveness. What we are really appreciating in "the object-in-itself," he suggests, is the godlike creator who has made and then abandoned it. Yet what we observe, both logically and chronologically, is the reverse: expressiveness is caught up and digested by the voracious new doctrine of objectivism. Proving that the New Critics are Romantics at heart, Abrams follows Romantic organicism into the objectivist trap. At the center of his diagram of the four orientations, and the only one that is "all-inclusive" (27), the objective orientation mediates and resolves the titular contradiction between the mimetic and the expressive.

25. Stanley Fish, "Anti-Professionalism," in *Doing What Comes Naturally*:

Change, Rhetoric, and the Practice of Theory in Literary and Legal Studies (Durham: Duke University Press, 1989).

26. I am assuming that Socrates' apparent endorsement of the technical knowledge (*techne*) of professions other than Ion's is merely a tactic for exposing Ion's true ignorance, and that representatives of the other professions would fare just as badly under his interrogation.

27. Compare with Freud's rhetoric in seeking to win jurisdiction over the interpretation of dreams, as in the essay anthologized in Hazard Adams's *Critical Theory Since Plato*. Freud begins with the words "We laymen" and proceeds to win over the general reader by claiming no expertise. Compare also with Lévi-Strauss's professionalizing argument about myth in "The Structural Study of Myth," anthologized in the sequel to Adams's volume: Hazard Adams and Leroy Searle, eds, *Critical Theory Since 1965* (Tallahassee: Florida State University Press, 1986).

28. Friedrich Schiller, *On the Aesthetic Education of Man*, ed. and trans. Elizabeth M. Wilkinson and L.A. Willoughby (Oxford: Clarendon, 1967), p. 210.

29. M.H. Abrams, *Natural Supernaturalism: Tradition and Revolution in Romantic Literature* (New York: Norton, 1971).

30. John Gross, *The Rise and Fall of the Man of Letters* (New York: Macmillan, 1969); Terry Eagleton, *The Function of Criticism: From "The Spectator" to Post-Structuralism* (London: Verso, 1984). This section draws on my "Oppositional Professionals," in Jonathan Arac and Barbara Johnson, eds, *Consequences of Theory*, Selected Papers from the English Institute. (Baltimore: Johns Hopkins University Press, 1989), pp. 5–7.

31. Terry Eagleton, *Literary Theory: An Introduction* (Minneapolis: University of Minnesota Press, 1983).

32. Williams begins his chapter on T.S. Eliot by provisionally suspending his explicit political differences with him and instead choosing to appreciate their common concern for "culture": "We can say of Eliot what Mill said of Coleridge, that an 'enlightened Radical or Liberal' ought 'to rejoice over such a Conservative'" (227). Although the chapter goes on to criticize Eliot's social philosophy quite sharply, Eliot remains an indispensable figure in the oppositional tradition Williams constructs – the tradition of our professional antecedents. To some extent, Williams and Eliot share the politics dictated by a shared professional narrative of legitimation.

33. John Ehrenreich, *The Altruistic Imagination* (Ithaca: Cornell University Press, 1985), p. 42. The parallel between social workers and university teachers of the humanities, as professionals or would-be professionals whose legitimacy is mediated through pre-existing bureaucratic institutions, is discussed further in the Conclusion.

34. Sherry Gorelick, "Class Relations and the Development of the Teaching Profession", in Dale Johnson, ed., *Class and Social Development: A New Theory of the Middle Class* (Beverly Hills, CA: Sage, 1982), p. 204.

35. David Bromwich, "Literary Radicalism in America," *Dissent*, 32

(1985). Bromwich develops this view at greater length in *Politics By Other Means: Higher Education and Group Thinking* (New Haven: Yale University Press, 1992).

36. Williams, *The Politics of Modernism*, pp. 153–7.

3. The Insistance of the Public in Postmodern Criticism

1. The adjective "Marxist" was not that day of my own choosing, in part because I anticipated its likely chilling effect. Though it might seem to offer an alternative explanation for the scene that follows, this term is interesting here above all for how relatively little it adds to the sense of oppositionality that already structured the self-consciousness of the representatives of the humanities, and the event as well.

2. This question points up to the unconscious continuity with Arnold, who of course claimed precisely that poetry was taking over the functions of religion.

3. On this topic see my "Death and Vocation: Narrativizing Narrative Theory," *PMLA*, 107:1 (January 1992), pp. 38–50.

4. See Evan Watkins, *Work Time: English Departments and the Circulation of Cultural Value* (Stanford: Stanford University Press, 1989).

5. See Fish, "Anti-Professionalism," for the path-breaking exposé of this paradox. My disagreement with Fish's interpretation will be explained below.

6. I do not want to imply, for example, as my substitution of "professional" for the adjective "political" in Fredric Jameson's title might seem to indicate, that the sort of negotiation with the public to which, as I argue, professional discourse is always already committed constitutes our one crucial political issue. Such negotiations do not define the profession's single, deep, ultimate truth; there are other politics and other truths. Nor must this one in fact be unconscious, repressed, inaccessible to intention and agency. In the Bate scene, for example, Bate's intention to provoke a crisis of professional rationale would seem to be perfectly conscious.

7. The field of texts that I am discussing, from overt "'mission' statements" (Evan Watkins's phrase) to diverse and covert scholarly subgenres, belongs to a discourse of legitimation that is usually associated with the Enlightenment tradition of Weber and Habermas. My discussion tries to open this tradition up to dialogue with other voices, including those of poststructuralism and cultural or "identity" politics.

8. Hayden White, "The Value of Narrativity in the Representation of Reality," *The Content of the Form: Narrative Discourse and Historical Representation* (Baltimore: Johns Hopkins University Press, 1987), and Jean-François Lyotard, *The Postmodern Condition: A Report on Knowledge*, trans. Geoff Bennington and Brian Massumi (Minneapolis: University of Minnesota Press, 1984).

9. Gerald L. Geison, ed., *Professions and Professional Ideologies in America* (Chapel Hill: University of North Carolina Press, 1983), p. 7.

10. Magali Sarfatti Larson, *The Rise of Professionalism* (Berkeley: University of California Press, 1977), pp. xii, 188, 231. Larson is among those sociologists who emphasize market control via expertise more than claims to public service as a source of professional power. But her examples and arguments also leave room for this alternative emphasis.

11. Thomas Haskell, *The Emergence of Professional Social Science: The American Social Science Association and the Nineteenth-Century Crisis of Authority* (Urbana, IL: University of Illinois Press, 1977).

12. Perhaps this outside seems so accessible because, as contrasted with esoteric professional knowledge, the domain of value too seems accessible.

13. This section is a revised version of my "Interdisciplinarity in Public: The Rhetoric of Rhetoric," *Social Text*, 25/26 (Summer 1990), pp. 108–18.

14. I.F. Stone, *The Trial of Socrates* (Boston: Little, Brown, 1988). As I wrote the preceeding lines, I reached across my word processor for my copy of Stone's book, which had found its way to the bottom of a large pile of books I was using for this essay. The pile collapsed, and the bust of Socrates at the end of the crowded bookcase smashed on the floor. The event was so much more coherent than anything else in my life that I vowed it had to be included, and here it is. Beyond the immediate symbolism of the coincidence – the shattered head as embodied result of or revenge for Stone's attack, or my assenting relay of that attack – there is a further appropriateness. The crowdedness of New York City apartments like mine, which means that writing must be done in a bedroom, not a study, with inadequate shelf space for books, papers, and reverential busts, belongs after all to the material circumstances and situatedness of intellectual production that philosophical universalisms like Socrates' have for so long led us to ignore. More pertinently still, it is this neglect of the irreducible discursive embodiedness of thinking that the rhetoric revival aims pre-eminently to undo.

15. S. Fish, *Doing What Comes Naturally*, p. 480. Among recent discussions, see, for example, Brian Vickers, *In Defence of Rhetoric* (Oxford: Clarendon Press, 1988); Steven Mailloux, *Rhetorical Power* (Ithaca: Cornell University Press, 1989); Patricia Bizzell and Bruce Herzberg, eds, *The Rhetorical Tradition* (Boston: St Martin's Press, 1990); John Bender and David E. Welberry, eds, *The Ends of Rhetoric* (Stanford: Stanford University Press, 1990); and Charles Bazerman and James Paradis, eds, *Textual Dynamics of the Professions* (Madison: University of Wisconsin Press, 1991).

16. It would be interesting to consider, however, how far the rhetoricity of advertising may have imposed itself as a new norm, expressing itself equally in (and thus leveling off the hierarchy between) academic high theory and consumer common sense.

17. Wherever you take it, the term rhetoric leads into the public domain. Rhetoric is what people like ourselves did before there was literature or, therefore, a specialized profession of literary criticism; it is the

bridge that now takes people like Fish himself across professional borders into the law; and in the form of the teaching of composition, it is the most visible public service rendered by a profession that has always defined its professional expertise (as Gerald Graff has shown) in terms of research rather than teaching.

18. More might be said about rhetoric as a bridge between communications and English, respectively one of the least and most prestigious university departments, and within English between composition and theory, the least and most prestigious branches of the department. Such reshufflings within the academy are unfortunately the business of no one in particular within the academy – hence our analytic tools are insufficient to deal with them.

19. Richard Rorty, *Consequences of Pragmatism* (Minneapolis: University of Minnesota Press, 1982), p. 61.

20. For further development of this argument, see my "Oppositional Professionals."

21. See Alan Wolfe, *Whose Keeper? Social Science and Moral Obligation* (Berkeley: University of California Press, 1989), pp. 31–52. Wolfe's resistance to the colonization of sociology by economics is mobilized in terms of moral values – a notable constituent of legitimizing discourse in the humanities disciplines, and in the present argument as well.

22. In *The Structural Transformation of the Public Sphere: An Inquiry into a Category of Bourgeois Society*, trans. Thomas Burger (Cambridge, MA: MIT Press, 1989), Habermas observes that "publicity" does not so much disappear as spread out over the entire social field, thereby losing the sharp oppositional edge that had defined its value. However accurate as a description of nineteenth-century liberalism, this provides a suggestive and uncomfortable analogy for disciplines which have recently seen their capital – for example, "the political" for political science, "the literary" for criticism – invested in a greater diversity of domains. What is the connection between oppositionality and value? Between scarcity and value? We would seem to need a disciplinary economics that would be able to calculate the returns on these inter- or extra-disciplinary investments, the interplay of abundance and scarcity in determining the value of disciplinary objects.

23. René Wellek, *The Attack on Literature* (Chapel Hill: University of North Carolina Press, 1982).

24. In a sort of performative *encore*, Fish enacts his point by using the same words again in the "Rhetoric" chapter of Frank Lentricchia and Thomas McLaughlin, eds, *Critical Terms for Literary Study* (Chicago: University of Chicago Press, 1990).

25. Hayden White, "The Tropics of History: The Deep Structure of *The New Science*," *Tropics of Discourse* (Baltimore: Johns Hopkins University Press, 1978); "The Metaphysics of Narrativity: Time and Symbol in Ricoeur's Philosophy of History," *The Content of the Form*; *Metahistory: The Historical Imagination in Nineteenth-Century Europe* (Baltimore: Johns Hopkins University Press, 1973).

26. It seems possible, on the other hand, that, unlike forensic and deliberative rhetoric, epideictic is distinguished precisely by *not* leading to action, by being a version of Fish's "no consequences." If this were so, then perhaps it has been all too well adapted to the humanities – and it's the other sorts of rhetoric we need.

27. For a reading of Bakhtin that anticipates some of the concerns of the present volume, see Ken Hirschkop and David Shepherd, eds, *Bakhtin and Cultural Theory* (Manchester: Manchester University Press, 1989).

28. As retrieved, for example, in Victoria Kahn's *Rhetoric, Prudence, and Skepticism in the Renaissance* (Ithaca: Cornell University Press, 1985).

29. Barbara Johnson offers an instructive contrast: a position of *necessity*, beyond praise and blame. Necessity, for Johnson, is the only thing that can get you beyond praise and blame, beyond the critical cycle (defined by Robert Young) in which you criticize Y for abusing text X, but only repeat the abuse of Y, which will then be pointed out by Z in defense of Y, and so on. According to Johnson, praise/blame *cannot be avoided* – and she praises those who accept its necessity, and blames those who fail to. See Barbara Johnson's two contributions to Robert Young, *Untying the Text: A Post-Structuralist Reader* (London: Routledge & Kegan Paul, 1981) along with Young's introduction and commentaries.

30. For the exchange, see *New Literary History*, 17:1 (Autumn 1985). When "Anti-Professionalism" was reprinted in *Doing What Comes Naturally*, the exchange was not included, and the essay appears in the book unmodified. For further commentary, see Fish's afterword to H. Aram Veeser, ed., *The New Historicism* (New York: Routledge, 1989).

31. Paul Bové, *Intellectuals in Power: A Genealogy of Critical Humanism* (New York: Columbia University Press, 1986).

32. Stanley Fish, "Dennis Martinez and the Uses of Theory," *Yale Law Journal*, 96 (1987), pp. 1771 ff.

33. In Derek Attridge, Geoff Bennington, and Robert Young, eds, *Post-Structuralism and the Question of History* (Cambridge: Cambridge University Press, 1987), p. 27.

34. Terry Eagleton, *Walter Benjamin: Or Towards a Revolutionary Criticism* (London: Verso, 1981), p. 101.

35. Renato Barilli, *Rhetoric*, trans. Giuliana Menozzi (Minneapolis: University of Minnesota Press, 1989).

36. John S. Nelson, Allan Megill, and Donald N. McCloskey, eds, *The Rhetoric of the Human Sciences: Language and Argument in Scholarship and Public Affairs* (Madison: University of Wisconsin Press, 1987). Nelson writes (413): "Rather than remain a discipline apart," rhetoric "must become a part of all other disciplines."

37. For contrast, see the case against interdisciplinarity argued by Stanley Fish in "Being Interdisciplinary Is So Very Hard to Do," *Profession 89* (New York: Modern Language Association, 1989), pp. 15–22. With his customary flair for paradox, Fish argues both against interdisciplinarity and for rhetoric, so often the leading concept in interdisciplinary projects. For Fish, interdisciplinarity is "impossible";

it is a state of hypothetical freedom from particular disciplinary constraints, enclosures, and authorities that is always only imaginary. The moral is "the impossibility of authentic critique" (21) or of any other "employment of [our] knowledge in the struggles of social and political life" (19). Interdisciplinarity is indeed impossible if one naturalizes and essentializes the disciplines so that any changes that happen to them can only do so for reasons internal to them, and there is nothing external to them but other, similarly essentialized disciplines. In such a universe of monads, what can the space between be but emptiness?

38. I am indebted for the notion of dispersed debts to Thomas Keenan.
39. If it is true that fields always depart from their official norms, then there ought to be a theory of *why* they always so depart. For deconstruction, whose vocabulary is invoked here, the answer is perhaps an unacknowledged debt to Freud. Behind the never-failing, otherwise inexplicable power of the minor, neglected term of an opposition to destabilize the major one lies the model of the return of the repressed.

4. Enchanted Enclaves, Family Romance

1. John Le Carré, *The Russia House* (New York: Bantam, 1988), p. 172.
2. Joseph Conrad, *Heart of Darkness: A Case Study in Contemporary Criticism*, ed. Ross Murfin (NY: St Martin's Press, 1989), p. 49. For a topical misreading, see the comments for Victor Strandberg, member of the National Association of Scholars, quoted in the *New York Times*: "The best social advice I've ever seen is a literary citation: 'Try to be civil, Marlow' – from Conrad's 'Heart of Darkness.' The Duke faculty should try to be civil about the N.A.S. controversy." "Duke: Scholars' Group Accused of Bias, Divides Faculty," *New York Times*, October 21, 1990, p. 45.
3. Karl Löwith, *From Hegel to Nietzsche*, trans. David E. Green (Garden City, NY: Doubleday, 1967), p. 285.
4. Peter Brooks, *Reading for the Plot: Design and Intention in Narrative* (New York: Vintage, 1984), p. 240.
5. Jameson, "The Vanishing Mediator," p. 11.
6. Franco Moretti, *The Way of the World: The Bildungsroman in European Culture* (London: Verso, 1987). Moretti's narrative of decline mirrors many others: for example, that of Habermas, in *The Structural Transformation of the Public Sphere*, and that of Lukács, who sees the fall from realism into naturalism as a fall into specialization. In "Narrate or Describe?" he writes that Balzac and Stendhal "were not 'specialists' in the sense of the capitalist division of labor," while Flaubert and Zola "became specialists in the craft of writing." In Arnold Kettle, ed., *The 19th Century Novel: Critical Essays and Documents* (London: Heinemann in association with the Open University Press, 1972), p. 70.
7. It is a remarkably faithful parallel to what Matthew Arnold did when

he stopped writing poetry himself because of the supposed inability of contemporary poetry to produce the right sort of action, and instead turned to the tradition of the Greeks, thus laying for literary criticism and dichotomous foundations of present emptiness and past plenitude and setting the discipline at a distance from public action while ostensibly honoring and cherishing it.

8. This argument is developed in Ross, *No Respect.*

9. I will not discourage anyone who wants to extend the same reflexive suggestion to me.

10. See, for example, Peter Lassman, Irving Velody, and Herminio Martini, eds, *Max Weber's "Science as a Vocation"* (London: Unwin Hyman, 1989), which argues that "the heroic attempt to preserve a purely non-evaluative social science collapses" (190). "If the 'iron cage' was closed so completely then Weber himself would not have been able to stand apart from it in order to describe it" (202). See also Lawrence A. Scaff, *Fleeing the Iron Cage: Culture, Politics, and Modernity in the Thought of Max Weber* (Berkeley: University of California Press, 1989), which speaks of Weber's "antiprophetic prophecy" (230).

11. Jameson seems unwilling to entertain the possibility that "rationalization," like the pseudo-Marxist or neo-Marxist concept of "reification," serves the professional purposes of leftists in the humanities while also betraying certain of their own political principles. See Chapter Five.

12. If the study of culture is the study of the lost mother, then the mediator remains: the lady doesn't vanish.

13. Nancy Armstrong, *Desire and Domestic Fiction: A Political History of the Novel* (New York: Oxford University Press, 1987); Mary Poovey, *Uneven Developments: The Ideological Work of Gender in Mid-Victorian England* (Chicago: University of Chicago Press, 1988).

14. Fredric Jameson, *The Political Unconscious: Narrative as a Socially Symbolic Act* (London: Methuen, 1981).

15. Aijaz Ahmad, "Jameson's Rhetoric of Otherness and the 'National Allegory,'" *Social Text*, 17 (Fall 1987).

16. Fredric Jameson, "Third-World Literature in the Era of Multinational Capitalism," *Social Text*, 15 (Fall 1980), p. 75 (pp. 66–88).

17. In Weber's work on religion, Jameson comments in "The Vanishing Mediator," the prophet comes between the magician, representing "personal" power and "immediate gain" (17), and the priest, who represents "bureaucratic" power. A rationalizing figure who belongs to the "'cooling off' or solidification of charisma" (26), the prophet "breaks down the traditional sacred rules" (16), but he does so by means of miracles, in "a noninstitutionalized affirmation of his own personal powers and vocation" (26). The prophet "propagates ideas for their own sake and not for fees" (26).

18. Davie, "Poet: Patriot: Interpreter," p. 27.

19. *The New Yorker*, December 10, 1980. There is more to say about parallels and intersections between Steiner and Williams beyond their common proximity to Blunt and their common interest in spies. (Steiner's novel *The Portage to San Cristobal of A.H.* is overrun with

secret agents.) Both writing careers began in the years after the Second World War, both began with specifically international books (Williams on Ibsen, Steiner on Tolstoy and Dostoevsky), and both turned very quickly to the question of whether, after the war, the concept of tragedy retained its usefulness. Their clandestine debate over tragedy was indirectly about the meaning of the war. The present essay points toward another, still more clandestine debate between them about internationalism and intellectuals.

20. *New York Review of Books*, January 12, 1986.
21. James Wilkinson, *The Intellectual Resistance in Europe* (Cambridge, MA: Harvard University Press, 1981), pp. 74–5.
22. Franco Moretti, *Signs Taken for Wonders* (London: Verso, 1983), is interesting on work as immanence and transcendence.
23. *Second Generation* (London: Chatto & Windus, 1964), p. 138.
24. Raymond Williams, *Politics and Letters: Interviews with New Left Review* (London: Verso, 1979).
25. On the theme of generations in Williams, see the excellent introduction to the *News from Nowhere* volume (No. 6, February 1989) on Williams.
26. *Loyalties* (London: Chatto & Windus, 1985).
27. J.P. Ward, *Raymond Williams* (Cardiff: University of Wales, 1981), p. 42. Since his death in 1988, Williams and his work have become the objects of increasing critical attention. Notable are Jan Gorak, *The Alien Mind of Raymond Williams* (Columbia: University of Missouri Press, 1988), the special collection of *News From Nowhere*, and a forthcoming volume by John Higgins.
28. *The Fight for Manod* (London: Chatto & Windus, 1979).
29. *Border Country* (London: Chatto & Windus, 1960).
30. *Drama from Ibsen to Eliot* (London: Chatto & Windus, 1952), p. 27.
31. Raymond Williams, *Modern Tragedy* [1966], rev. edn (London: Verso, 1979). George Steiner, *The Death of Tragedy* (New York: Knopf, 1961).
32. *The Volunteers* (London: Chatto and Windus, 1978), p. 136.
33. Quoted in Tony Barley, *Taking Sides: The Fiction of John Le Carré* (Milton Keynes: Open University Press, 1986), p. 85.
34. See my discussion of Alan Sinfield and the Second World War in the Conclusion.
35. Myron J. Smith, *Cloak and Dagger Fiction* (Santa Barbara: ABC/Clio, 1982).
36. Raymond Williams, *Writing in Society*, p. 18.
37. On *Writing in Society*, see my "English as a National Discipline," *Harvard Educational Review* 55:1 (February 1985), pp. 129–30. For Williams on work in general, see his "The Meanings of Work," in Ronald Fraser, ed., *Work: Twenty Personal Accounts* (Penguin in association with New Left Review, 1968) and *Towards 2000* (London: Chatto & Windus/Hogarth Press, 1983), pp. 85–7.
38. Terry Eagleton, "Resources for a Journey of Hope: The Significance of Raymond Williams," *New Left Review*, 168 (March/April 1988), p. 9.
39. *Writing in Society*, p. 17.

40. Theodor W. Adorno, "The Actuality of Philosophy," *Telos*, 31 (Spring 1977), pp. 113–33.
41. *Writing in Society*, p. 194.
42. See, for example, in *Writing in Society*: "Region and Class in the Novel," is the micro-history of the word "region." Before coming to mean "a subordinate area" (from *regere*, to direct), it had meant, Williams says, "a realm or kingdom or country" in its own right (from *regere*, to rule); that is, it had been unsubordinated, equal to all other territories. As etymology suggests, the subordination is arbitrary: some areas can be described as "regions" only if "certain other areas are not seen in this way." The Lake District is a region, but London is not. The innocent usage of the term "regional novel" in fact ratifies the supposed universality of the metropolitan center.
43. Terry Eagleton, *Criticism and Ideology* (London: New Left Books, 1976), pp. 22–3.
44. *The Country and the City* (London: Chatto & Windus, 1973).
45. Richard Johnson, "Three Problematics," p. 212.
46. Joan Scott, *Gender and the Politics of History* (New York: Columbia University Press, 1988), ch. 4.
47. It would be interesting to compare Agee's relation to Whittaker Chambers and the Alger Hiss case with Williams's complex ambivalence toward Blunt.
48. James Agee and Walker Evans, *Let Us Now Praise Famous Men* (New York: Houghton Mifflin, [1940] 1988).
49. Lionel Trilling, review of *Let Us Now* . . . in *Kenyon Review*, 4 (Winter 1942), p. 102.
50. *A Death in the Family* (New York: Bantam, 1957).
51. The obvious parallel is with culture as praised but also as lost.

5. The East is a Career

1. Edward W. Said, *Orientalism* (New York: Vintage, 1978). For an enlightening counterpoint see Deirdre David, "The East as Profession," paper delivered at CUNY conference on "The Professionalization of Victorian Life," May 4, 1990.
2. Jacques Derrida, "Sending: On Representation," trans. Peter Caws and Mary Ann Caws, *Social Research* 49 (1982), p. 304.
3. A notable exception is Jonathan Arac's "Introduction" to *Postmodernism and Politics* (Minneapolis: University of Minnesota Press, 1986), from which the Derrida quotation is taken. Arac argues persuasively that "the received belief that 'advanced' theorists are 'against' representation" is both mistaken and "damaging," especially given that "in the world . . . the power of representation is something sought, indeed passionately struggled for, by groups that consider themselves dominated by alien and alienating representations" (xxi).
4. Said himself does not claim that the peoples of the Middle East have had the same relation to dominant discourse as, say, aristocratic women in Europe.
5. The first position is articulated with far greater refinement in Bové. The

second figures, with significant variations, in Benita Parry, "Problems in Current Theories of Colonial Discourse," *Oxford Literary Review*, 9 (1987), pp. 27–58. (Parry is more centrally concerned with Gayatri Spivak and her supposed "deliberate deafness to the native voice where it is to be heard" [39]), in Dennis Porter, "*Orientalism* and its Problems," and in Homi Bhabha, "Difference, Discrimination and the Discourse of Colonialism," both of which are in Francis Barker et al., eds, *The Politics of Theory*, Proceedings of the Essex Conference on the Sociology of Literature, July 1982 (Colchester: University of Essex, 1983).

6. Aijaz Ahmad, *In Theory: Classes, Nations, Literatures* (London: Verso, 1992), pp. 196–7.

7. Jim Merod, *The Political Responsibility of the Critic* (Ithaca: Cornell University Press, 1987), p. 185.

8. Arac, *Postmodernism and Politics*, p. xxi.

9. Edward W. Said, *After the Last Sky: Palestinian Lives*, photographs by Jean Mohr (New York: Pantheon, 1986), p. 158.

10. "An Ideology of Difference," *Critical Inquiry*, 12:1 (Autumn 1985), p. 51. See also *After the Last Sky*: Mohr's photography "enables us to see Palestinians in the process of sustaining themselves, perhaps even of re-presenting themselves" (145).

11. "The Post-Colonial Intellectual," *Salmagundi*, 70–1 (Spring–Summer 1986), p. 49. See also discussion following, e.g. p. 55.

12. Here and at some later points I draw on my review of this book and of Said's *The Question of Palestine* (London: Routledge & Kegan Paul, 1980): "Homelessness and Worldliness," *Diacritics*, 13:3 (Fall 1983), pp. 69–77. For a critique see Catherine Gallagher, "Politics, the Profession, and the Critic," *Diacritics*, 15:2 (1986), pp. 37–43. The controversy continues in "Deformed Professions, Empty Politics," *Diacritics*, 16:3 (1986), pp. 67–72.

13. Sadik Jalal al-Azm, "Orientalism and Orientalism in Reverse," *Khamsin*, 8 (1980), pp. 9–10. For a related view see S.P. Mohanty, "Us and Them: On the Philosophical Bases of Political Criticism," *Yale Journal of Criticism* 2:2 (Spring 1989), pp. 1–31.

14. Claude Lévi-Strauss, "Anthropology: Its Achievements and Its Future," *Current Anthropology*, 7:2 (1966), p. 126; quoted in Dell Hymes, ed., *Reinventing Anthropology* (New York: Vintage, 1972), p. 64.

15. Clifford Geertz, *The Interpretation of Cultures* (New York: Basic Books, 1973), p. 346.

16 *Tristes Tropiques*, trans. John and Doreen Weightman (New York: Washington Square Press, [1956] 1978).

17. David Pace, *Claude Lévi-Strauss: The Bearer of Ashes* (London: Routledge & Kegan Paul, 1983), p. 4.

18. Claude Lévi-Strauss, "The Structural Study of Myth," *Structural Anthropology*, trans. Claire Jacobson and Brooke Grundfest Schoepf (Harmondsworth: Penguin, 1963).

19. Charles C. Lemert, *French Sociology: Rapture and Renewal Since 1968* (New York: Columbia University Press, 1981), p. 11.

20. Pace, p. 12.
21. Ivan Strenski, *Four Theories of Myth in 20th Century History* (Houndmills, Basingstoke: Macmillan, 1987), pp. 198–9.
22. Didier Eribon, *Michel Foucault* (Paris: Flammarion, 1989), p. 131.
23. Edward W. Said, *Beginnings: Intention and Method* (Cambridge, MA: Harvard University Press, 1975).
24. Michel Foucault, *Power/Knowledge: Selected Interviews and Other Writings, 1972–1977*, ed. Colin Gordon (New York: Pantheon, 1980), pp. 131–2.
25. Samuel Weber, "The Limits of Professionalism," *Oxford Literary Review*, 5:1–2 (1982), p. 72.
26. *The World, the Text, and the Critic*, p. 34.
27. Peter Brooks, *The Novel of Worldliness* (Princeton: Princeton University Press, 1969), p. 4.
28. *The World, the Text, and the Critic*, pp. 226–47.
29. One might also describe this narrative as the slow fall from revolutionary Marxism (Lukács) to academic Marxism (Goldmann) to self-critical academic Marxism (Williams) and, finally, to self-critical academic anti-Marxism (Foucault), or anti-Marxist academic self-criticism, or poststructuralism. In this version, some would see a rise rather than a fall.
30. It might be objected that there is a more restrictive sense of reification in Lukács, closer to Marx on commodity fetishism, which does not lend itself to the assumptions of the humanities as easily as does Jameson's Weberian version.
31. James Clifford and George Marcus, eds, *Writing Culture: The Poetics and Politics of Ethnography* (Berkeley: University of California Press, 1986), p. 112.
32. *Orientalism*, pp. 21–2.
33. Said, "Media, Margins, and Modernity," p. 196.
34. Eribon, p. 201.
35. *The World, the Text, and the Critic*, p. 240. Ironically, "distance" is Williams's own preferred word for what is *wrong* with professionalism: its rejection of communal, experiential proximity.
36. "Orientalism Reconsidered," *Cultural Critique*, 1 (1985), pp. 106–7 (pp. 89–107).
37. *The World, the Text, and the Critic*, p. 232.
38. Richard Johnson, "Culture and the Historians," p. 212.
39. "Third World Intellectuals and Metropolitan Culture," *Raritan*, 9:3 (Winter 1990), pp. 27–50.
40. Johannes Fabian, *Time and the Other: How Anthropology Makes Its Object* (New York: Columbia University Press, 1983), p. 69.
41. More will have to be written on the North African context for Derrida, Lyotard, Foucault, Cixous, Althusser. The influence of Mao's China is better known but not necessarily better understood. How does Maoist populism assort with high poststructuralism?
42. This also means, as in *Orientalism*, "preferring to analyze the verbal symptoms of power rather than its brute exercise, its processes and tactics rather than its sources; to analyze its intellectual methods, its

enunciative techniques rather than the morality of its holders" (48). As mediated autobiographical allegory, this narrative can be contrasted with the unmediated, directly autobiographical version – specialization as forced abandonment of the wholeness of personal background, experience, culture – that Said offers in *The Politics of Modernism*, pp. 179–80.

43. As Gerald Graff suggests in *Professing Culture*, the "method" that holds such communities together includes their controversies and self-contestations.

44. *The World, the Text and the Critic*, p. 126.

6. Comparative Cosmopolitanisms

1. I am grateful to Jean Franco, Dominick LaCapra, Satya Mohanty, Sara Suleri, Jennifer Wicke, Carolyn Williams, Bob Utley, and Larry Rothfield for kind invitations to talk through earlier versions of this chapter. A slightly different version of the first two sections appeared in *Social Text*, 31/32 (Summer 1992), pp. 169–86.

2. Anne Matthews, "Deciphering Victorian Underwear and Other Seminars," *New York Times Magazine*, February 10, 1991, p. 57. The sensational overstatement ("every possible course") is evidence that the *Times Magazine* is shooting to kill – as it does again, in its summary of current dogma in the Modern Language Association, when it pretends that culture and multiculturalism are natural antagonists locked in a one-on-one struggle to the death: "The 'classic books' approach to literary study is bankrupt. Multiculturalism is essential."

3. As the word "our" suggests, I am primarily interested here, as in this book as a whole, in addressing people who, like myself, earn an uneasy living from cultural work in professions and institutions that sometimes seem aimed against the political and ethical principles which give that work such meaning as it has. Those who work elsewhere, or who escape such contradictions between work and politics by sustaining their radicalism without the help or hope of tenure, will I hope pardon what may look like the self-indulgent narcissism of this exercise. Others will hopefully excuse what they may see as my evasion of personal detail.

4. Dinesh D'Souza, "Illiberal Education," *The Atlantic Monthly* (March 1991), pp. 51–79. On p. 54, D'Souza quotes (with approval) an article by Michael O'Brien in *The Chronicle of Higher Education*.

5. Outside the US, there are many exceptions to this rule. Robin Blackburn, for example, speaks of the new European union as "a rare and ambitious experiment, of great moment for that radical and democratic cosmopolitanism which might be able to contain and defeat those global forces of division and destruction that stalk the new world order." "The Ruins of Westminster," *New Left Review*, 191 (January/February 1992), p. 29 (pp. 5–35).

6. Donna Haraway, "Situated Knowledges: The Science Question

in Feminism and the Privilege of Partial Perspective," *Simians, Cyborgs, and Women* (London: Free Association Books, 1990), p. 188. Haraway's remarks leave the question of what precisely happens – how far the undesirable consequences of panopticism are undone – when bodies are *returned* to visibility – a question for so-called "experimental ethnography." Would a "panopticism" in which the viewer would be visible remain unacceptable? Would a cosmopolitanism which would be forced to know boundaries and bodies still be one?

7. V.S. Naipaul, "Our Universal Civilization," *New York Review of Books*, January 31, 1991, pp. 22–5.

8. Rob Nixon, "London Calling: V.S. Naipaul and the License of Exile," *South Atlantic Quarterly*, 87:1 (Winter 1988), p. 1 (pp. 1–37). Note the beautiful phrase "comprehensively uprooted," which recognizes diversity of uprootings and encourages discrimination of more or fewer, greater or lesser, uprooting, rather than an over-simple dichotomy of rooted-or-not.

9. Tim Brennan, "India, Nationalism, and Other Failures," *South Atlantic Quarterly*, 87:1 (Winter 1988), pp. 134–5 (pp. 131–46). Brennan usefully argues for a discrimination of nationalisms: "The cosmopolitan writers very often cannot accept the virtues of nationalism in this postcolonial setting, are unable to see it as a defensive bulwark, and therefore fail to distinguish between monstrosities like Pakistan or Kenya ... and Cuba and Vietnam" (144).

10. Tim Brennan, "The National Longing for Form," in Homi K. Bhabna, ed., *Nation and Narration* (London: Routledge, 1990), p. 63 (pp. 44–70).

11. George Boas, "Types of Internationalism in Early Nineteenth-Century France," *International Journal of Ethics*, 38:1 (1927), p. 152.

12. It seems possible that the vocabulary of "celebrity" functions in cases like this to tarnish a given writer obliquely, that is, to do so without invoking the vocabulary of *class*, which is more seriously contaminating, on the one hand, but also too visibly contaminating for one's allies as well as one's enemies, on the other, hence often unusable.

13. This point has been forcefully articulated by Stanley Fish in "Anti-Professionalism."

14. Chandra Mohanty, "Under Western Eyes: Feminist Scholarship and Colonial Discourses," *boundary 2* (12:3/13:1, Spring/Fall 1984), p. 340 (pp. 333–58). Reprinted in Chandra Mohanty, Ann Russo, and Lourdes Torres, eds, *Third World Women and the Politics of Feminism* (Bloomington: Indiana University Press, 1991). Subsequent quotes are taken from the original article.

15. One thinks of the extraordinary universalizing of Lyotard's use of the Cashinahua as figures for all of non-Western humanity in *The Postmodern Condition*.

16. Agency occupies much the same place in another equally classic polemic on behalf of Third World specificity, Kumkum Sangari's "The Politics of the Possible," *Cultural Critique*, 6 (Fall 1987), pp. 157–86.

17. For those of us who are involved in literary theory, this point will be

familiar as the burden of "intertextuality" – the arbitrariness of any text's limits, and the way the negotiating of those limits is also the negotiating of the text's meaning and value.

18. Simon Duncan and Mike Savage, "Space, Scale, and Locality," *Antipode* 21:3 (December 1989), p. 187 (pp. 179–206).

19. Neil Smith, "Dangers of the Empirical Turn: Some Comments on the CURS Initiative," *Antipode*, 19 (1987), p. 66 (pp. 59–68).

20. Gayatri Chakravorty Spivak, "Three Women's Texts and a Critique of Imperialism," *Critical Inquiry*, 12 (Autumn 1985), pp. 243–62.

21. Ulf Hannerz, "Cosmopolitans and Locals in World Culture," in Mike Featherstone, ed., *Global Culture, Theory, Culture and Society*, 7 (London: Sage, 1990), pp. 237–51.

22. James Clifford, review of Edward W. Said, *Orientalism*, reprinted in *The Predicament of Culture* (Cambridge, MA: Harvard University Press, 1988), pp. 255–76.

23. Reprinted in *The Predicament of Culture*, pp. 92–114.

24. Paul Rabinow, "Representations are Social Facts," in James Clifford and George E. Marcus, eds, *Writing Culture* (Berkeley: University of California Press, 1986). Rabinow offers "critical cosmopolitanism" as a desirable position: "Let us define cosmopolitanism as an ethos of macro-interdependencies, with an acute consciousness (often forced upon people) of the inescapabilities and particularities of places, characters, historical trajectories, and fates." "We are all cosmopolitans" (258).

25. James Clifford, "Travelling Cultures," in Lawrence Grossberg, Cary Nelson, and Paula Treichler, eds, *Cultural Studies* (New York: Routledge, 1992).

26. Ozick, p. 125. I discuss this passage at greater length in "Othering the Academy."

27. Hugh Harris, "The Greek Origins of the Idea of Cosmopolitanism," *The International Journal of Ethics*, 38:1 (1927), p. 1. Claude Lévi-Strauss, "Cosmopolitanism and Schizophrenia," *The View from Afar* (New York: Basic Books, 1985).

28. Elisabeth Burgos-Debray, ed., *I, Rigoberta Menchu: An Indian Woman in Guatemala*, trans. Ann Wright (London: Verso, 1984), p. 247.

29. Arjun Appadurai, "Global Ethnoscapes," in Richard G. Fox, ed., *Recapturing Anthropology: Working in the Present* (Santa Fe: School of American Research Press, 1991), p. 201 (pp. 191–210).

30. There is a great deal of pressure right now to reconsider the resistance to universals that for some time has seemed to be an article of faith on the cultural left. In a recent speech, Cornel West declared: "The power of the civil rights movement under Martin Luther King was its universalism. Now, instead of the civil rights movement being viewed as a moral crusade for freedom, it's become an expression of a particular interest group. Once you lose that moral high ground, all you have is a power struggle, and that has never been a persuasive means for the weaker to deal with the stronger." (*New York Times*, April 3, 1991, p. 1.) The paradox of a case for universalism based on

historical conjuncture and rhetorical advantage suggests how unsettled our relation to universalism remains. Without taking a position on universalism, I want to agree, however, that *some* sort of "high ground," some description of radically expanded and diverse cultural knowledge that is also of positive value and at least possible commonality, has got to be part of our self-definition and strategy. The term cosmopolitanism makes this point.

31. The word "secular" would probably be a matter of dispute.

32. Haraway, p. 191.

33. Jean Franco, "The Nation as Imagined Community," in H. Aram Veeser, ed., *The New Historicism* (New York: Routledge, 1989), p. 205 (pp. 204–12).

34. Sylvia Wynter's critique of California's new, insufficiently multicultural history texts uses the power of this slogan. Wynter calls for a new framework which "seeks to go beyond the model of a nation-state coterminus only with Euro–immigrant America, to one coterminus as a 'world' civilization, with all its peoples; and therefore, for the first time in recorded history, coterminus (as a land that's not been yet but must be) with humankind." Sylvia Wynter, quoted in Robert Reinhold, "Class Struggle," *New York Times Magazine*, September 29, 1991, p. 47. But see George Yudice, "We Are Not the World," *Social Text*, 31/32 (1992) for reservations about the hidden US nationalism of any such formulation.

35. It is possible, of course, that intellectuals are simply inconsistent – that they denounce cultural capital, on the one hand, while benefiting from their continued possession of cultural capital, on the other, and therefore suffering from a difficult conflict of interest.

36. "[N]ineteenth-century feminist individualism could conceive of a 'greater' project than access to the closed circle of the nuclear family. This is the project of soul making beyond 'mere' sexual reproduction," the ethical task of turning heathens into humans. Spivak, "Three Women's Texts," p. 248.

37. Sandra Gilbert and Susan Gubar, *The Madwoman in the Attic: The Woman Writer and the Nineteenth-Century Literary Imagination* (New Haven and London: Yale University Press, 1979).

38. Julie Abraham, reviewing the sequel to *Madwoman, No Man's Land*, called that work "a nineteenth-century novel about twentieth-century women's writing" (*The Nation*, July 2/9, 1988, p. 27). *No Man's Land: The Place of Woman Writers in the Twentieth Century*, Vol. 1, *The War of the Words* (New Haven and London: Yale University press, 1988).

39. Indeed, these are the raw material that professionals must work on, as the Jane-Eyre-like feminist critic works on and works through the angry activist or the neglected Third World woman; the neglect and the anger are constitutive.

40. If, as Harold Perkin writes in *The Rise of Professional Society: England Since 1880* (London: Routledge, 1989), "all professionals are laymen to the other professions" (3), then this zero-sum logic would not seem appropriate to society's multiplicity of roles or "subject positions."

41. In my own opinion, it is only professionals themselves who would ever

be tempted to propose, against all unlikelihood, that professionalism is the very center of injustice. And this, in the jeremiad mode, for reasons of professional self-flattery.

42. Jean Franco, "Dependency Theory and Literary History: The Case of Latin America," *Minnesota Review*, 5 N.S. (Fall 1975), p. 67 (pp. 65–80).

43. Robert Brenner, "The Origins of Capitalist Development: A Critique of Neo-Smithian Marxism," *New Left Review*, 104 (July–August 1977), pp. 25–92.

44. Fredric Jameson describes the concept of scarcity in Sartre as "the unanalyzable starting point ... of the world in which we exist," a starting point which also produces the "idea of total responsibility": "my very existence, in a world of scarcity, is a threat to my neighbor's existence, as is his for me. Thus Manichaeanism and violence have their source in the very contingent structure of the world of matter itself, and it is with the accents of an older rhetoric, the homo homini lupus, that Sartre evokes this absolute otherness imposed on human life by scarcity." "The idea of scarcity has struck many critics," he adds, "as being more Malthusian and Darwinian than Marxist." Fredric Jameson, *Marxism and Form* (Princeton: Princeton University Press, 1971), pp. 233–6.

45. See, however, D. Michael Shafer, *Deadly Paradigms: The Failure of US Counterinsurgency Policy* (Princeton: Princeton University Press, 1988), for the argument that imperialism both functions and fails by blinding itself to inconvenient truths.

46. Inderpal Grewal, "Reading and Writing the South Asian Diaspora: Feminism and Nationalism in North America," ms available from the author.

47. Williams, *Politics and Letters*, p. 170.

48. See my "Colonial Discourse: A Paradigm and its Discontents," *Victorian Studies* (Winter 1992), pp. 209–14.

49. This does not mean that defense of the canon, or more generally defense of the professional status quo, is the profession's only motive. It is no less fair to say that the threat to the canon which *requires* this defense also embodies a professional motive – here, the motive of extending the profession's representativeness. Which is to suggest that this Freudian/Hegelian zero-sum logic does as unconvincing a job on professionalism as it does on imperialism.

50. Benita Parry, "The Contradictions of Cultural Studies," *Transition*, 53 (1991), p. 41.

51. Parry, "Problems in Current Theories of Colonial Discourse," p. 35.

52. "Three Women's Texts," p. 243.

53. Gayatri Chakravorty Spivak, "Poststructuralism, Marginality, Postcoloniality, and Value," in Peter Collier and Helga Geyer-Ryan, eds, *Literary Theory Today* (Ithaca: Cornell University Press, 1990), p. 224.

54. Gayatri Chakravorty Spivak, "Can the Subaltern Speak?", in Cary Nelson and Lawrence Grossberg, eds, *Marxism and the Interpretation of Culture* (Houndmills: Macmillan 1988), p. 275 (pp. 271–313).

55. Bourdieu, "Les usages du 'peuple'," *Choses dites* (Paris: Minuit, 1987).

56. Pierre Bourdieu and Terry Eagleton, "In Conversation: Doxa and Common Life," *New Left Review*, 191 (January/February 1992), p. 119.

57. Pierre Bourdieu and Jean-Claude Passeron, *La Reproduction* (Paris: Minuit, 1970). Jacques Ranciere comments: "Toute l'opération se joue sur un seul concept: *l'arbitraire*." "L'ethique du sociologue," in Collectif "Révoltes Logiques," *L'Empire du sociologue* (Paris: La Découverte, 1984), p. 27. The introduction to this volume offers an analysis of Bourdieu's professional success that largely overlaps with my own.

58. The origin of capital, according to a well-known book on the subject, is surplus value, which is to say labor-power, and its changing organic composition (the proportions of organic and inorganic capital – the capital which comes directly from labor, and the capital which has taken the form of machines, buildings, infrastructure) is historically determined. Coming back to Bourdieu's metaphor, we would have to say that cultural capital is also composed of elements which come from below, as it were, and that its composition too is shifting and radically heterogeneous. It is not a divinity, but a battlefield. And the battle over it has nothing to do with disinterestedness.

59. I am suggesting only that, since *some* legitimation is unavoidable, attention should fall on a discrimination of authorities. Which would mean that the state needs a fresh and comparative look.

60. In the study of the university made in 1967 and later published as *Homo Academicus*, Bourdieu writes: "Plus on va vers le pole de la recherche, plus on voit s'accroître la possibilité d'un ećart entre le capital proprement symbolique et le statut universitaire, certains des intellectuels les plus prestigieux pouvant occuper des positions universitaires tout à fait mineures (comme, au moment de l'enquête, Louis Althusser, Roland Barthes ou Michel Foucault)." Pierre Bourdieu, *Homo Academicus* (Paris: Minuit, 1984), p. 145, n. 43. Note his will to ignore the paradox that he and Foucault both could occupy the most prestigious academic positions at the very heart of the state apparatus.

61. Bové reminds us that the Arnoldian tradition already brought culture and the state into close proximity: "The essential requirement of 'culture' is that it parallel, reinforce, and embody the political regulations of civil society and the state." Bové, pp. 252–3.

62. "What characterizes 'reproduction' over time," according to George Ross, "is that the upper classes always win." George Ross, "Intellectuals Against the Left: The Case of France," in Ralph Miliband and Leo Panitch, eds, *The Retreat of the Intellectuals: The Socialist Register 1990* (London: Merlin, 1990), p. 225, n. 46. Ross speaks of Bourdieu's "deep pessimism about change."

63. This issue in political theory requires more work. Within what borders, in what scale of unit, is democracy more or less possible?

Conclusion

1. Alan Sinfield, *Literature, Politics, and Culture in Postwar Britain* (Berkeley: University of California Press, 1989), p. 41.
2. "In order to retain their positions as intellectuals in the face of growing competition from mass culture, the group (New York intellectuals] sometimes acted and sounded like a professional organization intent on upholding the correct vocational standards.... They resented people experiencing art easily because, in effect, that rendered intellectuals useless. If one could experience culture without trouble, there was no need to employ an intellectual to interpret it for you ... Their attack on middlebrow culture was thus in part an extension of their attempt to maintain their central position as recognized intellectuals in a period of transformation." Neil Jumonville, *Critical Crossings: The New York Intellectuals in Postwar America* (Berkeley: University of California Press, 1991), p. 183.
3. Dietrich Rueschemeyer, *Power and the Division of Labour* (Cambridge: Polity Press, 1986), pp. 122–3.
4. Jonathan Culler, "Criticism and Institutions: The American University," in Derek Attridge, Geoff Bennington, and Robert Young, eds, *Post-structuralism and the Question of History* (Cambridge: Cambridge University Press, 1987), p. 87.
5. Evelyn Waugh, "Dr Wodehouse and Mr Wain," *The Spectator*, 24 February 1956, pp. 507–9. Thanks to my colleague William Vesterman for the reference.
6. John Gross, "The Man of Letters in a Closed Shop," *Times Literary Supplement*, November 15, 1991, pp. 15–16. Gross quotes Bernard Bergonzi's view that the "emergence of a new generation of university-based critics in the 50s" (Bayley, Davie, Hoggart, Kermode, Williams) did not mean the end of the man of letters. "It was not until a generation later that the true, unimpeachable professionals finally took over" (15). "The crowning triumph of professionalism, in this version of events, comes close to being equated with the coming to the fore of critical theory" (15). Gross is a moderate voice, admitting that "every discipline needs its specialized vocabulary" and wondering "why all the fuss?" However, he is angered by the "arrogance" of the argument (in George Levine et al., *Speaking for the Humanities* [New York: American Council of Learned Societies, 1989], Occasional Paper No. 7) that nonspecialized "amateurs-belletrists ... unselfconsciously sustain traditional hierarchies, traditional social and cultural exclusion, assuming that their audience is both universal and homogeneous." In the end he endorses Roger Kimball's view that all this is the self-serving theory of, by, and for "professional academic."
7. Louis Kampf and Paul Lauter, *The Politics of Literature: Dissenting Essays on the Teaching of English* (New York: Pantheon, 1970).
8. Richard Flacks, *Making History: The American Left and the American Mind* (New York: Columbia University Press, 1988), pp. 60–1. On the same subject see Paul Buhle, *Marxism in the United States*, 2nd edn (London: Verso, 1991), ch. 7, which departs

refreshingly from the narrative of institutionalization-as-decline.

9. Harold Perkin, "The Ebbing of the Tide in Academia", *Times Literary Supplement*, June 26, 1992, p. 7.

10. C. Wright Mills, *White Collar* (New York: Oxford University Press, 1953), p. 115.

11. James Livingston, "How to Succeed in Business History without Really Trying: Remarks on Martin J. Sklar's *Corporate Reconstruction of American Capitalism*", *Business and Economic History*, 21 (1992), 2nd Series, pp. 1–6. John and Barbara Ehrenreich's theory of the "Professional-Managerial Class" is an early and powerful reading of the Progressive heritage back from the perspective of 1960s middle-class radicalism: "the PMC emerged with dramatic suddenness in the years between 1890 and 1920" (18). And "the 'middle-class' left . . . is, to a very large extent, the left itself"(5).

12. I invoke Sinfield and left-culturism here rather than one of the New Class theories so as *not* to suggest that the real differences, the real opposition-ality of what the Ehrenreichs call "the professional-managerial class," is indeed that of a distinct class, indicating some profound rupture in the class structure of contemporary society. From the perspective similar to my own, Elliot A. Krause places "New Class" theories in the tradition of Weber and argues against them: "Evidence that the group acts for its interest and not at the behest of others is scanty . . . Weber never said experts wouldn't be needed in bureaucracies. But he clearly spelled out their role and its limits." Bureaucracies do not rule, he says, they are ruled, and there is room inside them for dissent that comes up from below: "professions in *any* context (even the bureaucratic) may march to a different drummer than goal-rationality." Elliot A. Krause, *Division of Labor: A Political Perspective* (Westport, CT: Greenwood Press, 1982), pp. 59, 60. See also George Ritzer, "Professionalization, Bureau-cratization, and Rationalization: The Views of Max Weber," *Social Forces*, 53:4 (June 1975), 627–34.

13. Terence C. Halliday, "Professions, Class and Capitalism," *Archives of European Sociology*, 24 (1983), p. 339 (pp. 321–46). See Novick, p. 50, for further critique of Larson.

14. Linda Cherrey Reeser and Irwin Epstein, *Professionalization and Activism in Social Work: The Sixties, the Eighties, and the Future*, with a foreward by Richard A. Cloward (New York: Columbia University Press, 1990), p. xv. A similar line is argued in Rick Spano, *The Rank and File Movement in Social Work* (Washington, DC: University Press of America, 1982). For radicalism in the professions more generally, see, for example, Ronald Gross and Paul Osterman, eds, *The New Professionals* (New York: Simon & Schuster, 1972) and Joel Gerstl and Glenn Jacobs, *Professions for the People: The Politics of Skill* (New York: Schenkman, 1976).

15. Rueschemeyer speaks of a "high devotion/low power syndrome": "Many social service occupations excel more in devotion to the welfare in their clients than in potentially threatening expertise" (136–7).

16. Myron Peretz Glazer and Penina Migdal Glazer, *The Whistle-Blowers:*

Exposing Corruption in Government and Industry (New York: Basic Books, 1989). An example is Demetrios Basdekas, one of their "professionals as ethical resisters," who brought his findings before the Senate and the newspapers when he was taken off a job by the Nuclear Regulatory Commission. According to the authors, "The combination of professional ideology, breach of trust by management, and ethical solidarity that drove Demetrios Basdekas to challenge his superiors at the NRC is repeated" in many other cases (82).

17. "The movement for corporate capitalism reconstructed American society during the years 1890–1916. In effecting a reorganization of property ownership and the market, and in attaining a revision of the law and of government–market relations, this movement established the fundamental conditions of what many historians regard as the mass-culture society and also as the organizational or bureaucratic society with its concomitant rise of a professional, managerial, and technical middle class." Martin J. Sklar, *The Corporate Reconstruction of American Capitalism, 1890–1916: The Market, the Law, and Politics* (Cambridge: Cambridge University Press, 1988), p. 441. The quotations are from Sklar, pp. 431–2, and from Livingston, p. 1.

18. As Herbert Gans suggests, the actual distribution of power can serve as an argument for as well as against professional autonomy: "In principle, I would argue that like other professionals, journalists should share their responsibility with others. But principles must acknowledge the real world, wherein the first and most energetic claimants to a share in news selection would be advertisers, powerful sources which prefer to exclude harmful publicity from the news, and the best organized or most vocal audience members. In a world of unequal power, the principle could well enhance the power of those groups which already exert pressure on journalists." Herbert J. Gans, *Deciding What's News: A Study of CBS Evening News, NBC Nightly News, Newsweek and Time* (New York: Vintage, 1979), p. 323.

19. Alan Dawley, *Struggles for Justice: Social Responsibility and the Liberal State* (Cambridge, MA: Harvard University Press, 1992), reviewed by Alan Brinkley, "The Progressive Impulse," *Times Literary Supplement*, May 29, 1992, p. 8.

20. Andrew Sayer and Richard Walker, *The New Social Economy: Reworking the Division of Labor* (Cambridge, MA: Blackwell, 1992), p. 7. "It is by underestimating the significance of an advanced division of labor that many socialists are able to see only the disadvantages of gesellschaft relations epitomized by market exchange, ignoring their liberating qualities, and to entertain utopian hopes for a gemeinschaft economy, in which modes of social organization, feasible within small, knowable communities, are imagined to be possible at much larger scales" (269).

21. To say American here is of course to raise the familiar specter of social democracy at home, neo-imperialism abroad.

22. Andrew Abbott puts the point thus: "In America it is ultimately through public opinion that professions establish the power that enables them to achieve legal protection. By contrast, on the Continent

the state itself has traditionally been the professions' public" (*The System of Professions*, p. 60).

23. George Yudice, "For a Practical Aesthetics," in Bruce Robbins, ed., *The Phantom Public Sphere* (Minneapolis: University of Minnesota Press, 1993).

Index

255